THE COSTS AND ECONOMICS OF OPEN AND DISTANCE LEARNING

D1519634

Open and Distance Learning Series

Series Editor: Fred Lockwood

THE COSTS AND ECONOMICS OF OPEN AND DISTANCE LEARNING

Greville Rumble

KOGAN PAGE

London • Stirling (USA)
Published in association with the
Institute of Educational Technology, Open University

9-97   #36916406

First published in 1997

Kogan Page Limited   and
120 Pentonville Road   22883 Quicksilver Drive
London N1 9JN   Stirling, VA 20166, USA

© Greville Rumble, 1997

British Library Cataloguing in Publication Data

A CIP record for this book is available from the British Library.

ISBN 0 7494 2381 1 hardback
ISBN 0 7494 1519 3 paperback

Typeset by JS Typesetting, Wellingborough, Northants.
Printed and bound in Great Britain by Clays Ltd, St Ives plc

Contents

Series editor's foreword

In the early pages of this book, Greville Rumble acknowledges that many people are put off by the mere mention of costs – they 'look at the budget and their eyes glaze over'. However, if you are prepared to put a modest amount of effort into considering the arguments, analyses and evidence provided here, you will accrue massive returns for your investment.

Greville Rumble has succeeded in assembling a book that teachers and trainers, managers and planners, and ultimately their learners, can benefit from. He not only discusses the arguments underlying the costs and economics of open and distance learning, he identifies and unpacks the component parts within these systems and explains their significance. Your previous ideas of recurrent and non-recurrent expenditure, of direct costs, indirect costs and overheads, will be clarified. The significance of cost drivers, economies of scale, break-even points and a host of other considerations will be expertly revealed and illustrated.

The initial chapters will provide you with the ideas, concepts and relationships that will enable you to cost particular activities. Other chapters will alert you to the factors to consider in designing open and distance learning courses, the choice of media and levels of student support. The issues of cost efficiency, cost effectiveness and cost benefit are revealed and skilfully illustrated. However, the procedures and techniques presented here do not represent mechanical processes. Greville repeatedly reveals why such costing and analyses require your continual judgement if valid assessments and conclusions are to be drawn.

I believe this book marks a significant point in our consideration of open and distance learning in teaching and training contexts; whether in schools, colleges and universities or in industry and commerce. I can think of no person better to present the issues than Greville. He shares his experience of undertaking numerous costing exercises, brings together a unique collection of evidence and references from around the world, and provides numerous examples and illustrations.

Many of us, I'm sure, have been tempted to make sweeping generalizations when commenting on the costs and economics of open and distance learning. I'm afraid that after reading this book you will not be tempted to do so again. Greville ends by saying that little can be concluded with certainty; that 'there is no substitute for management; for active involvement in planning and costing a project'. This book, I am sure, will not only persuade you that you need to be involved in such planning, it will give you the insights and confidence that will enable you to cost your own projects.

Fred Lockwood

Preface

This book is the result of many years of experience. In 1973 the Open University in the UK appointed me to head its Planning Office, a job which I held until 1978, and then again between 1985 and 1989. While there I developed an interest in the economics and costs of distance education. Over the years I have written and published much in these fields, and in writing this book I have inevitably drawn on work I have done elsewhere. I have also drawn on the work of friends and colleagues around the world. This preface, then, acknowledges this past, and my debts, to the following.

Professor Leslie Wagner (now Vice-Chancellor of Leeds Metropolitan University) and Professor Ralph Smith of the Open University for their early encouragement to work on the economics of the Open University, and the productivity of its academic staff. Professor Michael Neil and Mr Alan Tout, with whom I worked on the identification of the fundamental variables affecting costs in the Open University (Rumble, Neil and Tout, 1981). Dr Hilary Perraton and the Commonwealth Secretariat, for whom I wrote a report on *Costing Distance Education* (Rumble, 1986b). Mr Paul Northcott, Dr Louise Moran, and Deakin University, for whom I wrote a report on *Activity Costing in Mixed-Mode Institutions* (Rumble, 1986c). Janet Jenkins and the Commonwealth Secretariat, for whom I wrote a paper on 'The costs and costing of distance/open education' (Rumble, 1988). Geoffrey Crabb and Lesley MacDonald of the National Council for Educational Technology, and my co-authors Ken Dixon, David Lancaster and Philip Pearson, who worked on the handbook *Costing Open and Flexible Learning* (Crabb, 1990). Dale Holt and Deakin University, for whom I wrote two units for the Master of Distance Education programme's course on the *Management of Distance Education* (Rumble, 1991a, 1991b). João Oliveira and the International Labour Office and the World Bank, respectively, in connection with our preparation of case studies on distance education in the vocational field and in Latin America (Rumble and Oliveira, 1992; Oliveira and Rumble, 1992). Mr Claudio Dondi and SCIENTER (Centro di Ricerchi e Servizi Avanzati per la Formazione, Bologna), with whom I worked within the context of the DELTA Concerted Action on *The Economics of Flexible and Distance Learning* (SCIENTER, 1994).

Other debts are acknowledged through references, but I would wish in particular to acknowledge the fruitful interaction I have had over the years with Professor Anthony (Tony) Bates, now of the University of British Columbia, most notably in the studies that informed the Open University's Visiting Committee about the costs and capabilities of the technologies supporting distance education in the

Open University, and its Broadcasting and Audio-Visual Committee about the relative costs of video-cassettes and television, and audio-cassettes and radio.

Hilary Perraton, Thomas Huelsmann and Douglas L Adkins made a number of detailed comments on the manuscript, for which I thank them. Fred Lockwood, the Series Editor, continued to press me to write this book over the two and a half years during which I prevaricated in putting fingers to keyboard, and I have a debt to him and to the publishers, Kogan Page, for their patience.

Finally, I wish to thank my wife Anne who, once I had begun, not only put up with my obsessive immersion in the task of writing, but also read, commented on, and vastly improved the manuscript.

Greville Rumble
Nutley, East Sussex

Acknowledgements

The author and publishers are grateful to the following for permission to source tables and other material as follows:

Tables 11.1, 11.4, 11.6 and 11.7 – A W Bates (1995) *Technology, Open Learning and Distance Education,* Routledge, London, with kind permission of Routledge.
Tables 11.2 and 13.6 – Indira Gandhi National Open University.
Table 11.5 – D T Jamison, S J Klees and S J Wells (1978) *The Costs of Educational Media: Guidelines for planning and evaluation,* p.242 © 1978 by Sage Publications Inc. Reprinted by permission of Sage Publication, Inc.
Table 12.1 and material in Case Study 12.1 – Kogan Page.
Tables 13.1 and 13.5 – L Wagner (1977) 'The economics of the Open University revisited', *Higher Education* 1 (2), 159–83; Table III, © Elsevier Scientific Publishing Company, Amsterdam; and Table 13.2 – B Laidlaw and R Layard (1974) 'Traditional versus Open University teaching methods: A cost comparison,' *Higher Education* 3 (4), 439–68, Tables 2 and 3, © Elsevier Scientific Publishing Company, Amsterdam; with kind permission from Kluwer Academic Publishers.
Table 13.5 – Open and Distance Learning Association of Australia.
Tables 14.3 and 14.4 – Routledge.
Tables 15.2 and 15.3 – *International Journal of University Adult Education.*

Chapter 1

Introduction

The demand for education continues to rise. There are now over one billion children in school, one-fifth of the world's population. In 1950 the figure was nearer 300 millions (Delors *et al.*, 1996: 36–7). Third World countries have invested enormous sums in the expansion of primary, secondary and higher education but many countries lack the resources to expand education by traditional means. There has been a parallel increase in the demand for continuing education (ibid., 73). Developed countries see education and training as a key to remaining competitive and both private and public enterprises recognize the need to invest in the training and development of their workforces. But underlying this, there is pressure to find more efficient and effective ways of meeting demand. Educational and training providers are required to reduce their costs yet maintain quality. The cost of education and training is everywhere on the agenda.

Traditionally education and training have been labour intensive activities but, over the years, ways have been found both to increase the efficiency of labour and to substitute technology and capital for labour. The search for efficiencies in education has a long history and has included:

- the development and use of written texts as a means of instruction;
- the development of libraries as places where scholars and students can consult texts without the need for the presence of a teacher. Early examples include the libraries at Alexandria, established by Ptomely I (308–246 BC), and at Pergamum, founded during the reigns of Attalus I (d. 197 BC) and Eumenes II (d. 159 BC);
- the use of written examinations in the place of oral ones. In the eleventh century they were developed by the Chinese as a means of improving the efficiency of their selection procedures for entrance to higher education and the civil service;
- the development of printing with movable type faces, initially in Korea, where no less than three fonts had been developed by 1434, and then in Europe by

Gutenberg in Mainz in Germany in 1445. In Europe this was followed by the rapid spread of presses to meet the demand generated by the expansion of a secular reading public;
- the development in the eighteenth and nineteenth centuries of the classroom as the basic organizational unit of the school – a development that at the time represented an enormous increase in educational productivity.

While some efficiencies can be achieved through changes in the organization of labour and working practices, 'the key to productivity improvements in every economic sector has been through the augmentation of human efforts by technology' (Jamison *et al.*, 1974: 57). The early development of correspondence education, in Lund in Sweden in 1833 and by Sir Isaac Pitman in England in 1840, led to the creation of private, commercial, correspondence schools and colleges. Since then, governments have come to see distance education as a means of enrolling large numbers of students at a lower per capita cost than traditional institutions. The International Commission on Education set up by UNESCO under the chairmanship of Jacques Delors regarded distance education, already widespread, as a prime and unquestioningly promising means of meeting the growing demand for education (Delors *et al.*, 1996: 197, 198–9). The European Commission sought to encourage infrastructures and applications that help the development of cost-efficient and effective learning technologies (Van den Brande, 1993). Numerous distance teaching institutions have been set up with the specific intention of reducing the unit costs of education: Rumble (1986a: 59–60) points out that the planners of the Andhra Pradesh Open University in India, the Universidad Nacional Abierta in Venezuela and Everyman's University in Israel all specifically hoped that the use of distance teaching methodologies would lower the unit costs of higher education. Industry too has seen open learning as a way of reducing the per capita cost of training (Temple, 1991)

Of course, not all distance education systems are cheaper than the alternative, conventional means of teaching and training. There are social advantages to using open and distance learning methods that meet the needs of populations who could not otherwise be reached or avail themselves of educational and training opportunities. Very often, there is no intention to save money. Nevertheless, cost is frequently a major criterion in the decision to develop a particular system. Decision-makers want to know how much something will cost, and whether they can afford it. They need this information to set a budget, to cost change and to decide between two or more different options. The capital and operating costs of open and distance learning systems vary widely, depending on the technologies used. While the high levels of capital investment in many of these systems, and their high absolute cost, can often be justified because they reach large numbers of students, there is always the possibility that insufficient students will be attracted to the system to deliver economies of scale.

The activity of costing is therefore central to the planning and development of educational systems. Unfortunately, many people are put off by the mere mention of costs. They look at a budget and their eyes glaze over. Reports, conferences and workshops often indicate the need for a 'simple' costing tool that will help those who wish to develop distance and open learning courses. Yet, in fact, there is nothing intrinsically difficult about costing. All it requires is a certain degree of logic and care. The logic is mainly involved in considering the design of the system and identifying everything that might result in a cost being incurred. Also, since cost is related to the volume of activity, there is a need to identify those things that might cause costs to go up or down with a change in the level of activity. There is a further need to establish the cost or price of the inputs to the system. And, finally, the need for accuracy in any work involving figures should be obvious.

Over the years accountants have developed methods and conventions which are widely recognized and used, both as an aid to the process of costing and as a means of ensuring that the cost data derived from exercises is a fair reflection of the costs (actual or likely) of the activity. These conventions do change over time – the current emphasis on activity based costing being one example. Nevertheless, the existence of recognized methods and conventions is an enormous help to those required to cost a system.

Costing is, of course, undertaken within a context. This book aims to provide its readers with both the necessary technical tools to undertake costing, and information on the behaviour of costs in open and distance learning systems. The first part of the book (Chapters 2–9) provides an introduction to the basic concepts of costs and costing. The second part (Chapters 10–12) looks at the costs of designing, producing and distributing materials, and of supporting students. Because each medium has different cost characteristics, it makes sense in Chapters 11 and 12 to deal with the various media separately. Thus Chapter 11 covers text, audio, video, and computing, and Chapter 12 looks at audio-, video- and computer conferencing, as well as face-to-face tuition and other forms of student support. The third part of the book looks at particular aspects of the economics of distance and open learning (cost efficiency, cost effectiveness, cost benefit, and the issues around funding, demand and price), and the lessons that have been learnt over the years.

The title of the book refers to distance and open learning. These terms are not synonymous (cf Rumble, 1989a, 1990; Lewis, 1990). *Distance education* is a process of teaching-learning in which the learner is physically separated from the teacher. The geographical distances involved may be relatively small, or very large. Most definitions accept that there may be a degree of physical interaction between teacher and learner, but in comparison with the normal classroom experience the actual amount of face-to-face contact is usually much reduced or even nonexistent. Because of this, the teacher develops a range of learning materials to impart knowledge, skills and attitudes to the learner. The presence of such technical media (print, audio, video, computer-based) is a distinguishing feature of distance education. Students study these materials, generally alone, at times and in places of their own choosing. There are arrangements to test their knowledge, skills and attitudes through assignments that are sent to a tutor for marking, or marked by computer. Where tutors are involved, they record the marks and send the assignments back to the students, with comments on their progress and suggestions as to how they might improve their learning. The presence of such two-way communication in support of the student is what distinguishes distance education from teach-yourself-programmes and private study. This two-way communication may be asynchronous (the sending and receiving of the messages occurs at different times, as in postal communication), or it may be synchronous (happening at the same time, as in a telephone conversation). Early forms of distance education used technologies where there was a built-in delay between the sending and receipt of a message. Modern means can greatly reduce or even eliminate this delay.

Early forms of distance education used print and correspondence tuition which is why it was originally called *correspondence education*. The term *distance education* reflected the use of multi-media methods in addition to the methods of correspondence education, and finally achieved prominence when the International Council for Correspondence Education (ICCE), at its 1982 conference, changed its name to the International Council for Distance Education (ICDE).

Open learning is an imprecise phrase describing any form of educational provision in which the restrictions placed on students are minimized, and in which decisions about learning are taken by the learners themselves. These decisions may cover many aspects of the learning process, including whether or not to begin and continue to study, what to learn (selection of content/skills, selection of courses), how to learn (including choice of methods, routes through courses and media), where to study (not necessarily in a classroom), when to study (including when to start, how rapidly to progress and when to finish), how to be assessed, whom to approach for help, and what to do next. Institutional rules about who can enrol, how students progress and how they are assessed, are either relaxed entirely or opened up to provide for choice. Systems may be more or less open, depending on their design. Distance teaching methods can help course designers achieve some of the features of openness described above. However, distance systems are not necessarily open.

The term *flexible learning*, sometimes used more or less synonymously with open learning, also has no precise definition. The composite term *flexible and distance learning* (FDL) is also used, particularly by agencies of the European Commission.

Studying from materials is of course not restricted to distance learning. Traditional students have always had to use resources, principally libraries, particularly at the higher education level. The term *resource-based learning* describes schemes in which learners have some choice over the sources of information and support they will use through access to a range of resources. The use of resources allows learners, either individually or in groups, to study on their own, without the direct intervention of a tutor. *Independent learning* is a term used to describe approaches which allow this to happen. The term *self-study* may be used where students work through a book or other material that provides both content and sets of questions that enable students to check their own progress. Self-study is thus a form of independent learning. Flexible, open and distance learning may incorporate such approaches. Independent learning should not be confused with *individualized learning* in which the course is designed or tailored for the individual student.

Reflection suggests that distance education is a *method* of education whereas open learning espouses a *philosophy* of education. As a method, distance education is most usually contrasted with those forms of education, in the classroom, lecture hall, laboratory or study group, that are based on contiguity between the student and teacher. Sometimes called *contiguous education*, it is more usually and loosely described as *traditional* or *conventional education*, reflecting the paradigmatic nature of the school and its classroom in people's experience of education.

It helps to have a clear framework within which to approach costing. For most people working within organizations, the natural framework is set within the boundaries of the institution's budget. Managers are rightly concerned with the organization's income and expenditure, and with questions of internal efficiency and effectiveness. But there is a wider view, of concern to economists, that takes into account all the resources involved in the system.

This book assumes a *systems* approach to the costing of open and distance learning. This focus is deliberate. Human activities systems (such as educational and training organizations) comprise 'a number of activities linked together as a result of some principle of coherency' (Checkland, 1981: 111) that extend well beyond their organizational boundaries in ways that make it worthwhile for an observer to think about the activities as a whole. From an economic point of view, and even from a managerial one (for example, in pricing decisions), it is preferable to focus on a system rather than an institution (such as a school or university) because the actual organizational unit usually makes up only a part of the whole system. For example, in a school, the parents, likely employers of graduates, funding bodies and suppliers are all outside the organization but very much part of the system as a whole. Concentrating solely on the costs of the organization may be misleading. An organization's annual budget will not take account of many of its system costs, eg the costs that its students bear out of their own pocket, or the cost of broadcast transmission provided 'free' to the institution by state broadcasting agencies.

The systems framework used in this book was developed by Rumble in the late 1970s (cf Rumble, 1979), building on ideas expounded by Miller and Rice (1967). Any distance learning system involves two major *operating systems*: these are the systems which contribute directly to the input – conversion – output processes of the business. The first of these, the *materials subsystem*, involves the design, production, distribution (or delivery) and reception of course materials to support an agreed academic curriculum of awards and courses.

The *design* process incorporates curriculum planning, market research, the selection of media, the definition of teaching and assessment strategies, the authoring of texts and scripts, the development of audio-visual materials and the design of computer-based learning systems of various kinds. It also involves editing and graphic design. The end result is the master copy for each item of teaching and assessment materials. *Production* is the production of multiple copies of materials (texts, audio-cassettes, computer software disks, etc) from the master copies. *Distribution* is the process that gets these copies to their point of use. It may involve their physical distribution by post or courier, broadcasting or electronic transfer. *Reception* involves the receipt of the materials at their point of use (the home or a local resource centre) by their users (the learners and their tutors).

The second operating system is the *student subsystem* which recruits and enrols students; registers them on courses of their choice; collects fees and other payments; allocates them to tutors, local centres and examination centres; provides them with ongoing advice; arranges for their assessment; arranges tutorials and other points of contact; maintains their record; organizes graduation ceremonies; and provides transcripts and references.

Supporting the operating systems are two other subsystems: the *logistical system* procures and replenishes the resources required by the system (for example, human resources, finance, buildings and equipment). It encompasses the personnel, estates and buildings, maintenance, purchasing and finance functions, and includes that subsystem that recruits, inducts, develops, pays and manages the tutors. The *regulatory system* plans and manages the overall system, relating operating activities to each other, logistical activities to operating activities, and the activities of the organization as a whole to its environment. Figure 1.1, based on Rumble (1979: 62) illustrates the distance learning *system* as a whole.

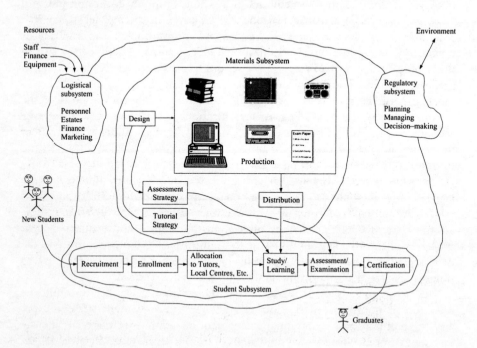

Figure 1.1 *A systems view of distance education*

Chapter 2

Budgets

Chapters 2 to 9 provide a basic understanding of how accountants and, in particular, cost accountants approach their work. This chapter explains:

- what a budget is, and how expenditure is usually categorized in budgets (Section 2.1);
- the difference between recurrent and non-recurrent expenditure (Section 2.2);
- the difference between capital and revenue (or operating) expenditure (Section 2.3).

2.1 Budgets

The central function of financial accounting is to record financial transactions in monetary terms and to analyse these to show their effect over a period of time. Normally *budgets* (a statement of the money it is planned to spend) and *financial analyses* (a statement of the money that has been spent) are drawn up for a fixed period of a year, though other periods of time may be used. Budgets and financial analyses are more meaningful if it is clear on what the money is being spent. By convention, expenditure is analysed into four categories:

- human resources;
- premises and accommodation;
- equipment and furniture;
- stocks, supplies, consumables and expenses.

Human resources covers staff on the payroll. Managers may want to draw a distinction between particular categories of staff (for example, academics/teachers, administrators and support staff). The costs covered include salaries (monthly paid) and wages (weekly paid) and *all* the other costs involved in hiring staff. These *on-costs* include insurance payments, employment taxes and staff benefits etc. Consultants on short-term contracts may be included here, particularly if they are paid on a salary or wage basis. If not, they are shown as an expense.

Premises and accommodation normally covers:

- the purchase of a building;
- the costs of putting up a building;
- rents;
- rates (a tax levied on the occupation or ownership of land);
- insurance of buildings and their contents;
- utilities (heat, light, water, power), waste disposal, telephone, fax, etc, *unless* these are charged to a particular department and treated as an expense;
- repairs and maintenance (direct labour plus materials, or outside contractor charges plus management and supervision costs);
- grounds and gardens;
- porters;
- security;
- cleaning;
- management and supervision of all these activities.

Equipment is a fixed asset (as are land, buildings and furniture). It covers plant, machinery and tools and is distinguished from consumables in that it is expected to have a useful life of more than one year. Equipment and furniture is usually held on an inventory (a list of all the items owned by the organization). Inexpensive items of equipment (such as staplers and computer disks) which may have a useful life of more than one year are treated as consumables.

Stocks, also called 'inventory', are holdings of goods and raw materials and components, work in progress (ie partially completed stocks), or finished goods (ie completed manufactured goods held for sale). Course texts and cassettes are examples of stocks, as is paper prior to its use in books. Supplies is material used in production for which it is impossible or not worthwhile determining the amount attributable to each unit of production. Examples include cleaning materials and lubricants used for machinery, and ink for printing. Consumables are materials used by the organization but not incorporated into its products (for example, office stationery). Expenses are the cost of something other than materials, supplies or labour. Examples include travel and postage costs.

The detail identified under each of these heading very much depends on the activities being costed and the needs of management. A typical departmental budget would be drawn up to reflect provision and expenditure on each of these categories. Table 2.1 shows how such a budget might traditionally be built up.

Each line of the budget would have a budget code to facilitate the attribution of expenditure to that category. The actual budgetary lines and the codes used need to be agreed by the finance department and the department's managers. Finance will wish to ensure that the coding structure enables them to abstract information required for accounting and control purposes, while managers will want to have the budget and expenditure coded in ways that help them manage

Table 2.1 *Departmental budget*

<table>
<tr><td colspan="4">Department of Continuing Education
Budget for the period 1.4.98–31.3.99</td></tr>
<tr><td></td><td>No.</td><td>Unit cost</td><td>Budget</td></tr>
<tr><td>Staffing</td><td></td><td></td><td></td></tr>
<tr><td>Academic staff</td><td></td><td></td><td></td></tr>
<tr><td>Head of department</td><td>1</td><td>40,000</td><td>40,000</td></tr>
<tr><td>Lecturers</td><td>3</td><td>25,000</td><td>75,000</td></tr>
<tr><td>Subtotal</td><td></td><td></td><td>115,000</td></tr>
<tr><td>Support staff</td><td></td><td></td><td></td></tr>
<tr><td>Administrator</td><td>1</td><td>20,000</td><td>20,000</td></tr>
<tr><td>Secretarial/clerical</td><td>2</td><td>15,000</td><td>30,000</td></tr>
<tr><td>Subtotal</td><td></td><td></td><td>50,000</td></tr>
<tr><td>Subtotal: all staff</td><td></td><td></td><td>165,000</td></tr>
<tr><td>Premises/accommodation</td><td></td><td></td><td></td></tr>
<tr><td>Central services charge</td><td></td><td></td><td>20,000</td></tr>
<tr><td>Subtotal</td><td></td><td></td><td>20,000</td></tr>
<tr><td>Equipment/furniture</td><td></td><td></td><td></td></tr>
<tr><td>Capital acquisition (computing equipment)</td><td>3</td><td>2,000</td><td>6,000</td></tr>
<tr><td>Subtotal</td><td></td><td></td><td>6,000</td></tr>
<tr><td>Stocks etc</td><td></td><td></td><td></td></tr>
<tr><td>Telephone</td><td></td><td></td><td>14,000</td></tr>
<tr><td>Stationery</td><td></td><td></td><td>1,500</td></tr>
<tr><td>Travel</td><td></td><td></td><td>4,500</td></tr>
<tr><td>Postage</td><td></td><td></td><td>3,000</td></tr>
<tr><td>Subtotal</td><td></td><td></td><td>23,000</td></tr>
<tr><td>TOTAL</td><td></td><td></td><td>214,000</td></tr>
</table>

their departments effectively. The level of detail varies enormously: for example, staff costs may be aggregated by department, shown by grades by department (as in Table 2.1) or be listed individually by name showing actual salary and on-costs.

Table 2.1 shows a *financial year* running from 1 April 1998 to 31 March 1999. This happens to more or less equate with the tax year in the UK, but it might equally have covered a different period – for example, the financial year may be coterminous with the calendar year. Sometimes funding bodies or legislation require institutions to adopt a particular financial year. In other cases there is freedom of choice. From a managerial point of view it is most convenient if the financial year reflects the activity year within the business, so that, for example, the end of one financial year and the beginning of the next does not come right in the middle of a coherent activity (for example, the academic year). Although financial periods are generally 12 months in duration, they may cover a longer or shorter period. This usually occurs where an institution is changing the phasing of its financial year for some reason, or where short-term projects are involved. For budget control purposes, financial years may be broken up into reporting periods, which can be based on calendar months, lunar months (of 28 days), or longer periods (often three months).

2.2 Recurrent and non-recurrent expenditure

The budget in Table 2.1 shows expenditure only for one year. But suppose it showed the expenditure for three years ahead (Table 2.2).

Table 2.2 *Recurrent and non-recurrent expenditure (at constant price levels)*

Year	Unit cost	1998/99		1999/2000		2000/1	
		No.	Budget	No.	Budget	No.	Budget
Staffing							
Academic staff							
Head of department	40,000	1	40,000	1	40,000	1	40,000
Lecturers	25,000	3	75,000	4	100,000	3	75,000
Consultant authors					23,000		5,000
Subtotal			**115,000**		**163,000**		**120,000**

The first thing to note is that in the second year there is an additional lecturer, who disappears in the third year. Years 2 and 3 also show a variable sum of money for consultant authors. Generally, significant elements of a department's budgets are allocated on the understanding that expenditure in one year will be continued in the next year. Such expenditure is known as *recurrent expenditure* (that is, it has occurred this year and it is expected that it will recur next year and in the years thereafter). Such on-going recurrent expenditure may be referred to as *baseline* expenditure.

In contrast, some expenditure is agreed for only a limited period. This is particularly true of expenditure on projects where, once the project is over, the staff leave (or are reassigned to other projects) and the expenditure finishes. In the example in Table 2.2 there is an additional lecturer for the middle year (1999/2000) only. The salary cost of the lecturer is *non-recurrent* (that is, it has been provided for only one year, and does not recur year after year). Expenditure on consultants is also non-recurrent.

How costs are analysed depends on what is being costed. Tables 2.1 and 2.2 present a departmental budget. Suppose that instead of the department itself, it is the department's courses that are being costed. In such circumstances, the costs of the staff would need to be allocated to particular courses. Even though from a departmental point of view the costs of the staff are ongoing (because they have long-term jobs with the department), from a course-costing point of view they would be treated as short-term project expenditure (see Table 2.3).

One of the cardinal rules of costing is that, before starting, the analyst must have a clear idea about the purpose of the exercise. This is very important since it will determine what information has to be collected and how it is analysed. Further, traditional departmental budgets and expenditure reports only provide some of the information needed. Analysts often have to get 'behind the figures'. This is particularly true when costing activities without the benefit of an *activity-based costing system* (see Chapter 7). In the absence of such a system, the only way to do this is to ask people about their activities, how they spend their time, and what it is that they do that affects costs. In the example in Table 2.3, for instance, the analyst would need to ask the lecturers to which course their time should be allocated.

Table 2.3   *Recurrent and non-recurrent expenditure*

Year	Unit cost	1998/99 No.	Budget	1999/2000 No.	Budget	2000/1 No.	Budget
Staffing							
Management function							
Head of department	40,000	1	40,000	1	40,000	1	40,000
Course expenditure							
Macroeconomics course							
Lecturers	25,000	1.5	37,500	1.5	37,500	1.5	37,500
The UK Economy 1960–95							
Lecturers	25,000	1	25,000	1	25,000		
Inflation in Latin America							
Lecturers	25,000	0,5	12,500	1.5	37,500	1.5	37,500
Consultant authors					23,000		5,000
Subtotal			**115,000**		**163,000**		**120,000**

2.3 Capital and revenue (or operating) expenditure

The departmental budget in Table 2.1 included some items for capital expenditure – in this case equipment. By its very nature, capital is a non-recurrent expense in the sense that a computer is expected to have a useful life of several years; a building is expected to last much longer. Of course, eventually equipment wears out and has to be replaced, but the point about capital expenditure is that, once bought, it has a useful life of more than one year. There are special considerations to be addressed in dealing with capital expenditure which are dealt with in Chapter 6.

Revenue expenditure (also called operating costs) is expenditure that will provide a benefit only during the current accounting period. Thus the benefits of expenditure on staff (salaries, wages), utilities, consumables and expenses are closely related to the period in which it is incurred, but it is not always so clear cut. Staff training is an investment in 'human capital' and is expected to be of long-term benefit to both the recipient and the employer, but from an accounting point of view such expenditure would normally be treated as an operating cost. Revenue expenditure may be, as noted, recurrent or non-recurrent.

Chapter 3

The classification of resources

Section 2.1 identified four categories of expenditure. This chapter enlarges on them.

3.1 Human resources

There are two basic ways of paying staff: either for their time or for their performance. Obviously, when costing an activity, it is important to know how people are paid, because the mechanisms of paying them are the engine that generates cost. Performance-based systems pay by result. Expected performance is usually set down in a contract and payment follows completion. Examples of performance related pay in open and distance learning include:

- paying an author a fixed sum for writing a text;
- paying an editor a fixed sum for editing the text;
- paying a tutor a sum for each script marked.

Staff on time-based systems are paid salaries (monthly) or wages (weekly). Salaries and wages may be determined *ad hoc* for each member of staff, or they may be on an incremental scale. Usually, management reflect the increasing experience of staff by paying them a little more each year. In incremental systems pay may increase virtually automatically by defined steps until such time as an individual reaches the top of the pay scale; alternatively, incrementation may be at the discretion of management. Either way, the year on year increase in cost is known as *incremental drift* and, in budgeting costs forward, it is important to take account of it. Where management determines pay on a case by case basis, it is important to establish how much money is being put aside for pay rises. Normally this is a set percentage of the salary/wages bill. Incremental drift and wage/salary drift is likely to be particularly high in young organizations where staff have been recruited at a young age. Later on, as people reach the top of the scale, or as a balance is struck between recruitment of new staff on lower salaries and the retirement of longer-serving staff who are paid more, incremental drift will cease to be a big problem.

In time-based systems, people are usually contracted to work for so many hours a week, for so many days a year. Such staff may have fixed hours and days of work. They may work 'full time' (a full week) or 'part time' (shorter hours). If they work more than their contract stipulates, they need to be paid more – and provision has to be made for overtime payments.

Some time-based staff, particularly professional staff, may have no set hours of work stipulated in their contracts. Equally, they may be so motivated or under such pressure that they work long hours. While this may seem excellent, it can be exploitative and cause stress. Further, in looking to the future and forecasting future levels of activity (for example, output of printed course texts) or future staffing requirements given an expansion in the number of courses to be offered, it is unreasonable to assume that staff will work long hours in the future. Hence, in projecting staffing costs forward, it should be assumed that staff will take their holidays and will not work unreasonable hours. Time-based staff usually have 'on-costs' in the form of insurance, taxes, pension contributions etc. Performance-paid staff may not have the same on-costs. Time- and performance-based pay systems can be combined.

There are various ways of computing salary costs. The most accurate is to take the actual salary and on-costs of all the individuals in employment but, of course, this information is confidential and may not be readily available. Also the cost of new or vacant posts may have to be estimated for budgetary purposes. In such cases it is usual to take the average salary/wage cost for the grade of staff. However, if large numbers of people are near the top end of the salary range, use of the average salary cost may inflate staffing costs in situations where a new department is being set up with young staff, or existing staff who are retiring are replaced by younger people near the bottom end of the salary range. In such circumstances different figures may have to be used.

When costing a project or a particular activity, it is probable that only the time spent on that activity is relevant. Academic staff may have a number of duties: these are normally teaching, research and administration. It is unlikely that they will spend all their time on one activity. In trying to establish the cost of developing a course, it is necessary to discover what proportion of their time is spent on that activity as opposed to others. There are different ways of doing this. Sometimes there is an expectation that staff spend a certain proportion of their time (together with the associated holiday time) on particular activities (40 per cent research, 40 per cent teaching, 20 per cent administration), and these proportions can be used to calculate costs. But in open, flexible and distance learning systems academics may well be relieved of some of their duties in order to concentrate on developing courses. Also, the amount of time an individual spends on administration may vary a lot. Senior academics may spend a great deal of their time on it while junior staff do little administration.

The question then arises, how is it possible to check that staff are spending their time on activities in the proportions laid down by contract or custom and practice? One approach is to rely on their memories, faulty as these may be, and ask them after the event to estimate how much time they spent on each activity. If staff have kept a rough diary of how they spent their time, this can be a great help – and indeed, diary exercises (in which staff are asked to record how they spent their time) can be a good way of establishing the proportions of time spent on major activities such as teaching, research and administration. Sometimes staff have to book their time to projects: lawyers and accountants frequently book time to clients, and some staff working in open, flexible and distance learning (for example, editors, graphic designers) may be used to a similar discipline. This is the best way of establishing the time actually spent on a project. But many staff do not do this as a matter of course. Some find reporting the time booked to projects an intrusion. They may misrepresent the hours spent on projects to hide idle time, or they may forget to book the time regularly. Nevertheless, as Chapter 7 points out, establishing the cost of activities may be important. The only way of doing this is to allocate people's time to different activities.

Throughout, there is a need to bear in mind the purpose to which the costings will be put. Suppose it is established that a particular academic spent an average of 65 hours a week over a three-month period on a particular course. In estimating how much time would be required to do a similar job in the future, it would be important to know that he or she spent this number of hours on the job. An allowance for buying in that amount of time could be included in the budget. But suppose that academics have no set hours of work, and their weekly pay is unaffected by the number of hours they work. In establishing historic costs, the fact that he or she spent 65 hours a week on the work would be irrelevant. But the historic cost could not be used as an accurate projection of reasonable costs for a similar job in the future. Costing is not a mechanical task: it requires continual judgements to be made as to what is a reasonable approach in any given circumstances.

Because education and training are such labour-intensive tasks, the costing of staff time is clearly an important element in the total cost picture, and it pays to get it right.

3.2 Premises and accommodation

Premises cover land and buildings and may be acquired in the following ways.

- Purchase (in which case they are treated as a capital cost). There may be money available to purchase them outright, or money may need to be borrowed to do this. In the latter case, the cost of borrowing (interest) appears as a revenue expense.

- Obtained by gift (in which case they are 'free' to the recipient institution). However, they do have a value (their value if they were to be sold), and this value would be reflected as a fixed asset in the accounts.
- Rented (in which case they are a revenue expense).

Once land and buildings are purchased, the costs are regarded as *sunk costs* and are not regarded as relevant to current decision-making. Whether this is acceptable or not depends on the questions being asked. Within an institutional context, there is often no need to consider the costs of the buildings and land. They exist and are in use. But when considering setting up a new department or a new institution, the cost of land and buildings becomes a very important consideration. In such circumstances there may be a choice between building or renting, and the relative cost of capital expenditure now against on-going revenue expenditure on rents may be important. Economists take the view that one always needs to take into account the cost of capital – a problem discussed in Chapter 6.

Buildings, accommodation and land incur annual running costs of the kind mentioned in Section 2.1. These costs may be easily identifiable, particularly where a building 'belongs' to a particular project and where all the service charges associated with that building are charged to the occupiers. But often this is not the case. Buildings on a campus may be occupied by a number of departments and the occupiers, even within a single department, may be involved on a range of projects. How can the costs be apportioned to a particular group of staff or project?

The answer to this question depends on the information available. It might be possible to obtain the service costs of a particular building, or, alternatively, only the general service cost across the whole of a campus. To apportion accommodation costs to a project, there are two options.

1. Calculate the cost of services per square metre. To do this, divide the total cost of premises by the number of square metres of space. Find out what area is occupied by people engaged on the project. Check that they are spending 100 per cent of their time on the project, and if not, adjust accordingly; and then calculate the cost of space attributable to the project.

    The costs of space may vary according to its use: office accommodation, common areas such as corridors, stairways and common rooms, laboratories etc. Sometimes it is better to separate out common space from the cost of 'operational' office space. In such cases one might determine the number of square metres of office accommodation (and lecture rooms etc) and its cost, and charge this in total to the project; but cost common areas such as common rooms and corridors separately, and apportion a proportion of their costs to the project, on the grounds that they are used by everyone. Example 3.1 shows how accommodation costs can be calculated using this approach.

Example 3.1

The total service cost of premises in the firm is £752,000 per year. There are 3,423 square metres of floor space. The cost per metre per year is therefore £219.69. The training department occupies 370 square metres, so the total cost to the department is £81,285.30. The department has a number of courses on offer. These are quantified in terms of training hours. At present the department is delivering 8,400 training hours. Thus the cost per training hour of space is £9.68. The current project is for a 50-hour course. So the attributable cost for space for this course is £484.

Note that if more training hours are offered, the cost per hour (the unit cost) comes down. If less training hours are offered, it goes up.

2. Alternatively, calculate the cost of space per member of staff by dividing the total cost of the space by the number of employees. Find out how many staff are involved on the project. Check whether 100 per cent of their time is spent on the project, and if not, adjust accordingly. Then calculate the cost of space per member of staff.

The cost of grounds is probably best apportioned across all staff. However, there may be reasons for not adopting this approach – where, for example, some part of the grounds is used by a particular department.

As the above examples show, apportioning costs is not an exact science. There may be several ways of doing it, and it is advisable to talk to the people who are involved in the project, to those who have commissioned the cost study, and to the finance department, discussing the pros and cons of each method. Once there is agreement on a particular method, it must be used consistently for the particular exercise.

If accommodation costs are not known (because there is no building in place as yet), the cost of renting a building or part of a building of the size needed can be used as a *proxy price*. This is a way of valuing any item which is in short supply or unavailable at the time one is seeking to establish a price for that item.

3.3 Equipment and furniture

Equipment may be bought or rented. Rented equipment is treated as a revenue cost. Furniture is usually bought unless it is provided in the context of rented furnished office space, in which case it is treated as part of the rental cost. Cheap items of equipment are treated as a consumable (see Section 2.1). Equipment and furniture can usually be treated as sunk costs. However, they cannot be ignored entirely, because of the need to:

- reflect their residual value as an asset in the accounts; and
- plan for the purchase of replacement equipment and furniture. Neither lasts forever. The replacement cost of equipment is problematic. Straight replacement is rarely possible or even wise, particularly in the case of equipment where technological advances are being made rapidly (as in computing). Fortunately, in such areas, even though specifications are rising, the cost of equipment is coming down. Each year that passes, one gets more computing power for one's money. The best approach to use is to cost equipment at its replacement value, recognizing that the new equipment will almost certainly be much better than the equipment being disposed of.
- Equipment and furniture may have a second-hand value. Any income should be included in the budget.

Frequently there is a direct relationship between the need to buy in equipment and furniture and the creation of new jobs on the establishment. If there are a lot of people working part time, the total cost on salaries may be the same as if fewer staff are working full time, but more desks, computers, telephones and office space may have to be provided because they all work at the same time (many woman with part-time jobs work in the mornings, when young children are at school).

3.4 Stocks, supplies, consumables and expenses

In general, the costing of consumables or expenses does not cause problems. Estimating their cost involves both deciding on the volume (of postage, travel etc) and the unit cost per volume. Equally, there is little problem about budgeting for the purchase of stocks and supplies: one decides what is needed and finds out the likely cost of acquiring it. This in effect means establishing a *standard price* for each item and using it to forecast budgetary needs.

There are, however, problems with deciding what particular projects should be charged when they use stocks or inventory. The problem particularly arises when stocks and supplies are bought in and stored prior to use. By the time they are taken out of store there may well be a difference between the price at which they were originally bought and the price of replacing them. This being so, which cost should be charged to a project: the old price, or the new one? Using the standard price may be fine for back-of-the-envelope calculations but it is not a satisfactory way of recording actual costs.

Historically there are a number of answers to this problem. The *replacement price* method uses the replacement price on the day of issue of the materials from stores. So, for example, if the replacement price was £0.64 on 7 November when the stores were taken out, this would be the price charged to the project. This method is not recommended because the price charged to the project does not reflect the actual price, so fictitious profits and losses can be made in the books.

The *average price* method calculates the total price paid for all the items in the inventory and divides this by the number of items in the inventory to arrive at an average price per item. Thus if there are 1000 items, of which 300 cost £0.64, 400 cost £0.65, and 300 cost £0.69, the total paid for the items would be £659 (Table 3.1).

Table 3.1   *Cost of items in an inventory*

Number	Unit price (£)	Total cost (£)
300	0.64	192
400	0.65	260
300	0.69	207
1000		659

The average price is £0.659 (£659 ÷ 1000). All stocks issued would be charged at this price. Every time old stock went out, or new stocks were bought in, the average price would be recalculated. This method has the advantage that no fictitious prices are involved. There may however be some slight rounding errors.

A method that is actually based on price paid is the *first in, first out (FIFO)* method. This assumes that the stores will always issue the oldest stock first (which is good stocktaking practice anyway). It uses the price of the first delivery of materials to the stores, until such time as that consignment has been used up, when it uses the price of the next delivery. It does not matter whether the price goes up or down. Assume that the stores records showed the following receipts and issues of C60 audio-cassettes (Table 3.2).

Table 3.2   *Stores records – receipt and issue of C60 audio-cassettes*

Date	Item by type	Stock purchase	Price	Stock value	Issue to Course	Number issued	Balance in stock
2 May	C60	6000	£0.62	£3720			6000
3 May	C60				L165	4800	1200
4 May	C60	2500	£0.65	£1625			3700
4 May	C60				M243	3200	500
7 May	C60	3400	£0.64	£2176			3900
7 May	C60				S840	3600	300

How much would each course be charged? Under this system, all the stock issued to L165 would be charged at £0.62 per cassette, so the cost to the course would be £2976. The stock issued to M243 would be charged at two prices: the first 1200 cassettes issued would be charged at £0.62, since this is the balance of the stock bought in on 2 May; the remaining 2000 cassettes issued would be charged at £0.65, the price paid for the stock bought in on 4 May. So the total cost to the course would be:

$$[1200 \times £0.62] + [2000 \times £0.65] = £2044$$

I suggest that the following methods are used:

- for cost projections, either the standard price or average price;
- for back-of-the-envelope costings, either the standard price or the average price;
- for accurate charging of costs to projects, the first in, first out method.

Chapter 4

A basic framework for analysing revenue costs

This chapter is crucial for an understanding of costs and costing. It introduces the following concepts:

- Cost (Section 4.1);
- Cost units, unit costs and cost centres (Section 4.1);
- Total cost (Section 4.1);
- Direct costs, indirect costs and overheads (Section 4.2);
- Fixed costs, variable costs and semi-variable costs (Section 4.3);
- Cost drivers (Section 4.4);
- Variable costs, linearity and economies of scale (Section 4.5);
- Committed costs and managed costs (Section 4.6).

4.1 Cost

Cost is the actual or notional expenditure of money incurred on, or attributable to, a specific thing or activity. If I travel from my office to London, and I am asked how much it would cost, I would say that the cost of my rail fare is about £16.00. That is, I have a *notional cost* in my mind. (Actually, it can be all kinds of prices, from £7.80 to £22.60, depending on the rail company, the route and the time of day, which just goes to show that I can get the notional cost of this simple activity very wrong indeed!) Once I have made the journey, I know how much it cost me. At that point I have an *actual cost* as opposed to a notional cost.

Institutions exist to produce products or provide services. This output can be measured. Examples might include a 60-minute audio-cassette, a 48-page text, a one-hour tutorial, a student, a graduate. A *cost unit* is a measured amount of product or service used for the expression of the costs of that product or service. What is important about a cost unit is that it reflects a *measured* amount of a product. In steel making, this is easy because the measured amount of product is usually a tonne of steel.

Often it is not that straightforward. A graduate may be the 'product' of a course of study lasting a variable number of years – say three, four or five years. One would expect the cost of a graduate emerging from a three-year course to be rather less than one emerging from a five-year course. So one may have to seek to define a measure for something as nebulous as a graduate. For example, there is an emerging consensus in the UK that a full-time university level undergraduate course will involve a student in 1200 study hours in a year, over three years. Thus a 'standard' undergraduate degree may be equated with 3600 study hours. A four-year course (4800 study hours) would therefore be equivalent to 1.33 'standard' degree courses. This provides a basis for making cost comparisons between different degrees. In this case the comparison would be made using a 'standard' degree as the cost unit used for costing purposes. A *unit cost* is the cost of one measure of output (one one-hour tutorial, one 'standard' graduate equivalent etc).

As well as attributing costs to cost units, one can also attribute them to locations, functions or items of equipment. These are referred to as *cost centres*. A cost centre may be an institution (for example, the Open University), part of an institution (eg the Centre for Modern Languages), a piece of equipment (eg the reprographics machine in the Centre for Modern Languages) or a person (the vice-chancellor).

The *total cost* is the sum of all the costs attributed to the cost unit or cost centre under consideration. For example, it might be the total cost of the Open University, the Centre of Modern Languages, or the *Introduction to French* course (all cost centres), or a graduate in modern languages (a cost unit).

4.2 Direct costs, indirect costs, and overheads

When considering the cost of producing products and services, some costs can usually be identified with a particular product or service, as distinct from other products and services. For example, my *Introduction to French* course uses interactive CD-ROM to teach basic grammar. The actual CD-ROM has been specially designed and produced for this course, thus the cost of designing, producing and distributing the CD-ROM to students is directly related to the course. In respect of the cost of this course, such costs are called *direct costs*.

Direct costs are made up of a number of elements.

- Direct materials are the raw materials or components that become part of the finished goods, or are used in the delivery of or supplied with and can be attributed to a particular product or service. This includes material wasted during the manufacturing process, as well as the costs of packaging etc.

- Direct labour is the cost of work done by people where that work can be attributed to a particular product or service.
- Direct expenses are items such as subcontracted work or special tools or equipment associated with a particular product or service.

On the other hand, in my example, the equipment which the students use to play the CD-ROM in a tutorial is used by a number of students, studying various courses. The costs cannot be identified with a particular course. Therefore, the costs have to be shared across a number of courses. Costs that cannot be directly attributed to one product are often referred to as *indirect costs*. In accountancy this term is usually restricted to indirect production costs; economists may use it more loosely to cover the indirect costs of a product including the sales cost, production overhead costs, distribution costs and administrative overheads of production. Accountants in manufacturing and service industries usually use the term *overhead* here, to describe any cost other than a direct cost identified with producing a service or product. (There is scope for confusion because the term *overhead costs*, which is also used, technically applies only to the sum of indirect expenses, indirect labour cost and indirect material cost – all of these being production costs. The term *overhead* refers to selling and administrative costs as well as production overhead costs. To avoid confusion some writers refer to '*production* overhead costs' and 'overheads'.)

4.3 Fixed costs, variable costs and semi-variable costs

Institutions providing products or services respond to demand. As the volume of services or products supplied rises or falls, so the total cost of providing those services or products rises or falls. However, some costs tend to be unaffected by these increases or decreases in the level of activity. For example, a university only ever has one vice-chancellor. Changes in the level of activity will not affect the number of vice-chancellors it has. Costs that do not increase or decrease with changes in the level of activity are known as *fixed costs*. (Of course, in one sense, there is no such thing as a fixed cost. If the activity is closed down completely, the cost disappears.)

On the other hand, what appears to be a fixed cost in one circumstance is not a fixed cost in another. Major expansion or contraction may alter the situation. For example, the cost of the finance department may have been unchanged for years, even though there has been a gradual growth in the number of students enrolled on courses. In such circumstances it is possible to act as if the costs of the department are fixed. If, however, the college suddenly expanded in size, the number of staff in the finance department might have to be increased to cope with the increased number of financial transactions that need to be handled. Costs that seemed to be fixed for a certain range of activity (say, the financial transactions arising from a student population of from 11,000 to 13,000 students) suddenly become variable because student numbers have doubled. Such costs are *semi-variable costs*, reflecting the fact that they may vary with significant changes in the level of activity. The range of activity in which costs are unchanged is known as the *relevant range*.

Other costs will vary proportionately with a change in the level of activity. For example, every time a student is added to the roll, there is an additional student generating assignments that have to be marked and mailings that have to be sent out. The overall costs of marking assignments or sending out materials are directly affected by increases or decreases in the number of students enrolled. Such costs are called *variable costs*. In other words, every time one unit of output is added, the cost goes up by the cost of that unit. The cost of adding just one unit of output is called the *marginal cost*.

In point of fact, different costs are affected by different changes in the volumes of activities. Thus, while the costs of marking assignments may go up with every additional student enrolled, the costs of face-to-face teaching will only go up each time a threshold is crossed and an extra class has to be set up. If the average class size is 20, then it seems likely that the class size would just be increased if an additional five students enrolled; but if 15 more students enrolled, another class might be formed. On the other hand, an additional 5000 students might be enrolled before a new records clerk was needed. In practice what is treated as variable and what is treated as semi-variable costs may be a matter of expediency. The costs of administration might be treated as a semi-variable cost, only 'releasing' additional money each time a threshold had been passed. On the other hand, it might be too complicated to account separately for every threshold (of 20 students) that triggers the establishment of another tutorial group, and instead treat tutorial costs as if they were variable with the number of students enrolled.

It may help to see these concepts portrayed graphically. In the graphs that follow, the vertical or y-axis is a monetary value (£), and the horizontal or x-axis is a measure of volume of activity or output (in this case, number of enrolled students). Where there is no relationship between the increasing volume of activity (students enrolled and the costs of the operation), such that the costs are fixed relative to enrolments, the total cost will be shown as a flat line parallel with the x-axis (Figure 4.1). An example would be the cost of transmitting television programmes, which is unrelated to the number of viewers.

Graphical representation of variable costs will show the total costs of the organization rising as the number of students increases. For an organization where each enrolled student incurs a direct cost of £x spent on teaching, there is a linear growth in costs (Figure 4.2).

Of course, the total costs of an organization are made up of fixed, variable and semi-variable costs, and a graphical representation of this situation would show the fixed costs (possibly with quantum jumps in value as semi-variable cost thresholds were passed), plus, on top of the fixed costs, an increase in the total variable costs that has a direct linear relationship with the increase in student numbers (Figure 4.3).

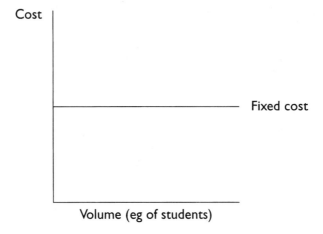

Figure 4.1   *Graphical representation of fixed costs*

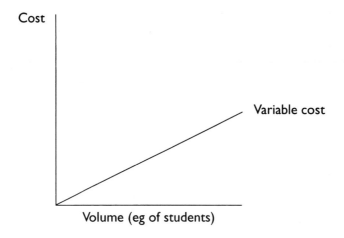

Figure 4.2   *Graphical representation of variable costs, where the relationship between cost and volume is linear*

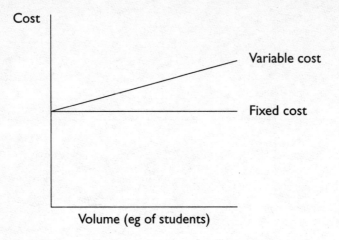

Figure 4.3   *Graphical representation of fixed and variable costs*

Example 4.1 provides a fictional scenario in which to explore these concepts.

Example 4.1: Fixed, variable and semi-variable costs

Open Training is a small training organization teaching computing skills. In 1995 it had a director of training, an administrative secretary and five trainers, and used hired accommodation comprising five teaching rooms and an administrative/social area. There were 50 students grouped in classes of ten. Each student is provided with books and materials worth £720. Open Training provides each pair of students with a workstation so there were 25 student workstations, each of which cost £2000.

Towards the end of the academic year, the director decided that she wanted to expand and increased the class size to 12 (ten additional students in all). The net additional costs are therefore:

- a non-recurrent £10,000 to provide five more workstations. (This is a non-recurrent cost (since the workstations will last for several years) that is variable with each pair of students. It can be regarded as a semi-variable cost.);
- an additional recurrent variable cost of £7200 for the materials provided for each student.

During 1996 the director decided to expand more significantly to meet the demand for Open Training's courses. Another 30 students are to be taken on. This would add six students to each group, and the director decided that this would be too much, since group size would then be 18. Accordingly, she decided to reduce the group sizes to ten students again by creating four more groups. The additional costs of this change are:

- a non-recurrent cost of £30,000 for the additional workstations – treated as a semi-variable cost;
- an additional £21,600 for materials – which is a variable cost;
- four additional trainers, also treated as a semi-variable cost;
- the additional costs of hiring four more training rooms – again, an increase in semi-variable costs.

Table 4.1 identifies the fixed, variable, and semi-variable costs involved, and the factors pushing up costs. This is a very simplified example, and in real life the costs would be driven by a wider and more complex set of cost drivers.

Examination of Table 4.1 shows that:

- certain items are *fixed costs* irrespective of the volume of activity (for example, the director). Her administrative secretary, and the administrative offices, are shown as fixed, indicating that neither of the expansion plans takes these costs outside of their relevant range. Obviously, if the number of administrative transactions increased, there would be a need for more staff, and this might in turn trigger a need for more space.
- some items of expenditure do not change between the base scenario and the modest growth scenario: for example, there is no need to increase the number of trainers or teaching rooms. However, significant expansion leads to a need for more trainers and more teaching space. These are *semi-variable costs*.
- some items of expenditure increase in direct proportion to the number of learners. This is true of the workstations and the materials. The materials, which are given to the students to keep, are a recurrent *variable cost*. The workstations, used by pairs of students, are retained by the institution for use with the next batch of students. Once bought they are available for future students to use. They are a capital *semi-variable cost*.

4.4 Cost drivers

A cost driver is anything that, following a change in its volume, causes the overall cost to change. In Example 4.1 the costs are being driven up (in this case, it is *up*, but it could equally well be *down*) by various factors.

- In the case of the materials, these are given to each student or trainee. Therefore the total expenditure (total cost) on materials depends on the number of *students/trainees* enrolled (ie in respect of materials, the *cost driver* is the number of students or trainees enrolled in the system).
- In the case of the workstations, the driver is the number of *pairs of students* at any one time.
- Each group needs both a classroom and a trainer. Thus the number of *groups* is yet another cost driver.

Table 4.1 Expansion of a training system

Item	Unit cost	Nature of cost and cost driver	Base scenario Vol.	£	Modest growth Vol.	£	Large growth Vol.	£
Staff								
Director	40,000	Fixed	1	40,000	1	40,000	1	40,000
Admin/secretary	20,000	Semi-variable, driven by the number of administrative transactions	1	20,000	1	20,000	1	20,000
Trainers	25,000	Variable (groups)	5	125,000	5	125,000	9	225,000
Accommodation								
Teaching	4,000	Variable (groups)	5	20,000	5	20,000	9	36,000
Offices	20,000	Fixed (but variable in the long term with staffing)		20,000		20,000		20,000
Equipment								
Workstations	2,000	Variable (student pairs)	25	50,000	30	60,000	45	90,000
Stocks								
Materials	720	Variable (students)	50	36,000	60	43,200	90	64,800
TOTAL				311,000		328,200		495,800
Net increase						17,200		167,600

Correctly defining what is driving the costs is crucial to costing expansion (or contraction).

4.5 Variable costs, linearity and economies of scale

Variable costs go up or down with each increase or decrease in the number of *cost units* of the cost driver involved. In Table 4.1, every time another trainee is enrolled the total cost goes up by one trainee cost unit or £720. If there are two trainees, the cost goes up by twice this amount; if three, by three times and so on. Where costs vary directly up or down with changes in the level of activity, the relationship is a *linear* one (ie, it goes up or down at a constant rate) (see Figure 4.2).

However, variable costs may not actually be linear. Very often, the rate of increase in cost decreases as the volume of activity rises. This is because what is apparently a direct cost actually hides a mix of fixed and variable costs. Take the cost of print: when books are printed the actual cost of the book is made up of direct materials cost (eg paper), which is variable with the number of books, and direct labour costs, some of which may be spent setting up the machines to print the book, and others running the machines during printing. Obviously, the set-up time bears no relationship to the number of copies printed, while the running time does have such a relationship. As a result, other things being equal, the unit cost of a book will tend to be higher where small numbers of books are printed, and lower where large numbers are printed. This means that the average cost of producing a book falls as the number of books produced rises. In other words, there are *economies of scale*. Economies of scale occur wherever the unit cost of production of goods or services does not rise in direct proportion to the increase in output of the goods or services. A graphical representation of such a situation might show the total cost curve beginning to flatten off as economies of scale are achieved (Figure 4.4).

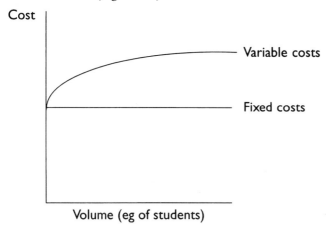

Figure 4.4   *Variable costs taking account of economies of scale (one of many possibilities)*

Example 4.1 treated the cost of the materials given to the students as linear. This would be acceptable when calculating the cost of the increase from 50 to 90 trainees, but it is likely that very large-scale expansion would trigger economies of scale in printing. The existence of economies of scale is widespread and is one of the reasons why assuming linearity in variable costs can lead to very considerable inefficiencies (in the sense that more money than is needed is allocated to fund an increase in the level of activities).

4.6 Committed and managed costs

Fixed costs are often divided into committed or managed costs. *Committed costs* are those which cannot be eliminated or cut back without a major effect on the enterprise's objectives or profits. Such costs remain constant even if the operation is reduced. In Example 4.1 the amount of accommodation used had to be increased. Once this had been done, the cost is committed – either through building additional accommodation or by having rented it on a lease that might be difficult to cancel. In either case, it can prove difficult to get rid of the accommodation once acquired.

On the other hand, there are costs which can be reduced fairly easily without any immediate major disruption to the objectives or profits of the organization. These are *managed costs*. In the short term, advertising and marketing costs, staff training costs, minor works expenditure etc can be reduced easily. Of course, in the longer term, their reduction would be very short-sighted since markets may be eroded, staff fail to develop, and buildings and equipment deteriorate.

4.7 Summary

Most of the concepts needed for costing a project have now been introduced. Chapter 2 introduced the basic four categories into which cost accountants divide expenditure. These are human resource or staffing costs, premises and accommodation costs, equipment and furniture costs, and the costs of stocks, supplies, consumables and expenses.

Costs arise from activities. Budgeting is the process of setting aside money to pay for activities. A *budget* is a plan, largely though not exclusively formulated in financial terms. Some items of expenditure will recur from year to year. These are *recurrent* costs. Others are met in a particular year and are unlikely to recur in the next year. These are *non-recurrent* costs. It is obviously important to know whether a particular cost will recur or not. Something that has a useful life of more than one year is a *capital* item. All other costs are *revenue* costs. While revenue costs can be either recurrent or non-recurrent, capital costs, by their very nature, are non-recurrent. However, capital goods will eventually wear out and have to be replaced.

As Section 4.1 made clear, costing is normally undertaken to determine the cost of outputs (cost units) or of cost centres. It is very important to be quite clear what it is one is costing. Budgets are usually drawn up on the basis of cost centres – a particular institution, department, person or machine. Money is spent on things or activities which are measured in cost units. The cost of one such measured cost unit is referred to as the unit cost of that item or activity.

In general, capital costs are committed costs. Recurrent revenue costs may be more or less committed, or more or less managed. The degree to which they are committed or managed depends on how easy it is to get out of the commitment. For example, with human resources one is more committed to permanent, core staff than one is to casual, peripheral staff. Overall, the more the costs are managed, the greater the *flexibility* and the greater the cost of management.

Any activity will involve both direct and indirect costs. Direct costs are variable with increases or decreases in the volume of output. Indirect costs are either fixed or semi-variable in their behaviour. Identifying what drives costs up or down (the cost driver) is crucial to the analysis of costs.

Chapter 5

Volume and its relationship with fixed and variable costs

This chapter:

- explores the impact of volume on fixed, variable and total costs (Section 5.1);
- introduces the concept of average costs (Section 5.2);
- looks at the behaviour of average costs (Section 5.3);
- explores the concept of marginal cost (Section 5.4);
- explores the concept of break-even (Section 5.5).

5.1 The impact of volume on fixed, variable and total costs

Fixed costs are costs which do not vary with any change in the level of activity or output. Variable costs do change. These costs can be plotted on a graph, as seen in Figures 4.1 (fixed costs) and 4.2 (variable costs). Some costs remain stable for a range in the volume of activities only but once the level of activity exceeds a threshold, they go up in steps. Such costs are semi-variable. Example 5.1 brings out the fixed, variable and semi-variable costs of the operation.

Example 5.1 Fixed, semi-variable and variable costs with changes of volume

The Forest College offers a range of courses to gardeners and estate workers. The course on *Garden Design* provides each student with course books and stationery (value £23). Each student also does four assignments, for which their tutor is paid £15 each. There are postage and packing costs of £5.70/student.

The college has a small administrative staff and for the purposes of calculating fees, their salaries and associated costs, including expenses, are shared equally between the 23 courses currently offered by the college. Each course is charged £6120. In addition, courses are charged accommodation and utilities costs (£1970). The college also invested £100,000 in the development of the course. In order to recoup this development cost the college, assuming that the course will have a five-year life, 'charges' the course a 'development costs recovery tax' of £20,000 each year.

The college keeps records on its students, and corresponds with them on administrative and other matters. The cost of the student services division is in part charged out directly to courses as a per capita student charge for postage and telephone (£11 per student) and partly apportioned to courses on the basis of a charge for overheads of £2500 towards the costs of clerical staffing and associated expenses for each 500 students or part thereof enrolled on the course.

The course currently has 837 students on it, but it is expected that demand will grow to around 1400–1700 next year. The course director has been asked to prepare a budget for the course, based on current student numbers, and assuming growth to 1000, 1350 and 1700 students.

Table 5.1 shows the budget prepared by the course director. It identifies costs under the headings of fixed, semi-variable and variable.

If this increase in cost is plotted graphically, instead of the totally 'flat' fixed cost shown in Figure 4.1, there would be a series of step increases in cost corresponding to the increases in semi-variable costs; and on top of this, a linear increase corresponding to increases in the number of students. This stepped increase in fixed costs arises because of the presence of semi-variable costs. In our example courses are charged a 'tax' of £2500 for every 500 students or part thereof enrolled on that course, as shown in Table 5.2.

In calculating the total costs of a project, allowance needs to be made for the existence of semi-variable costs. The example given above is simplistic. First, a number of semi-variable costs may be involved – not just one – and each of these might have different relevant ranges. Second, while there are cases where increases in semi-variable costs are triggered regularly as volume rises (as happens, for example, in all cases where human resources are tied to a staff:student ratio), it is more likely that step-increases in cost are triggered at irregular intervals.

Table 5.1 *Expansion of the Garden Design course*

Item	Unit cost	Student numbers 837	1000	1350	1700
Variable					
Course materials	23.00	19,251.00	23,000.00	31,050.00	39,100.00
Assignments	60.00	50,220.00	60,000.00	81,000.00	102,000.00
Postage and packing (materials/ assignments)	5.70	4,770.90	5,700.00	7,695.00	9,690.00
Student services per capita charge	11.00	9,207.00	11,000.00	14,850.00	18,700.00
Sub-total	**99.70**	**83,448.90**	**99,700.00**	**134,595.00**	**169,490.00**
Semi-variable					
Student services staffing costs charge		5,000.00	5,000.00	7,500.00	10,000.00
Sub-total		**5,000.00**	**5,000.00**	**7,500.00**	**10,000.00**
Fixed costs					
Recovery tax (recovers development costs)		20,000.00	20,000.00	20,000.00	20,000.00
Central administrative staffing/expenses		6,120.00	6,120.00	6,120.00	6,120.00
Accommodation and utilities		1,970.00	1,970.00	1,970.00	1,970.00
Sub-total		**28,090.00**	**28,090.00**	**28,090.00**	**28,090.00**
TOTAL		**116,538.90**	**132,790.00**	**170,185.00**	**207,580.00**

Table 5.2 *Semi-variable costs within Example 5.1*

Range in number of students	'Tax' charged
1 to 500	£2,500
501 to 1,000	£5,000
1,001 to 1,500	£7,500
1,501 to 2,000	£10,000
etc	etc

5.2 Average cost

The total cost (TC) can be expressed as being equal to the sum of the fixed costs (F) (including the semi-fixed costs related to the particular level of activity occurring) plus the variable cost per unit (V) times the number of units (N) (Equation 5.1):

$$TC = F + VN \qquad\qquad \text{[Eq. 5.1]}$$

Another important concept can now be introduced, that of *average cost*. The average cost is derived by dividing the total cost by the number of units. Equation 5.2 shows this, where:

$$AC = TC/N \qquad\qquad \text{[Eq. 5.2]}$$

where

AC = average cost per unit
TC = total cost
N   = number of units

Alternatively, using Equation 5.1, the average cost can be expressed in terms of the fixed and variable costs (Equation 5.3):

$$AC = V + (FC/N) \qquad\qquad \text{[Eq. 5.3]}$$

where

AC = average cost per unit
V   = variable cost per unit
FC = fixed cost (including for these purposes both the true fixed costs and the semi-variable costs)
N   = number of units

Return to the case of the Forest College in the previous section. Table 5.1 shows the total cost involved. By applying Equation 5.2, the average cost per student is derived by dividing the total cost by the number of students (Table 5.3).

Table 5.3 *Average costs*

Student numbers	837	1000	1350	1700
Total costs	116,538.90	132,790.00	170,185.00	207,580.00
Average cost per student	139.23	132.79	126.06	122.11

It is easy to check that Equation 5.2 gives the same result. From Table 5.1, the variable cost per group-year is £99.70. Taking as an example the situation where there are 1350 students, the total fixed + semi-variable costs involved is £35,590 (Table 5.1). Applying Equation 5.3 gives:

$$\begin{aligned} AC &= V + (FC/N) \qquad\qquad\qquad\qquad\qquad \text{[Eq. 5.3]} \\ &= 99.70 + (35{,}590 \div 1350) \\ &= 99.70 + 26.36 \\ &= 126.06 \end{aligned}$$

5.3 The behaviour of average costs

As a general rule, the fixed costs of distance education systems are high when compared to traditional education, but the variable costs per student are low. The result is that, when plotted on a graph, the average cost per student falls as student numbers increase (Figure 5.1). However, whereas the rate of decline in average costs is relatively large to begin with, it quickly falls off.

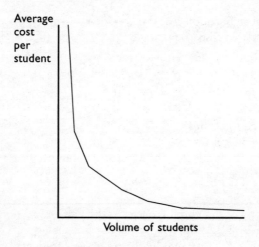

Figure 5.1 *Graph plotting average costs*

The behaviour of the average cost curve shown in Figure 5.1 is typical of average costs in general, and illustrates the fact that the most significant economies of scale are reaped in the early stages of expansion.

The overall effect of changes in the level of activity on fixed and variable costs is shown in Figure 5.2.

C		ACTIVITY INCREASES	ACTIVITY DECREASES
O	**Fixed costs**		
S	• in total	unchanged	unchanged
	• per unit	decrease	increase
T			
S	**Variable costs**		
	• in total	increase	decrease
	• per unit	unchanged	unchanged

Figure 5.2   *Effect of changes of activity on fixed and variable costs*

5.4 Marginal costs

The *marginal cost* of a product or service is the additional cost incurred in producing one more unit of the product or service. The marginal cost is often equated with the direct cost. For an example, return to Table 5.1 and consider the marginal cost of adding one student (say, increasing the number of trainees in a group from 837 to 838). In this particular example, the answer would be the cost of the materials given to the student and any other direct costs. This is £99.70. On this basis, the *incremental* cost (ie the additional cost of adding several students – say, eight) would be £797.60. The actual value of the marginal cost may vary. For example, given the way in which the 'tax' works in Example 5.1, the marginal cost of moving from 1000 to 1001 students would be £2599.70.

The concept of marginal cost is very useful when considering small expansions. However, at some point additional semi-variable indirect or overhead costs are likely to be required (in the above example, additional administrative support), and for this reason the concept of marginal costing is irrelevant in the case of large-scale expansion.

The relationship between total cost, average cost and marginal cost, is shown in the (simple) example in Table 5.4.

5.5 Break-even

As noted, the costs of an activity may be made up of both fixed and variable costs. Later on, in Chapter 11, it will become clear that each media and each technology has a different cost structure – that is, the relative balance of fixed and variable costs is different. One medium may have a high fixed cost, while another may have a low fixed cost; on the other hand, the first medium may have a high variable cost per unit of output, while the other may have a low variable cost, or even none at all.

Table 5.4 *Relationship between total, average and marginal costs*

Number of students	Total cost (£)	Average cost (£)	Marginal cost (£)
1	100	100.00	
2	190	95.00	90
3	270	90.00	80
4	370	92.50	100
5	460	92.00	90
6	550	91.67	90
7	670	95.71	120
8	770	96.25	100
9	850	94.44	80

Example 5.2: Comparative costs to show break-even point between broadcast transmission and video-cassette distribution

Medic Update is a programme that aims to keep medical practitioners up to date with developments in medicine and treatment. Much of the material is suitable for video. Transmission of a single 30-minute programme via satellite to practitioners in remote communities costs $427. Using E-180 cassettes, it is possible to copy six programmes on to a video-cassette, and send copies to the practitioners. The cost of buying a cassette ($6.99), copying the programme ($1.23), packaging it ($0.78) and sending it to the practitioner by courier service ($3.80) comes to $12.80. Each video-cassette contains material equivalent to transmitting six programmes at a total cost of $2562. The company wishes to know the number of practitioners to which it can send video-cassettes before it becomes cheaper to transmit the programmes and rely on the practitioners to record them off-air.

In Example 5.2 the comparison is between the cost of satellite transmission, which is a fixed cost in relation to the number of learners covered, and the variable cost of sending video-cassettes to each learner. The fixed cost is $2562; the variable cost per learner is $12.80. The number of practitioners to which it can send video-cassettes before it becomes cheaper to transmit the programmes is obtained by dividing the cost of transmission by the cost of sending out a video-cassette. This gives a break-even point at which the cost of the two options is the same. If there are less than 200 learners, it is cheaper to send out video-cassettes; if there are more than 200 learners, it is cheaper to transmit the programmes by satellite.

One can generalize this result by using the formula:

$$B = F \div V \qquad \text{[Eq. 5.4]}$$
$$= 2562 \div 12.80$$
$$= 200.16$$

where

B = the break-even point (in this case the break-even number of learners)
F = the fixed cost of transmitting the programmes
V = the variable cost of sending a video-cassette to each learner

One can also represent this situation graphically, as in Figure 5.3.

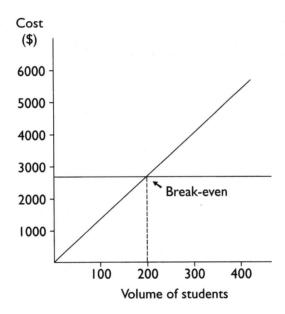

Figure 5.3   *Comparative costs to show break-even point between broadcast transmission and video-cassette distribution (based on Example 5.2)*

Suppose, however, that both options involve fixed and variable costs. Example 5.3 provides such an example.

Example 5.3: Comparative costs to show break-even point between traditional and open learning courses

Stonehill College of Advanced Technology teaches a course on the psychology of paranormal experiences using traditional means. The fixed costs of putting on this course for 20 learners is £720, with a variable cost of £1492 per learner. The college has decided that it will expand the course to 48 students to meet demand, but it is reluctant to expand staffing levels and provide more accommodation to teach the course using traditional means. By utilizing open learning approaches, it can bring down the variable cost of teaching the course to £329. However, this will involve an investment in the development of open learning materials of £37,878. In addition to these considerations, there is a political value in reducing the per capita cost of teaching. The principal of the college has asked the course chair how many students are needed to break-even such that the per student cost of teaching is less by open learning means than by traditional means.

The break-even point is calculated using the Equation 5.5:

$$B = \frac{F_1 - F_2}{V_2 - V_1} \qquad \text{[Eq. 5.5]}$$

where

B = the break-even point (in this case, the number of students enrolled)
F_1 = the fixed cost of teaching the course by open learning means
F_2 = the fixed cost of teaching the course by traditional means
V_1 = the variable cost of teaching by open learning means
V_2 = the variable cost of teaching the course by traditional means

such that:

$$
\begin{aligned}
B &= (F_1 - F_2) \div (V_2 - V_1) \\
&= (37878 - 720) \div (1492 - 329) \\
&= 31.95
\end{aligned}
$$

In other words, the college needs to increase its enrolment from the present 20 students to 32 students to pass the 'break-even' point at which teaching by open learning methods will prove to be cheaper than traditional methods.

5.6 Conclusion

This chapter, like the previous one, has introduced some key concepts which form the basis for costing and for analysing the behaviour of costs, including the average cost curve, which plots the average cost per student against the number of students in the system. As Figure 5.1 shows, in distance education systems this curve tends to fall steeply with early increases in student numbers, before flattening out. When considering figures giving the average cost per student in any open or distance learning system, it is always worth asking where the institution is on the average cost curve. Is it high up on the curve, able to achieve considerable additional economies of scale with expansion? Or have most of the economies of scale already been reaped?

Chapter 6

The treatment of capital costs

Capital expenditure, as noted in Section 2.3, is expenditure incurred on items that, once bought, provide benefits that last beyond the accounting year within which they were bought. The main items of capital expenditure are buildings, furniture and equipment. Very small pieces of equipment with a useful life of years – for example, a stapler or a hole-punch – cost so little that they are conventionally treated as consumables, but in general items that have an expected lifetime of more than one year are treated as capital costs; those with an expected lifetime (ie period of use) of less than one year are treated as recurrent costs.

Suppose a government minister is wondering whether to put money into an expansion of traditional education or into distance learning. While a decision to expand traditional education will require more classrooms, the major cost will be the recurrent costs of paying the salaries of additional teachers. Opting for a distance education ETV (Educational Television) based solution is likely to incur less recurrent costs but significant capital costs (to build studios and print shops, buy in printing and studio equipment and pay for the development of learning materials). Buildings generally have a useful life of many years (often taken to be 50 years), while equipment and furniture have a more limited life (audio-visual and computing equipment may last 3–4 years; furniture, 10–15 years). Given the different cost ingredients involved, how is the minister to form a judgement about the relative benefits of opting for one kind of solution as opposed to another? Some common measure of the cost of capital is needed to enable decision makers to compare the options available.

The basic approach to this problem is to spread the cost of capital goods over their lifetime. The cost of capital may be simply *depreciated*, or it may *annualized*, which involves taking account of the opportunity cost of using the capital, as well as its annual depreciated value. In general, economists prefer to annualize capital costs, although there are arguments against this course of action in the case of public expenditure decisions.

6.1 Depreciation

Depreciation is the technical term given to the monetary value of the wearing out or loss of value of capital goods arising from use, the passage of time and technological or market obsolescence. For example, suppose I bought my computer three years ago for £2000 and decided that it would have a useful life of four years. The annual depreciated cost of the computer is £500. This value is obtained by dividing the cost of the computer by the expected number of years of useful life. After three years, the total depreciation (loss of value) is £500 × 3 − £1500. Subtracting the total depreciation to date from the original historical cost or estimated historical value of the capital good gives me the *written down value* (also called the *net book value*) of the item in a particular year. In this case the written down value is £2000 − £1500 = £500. The written down value is the current value of capital items as reflected in a register of fixed assets.

Depreciation allows comparison of like with like. As an example, consider the comparison of the capital costs of expanding a traditional educational programme with the costs of setting up a distance learning programme. Assume that the traditional programme requires a new building costing £800,000, whereas the distance programme requires new buildings costing £500,000; audio–visual production equipment costing £600,000; desk top publishing equipment costing £60,000 and printing equipment costing £120,000. Table 6.1 shows how these two systems might be compared using the expected life of the buildings and equipment shown in column three of the table. The actual capital cost of setting the distance programme is significantly greater than that of the traditional programme (1.6 times as great), but the annual depreciated cost of the distance programme is significantly greater (8.48 times as much) because so much of the equipment has to be replaced regularly.

6.2 Social discount rate

The social discount rate acts in much the same way as *opportunity cost* in private enterprise. An opportunity cost is the value of that which must be given up to acquire or achieve something. For example, if a firm buys a replacement piece of equipment today out of its undistributed profits, in the expectation that it will use only 70 per cent of the power consumed by the previous equipment, the cost of the machinery is not just the outlay on its purchase (say £100,000) but also what could have been earned or saved by putting the money to another

Table 6.1 *Example of depreciation of capital*

Equipment	Actual cost (£)	Years of life (years)	Annual depreciated cost (£)
Traditional approach			
Buildings	800,000	50	16,000
Total	800,000		16,000
Distance learning approach			
Buildings	500,000	50	10,000
Audio-visual production equipment	600,000	7	85,714
Desk top publishing equipment	60,000	3	20,000
Printing equipment	120,000	6	20,000
Total	1,280,000		135,714

use. The firm might have put the money out on loan and earned interest on it (of, say, 5 per cent per annum). Or it might have had an overdraft costing 10 per cent per annum, which it could have paid off. In this latter case, if the money had been used to pay off the overdraft, the saving would have been £10,000 per year. The saving on power consumption would need to be greater than £10,000 per year to make the investment in new equipment a better investment than elimination of the overdraft.

Societies do not operate wholly like firms, but many economists would argue that 'application of the social discount rate reflects a value judgement concerning the cost to society of withdrawing resources from consumption now in order to have more consumption later' (Jamison *et al.*, 1978: 32). They therefore argue that the treatment of capital costs outlined in Section 6.1 is insufficient. There is a cost (interest charge) involved in having capital tied up in a project. Therefore account must be taken of:

> the foregone income on such an investment that could have been realized had the resources been invested... Because of the foregone opportunities represented by the sunken investment of the undepreciated portion of the facility, we calculate the cost to us of that investment of that amount. Accordingly, the second part of the annual cost of a facility is determined by applying a rate of interest to the undepreciated portion of the facility – that is, the value of the facility that remains after taking account of its past depreciation (Levin, 1983: 68–9).

This is known as the *opportunity cost* of capital. Levin (1983: 69) summarizes the approach to determining the annual value of capital goods as follows.

1. Determine the replacement value of the facility.
2. Determine the life of the facility.
3. Divide the replacement value by the number of years of life to obtain the cost of depreciation for each year of use.
4. Multiply the undepreciated portion by an appropriate interest rate to obtain the opportunity cost of having resources invested in the undepreciated portion of the facility.
5. Add the annual cost of depreciation and the annual interest forgone on the remaining investment to obtain the annual cost.

6.3 Annualization factor

The approach in Section 6.2, while valid and used in businesses to estimate the annual cost of facilities and equipment, suffers from the serious problem that the cost estimate depends crucially on the age of the facilities (Levin, 1983: 69). This is because the opportunity cost will be higher, the greater the undepreciated portion of their value outstanding. However, the value of the services received does not depend upon the age of the buildings and equipment used, and therefore may not differ substantially from one year to another. Therefore, it is better to 'annualize' costs by estimating an average of the combination of depreciation and interest on the undepreciated portion over the life of the facility. The formula most often used to take account of both the cost of depreciation and the opportunity cost of interest forgone is the formula for calculating the annualization factor (Equation 6.1):

$$a(r,n) = \frac{r(1+r)^n}{(1+r)^n - 1} \qquad \text{[Eq. 6.1]}$$

where $a(r,n)$ is the annualization factor, n is the life of the capital equipment, and r is the prevailing rate of interest. Returning to my computer, the annualized cost of a computer with a four-year life that I bought for £2000 in conditions where I can get 4 per cent for my money is:

$$a(r,n) = \frac{r(1+r)^n}{(1+r)^n - 1} \times £2000$$

$$= \frac{0.04(1+0.04)^4}{(1+0.04)^4 - 1} \times £2000$$

$$= \frac{0.04\,(1.1699)}{1.1699 - 1} \times £2000$$

$$= \frac{0.046796}{0.1699} \times £2000$$

$$= £550.86$$

Thus, the total future value of the present decision to invest £2000 in a computer is £550.86 per year over four years, or £2,203.44.

To avoid tediously having to calculate this value every time, the value of the annualization factor can be derived from annualization tables (Table 6.2).

Table 6.2   *Values of the annualization factor* a(r,n)

Life of capital equipment in years (n)	Interest rate (r)				
	0%	**5%**	**7.5%**	**10%**	**15%**
1	1.000	1.050	1.075	1.100	1.150
2	0.500	0.538	0.557	0.576	0.615
3	0.333	0.367	0.385	0.402	0.438
4	0.250	0.282	0.299	0.315	0.350
5	0.200	0.231	0.247	0.264	0.298
6	0.167	0.197	0.213	0.230	0.264
7	0.143	0.173	0.189	0.205	0.240
8	0.125	0.155	0.171	0.187	0.223
9	0.111	0.141	0.157	0.174	0.210
10	0.100	0.130	0.146	0.163	0.199
15	0.067	0.096	0.113	0.131	0.171
20	0.050	0.080	0.098	0.117	0.160
25	0.040	0.071	0.090	0.110	0.155
30	0.033	0.065	0.085	0.106	0.152
40	0.025	0.058	0.080	0.102	0.151
50	0.020	0.055	0.077	0.101	0.150

The figures in Table 6.1 can now be recast to take account not only of depreciation but also of the opportunity cost of capital (see Table 6.3). In Table 6.3, I have chosen an interest rate of 7.5 per cent. In general, the interest rates should reflect the likely rate available on the open market. In this example, the capital costs of the distance option are shown to be higher. However, it is possible that this higher capital cost may be offset by lower operating costs.

Table 6.3   *Example of annualization of capital where r = 7.5%*

Equipment	Cost (£)	Years of life (years)	Value of a(r,n)	Annualized cost (£)
Traditional approach				
Buildings	800,000	50	0.077	61,600
Total	800,000			61,600
Distance learning approach				
Buildings	500,000	50	0.077	38,500
Audio-visual production equipment	600,000	7	0.189	113,400
Desktop publishing equipment	60,000	3	0.385	23,100
Printing equipment	120,000	6	0.213	25,560
Total	1,280,000			200,560

Eicher (1980: 13) has argued that there are problems with annualizing capital costs.

1. The need to distinguish clearly between the cost of depreciation and the opportunity cost of capital. Obviously, Eicher says, it would be absurd to apply the total cost of a building to the first year of the project. To make a proper comparison of cost, the capital costs should be depreciated to compare the annual depreciated cost (as was done in Table 6.1). This has a practical benefit.
2. Second, it is by no means clear that the opportunity cost of capital expenditure should be taken into account. The use of interest rates to establish the opportunity costs of capital assumes that there is an alternative use to which the money can be put, but in point of fact public bodies funding educational projects rarely have a choice between buying buildings and equipment, and lending money to a bank to obtain interest on the investment. The decision to use interest rates does not rest on a sound theoretical basis for public finance decisions.

While I find Eicher's view convincing, the balance of opinion among economists favours the use of the annualization factor.

6.4 Investment in course materials

Just as the purchase of land, buildings and equipment is an investment for the future, so the development of course materials is an investment that pays off over the life of the course. It makes as little sense to charge the total cost of developing a course to the first year of the course as it does to charge the cost of a building to the first year of the project.

The costs of developing course materials can be discounted over the life of the course and, if desired, annualized. Consider, for example, a course where the development costs are spread over three financial periods (years 1 to 3 inclusive), as in Table 6.4; and the course is presented for four years (in years 3 to 6 inclusive). The actual cash outlay on developing the course is shown in line 1 of the table: the main development occurs in years 1 to 3 and costs £200,000. The depreciation of these costs presents some minor technical problems. With a straight purchase the investment would be depreciated from the date of purchase, but the course is, in fact, still being developed in the second and third years of the project. Since the costs of development are 'used' throughout the life of the course (years 3 to 6 inclusive), it seems appropriate to charge the depreciated amount to each year the course is offered to students. In this fictional example, however, there has been some minor redevelopment of the course in year 5 (costing £14,000), affecting the course's presentation in years 5 and 6, and so this sum too needs to be depreciated over the remaining life of the course. The depreciated value of the investment is therefore shown in line 2.

Line 3 of the table shows the annualized cost of the investment. Assuming an interest rate of 7.5 per cent, the annualization factor over four years is 0.299, and this has been applied to the original investment of £200,000; an annualization factor of 0.557 has been applied to the redevelopment costs. The total annualized value of the course's development is shown in line 4.

Table 6.4 *Fictional costs of developing and presenting a distance-taught course (£): depreciation and annualization of development costs*

	Year of project					
	1	2	3	4	5	6
1. **Cash flow**	38,000	146,000	16,000		14,000	
2. **Depreciated costs**			50,000	50,000	57,000	57,000
3. **Annualized cost**						
(a) original development			59,800	59,800	59,800	59,800
(b) redevelopment					7,798	7,798
4. **Total annualized cost**			59,800	59,800	67,598	67,598

Either the depreciated or the annualized costs of the course can then be set against student numbers to derive a capital cost per student. Table 6.5 takes the costs of the course and works out the average capital cost per student on the course, using both the depreciation method and the annualization method of dealing with course development costs. The average student costs are valid for the number of students shown in line 1 of the table. If the number of students rose or fell, the average cost per student would also rise or fall as the depreciated/annualized cost was spread over more or less students, and the example shows this. For the purposes of costing the course, the annualized or depreciated capital costs are treated as a fixed cost per year, to be spread over the number of students enrolled in that year.

Table 6.5   *Fictional costs of developing a distance-taught course (£): derivation of per capita student cost of capital*

	Year of presentation			
	3	**4**	**5**	**6**
1. Number of students	567	523	487	462
Depreciated cost method				
2. Depreciated costs	50,000	50,000	57,000	57,000
3. Depreciated cost per student	88.18	95.60	117.04	123.38
Annualized cost method				
6. Total annualized cost	59,800	59,800	67,598	67,598
7. Annualized cost per student	105.47	114.34	138.80	146.32

Two further points may be made: first, many institutions have a clear idea of how many years they will present a course when it is being developed, but often the life of a course is extended. Technically, the depreciated cost of capital should be written off over the expected life of the product, so that, in accounting terms, where the life is extended, then the course has no remaining depreciated value. This seems a perfectly sound approach.

Second, in a retrospective cost study, the full depreciated or annualized cost of the course over its presentation (£214,000 and £254,796 respectively), divided by the total student population over the life of the course (2039), gives an average capital cost per student per year of £104.95 (depreciation method) and £124.96 (annualization method).

6.5 Conclusion

In comparison with traditional forms of education where, over a given period of time, recurrent costs are high and capital costs are usually fairly low, distance education generally involves much higher levels of expenditure on buildings, equipment and the development of learning materials. This expenditure will benefit the institution for several, perhaps many years. When comparing the costs of traditional and open/distance learning systems, the capital costs in both systems must be treated in a manner that allows a fair comparison. The depreciation of capital costs (that is, the spreading of capital costs over the years during which an item of capital expenditure gives benefit) is a first and absolutely necessary step. But this alone is not necessarily enough. Any economic comparison will seek to take account of the social discount rate of capital, by using the annualization factor explained in Section 6.3. The annualization of capital costs is particularly important when trying to compare the future costs of different options as a precursor to making a decision on whether to address an education problem by using traditional, labour-intensive or non-traditional, capital-intensive methods.

Chapter 7

Overheads

Section 4.2 introduced the concepts of direct and indirect costs. While direct costs can be traced to individual products and services, this is not possible with indirect costs, often referred to as overheads. Yet overheads need to be taken into account in fixing the price of products and services. The attaching of overhead costs to products and services is thus a major challenge for cost accountants.

7.1 Direct and indirect costs and their relationship to products and services

Dealing with direct costs within the context of distance education is fairly straightforward. Many of the costs arising from the development, production, distribution and reception of learning materials, and from teaching students on courses, can easily be budgeted and accounted for against particular courses. So, for example, there may well be identifiable course budgets for items such as the following:

- production of printed materials;
- copyright clearances;
- graphic design and development of printed materials;
- editing of printed materials;
- television programmes associated with the course;
- audio-cassette production;
- audio-cassette copying;
- postage for course mailings;
- marking of assignments associated with the course;
- face-to-face tuition.

It is therefore relatively easy to identify the direct costs associated with the development, production and presentation of a course because these costs can readily be 'attached' to individual courses. The process of allocating costs that are readily identifiable as 'belonging' to a cost centre, product, or customer is called *cost allocation*. In saying that this is relatively straightforward, I do not want to suggest that it is without problems. As noted in Section 3.1, there are often difficulties in getting professional staff to allocate their time to particular projects. Without their cooperation it can be difficult to establish the direct labour cost of developing a course.

Other budgets and expenditure will be coded to activities that have a more tenuous relationship with particular products and services. The areas of expenditure where this is likely to be true would include, for example:

- the general management of a production department, and any associated expenses incurred by such management;
- the senior management of the institution;
- specialist functions such as planning, finance, personnel, estates and buildings management;
- any costs that cannot easily be charged out to products or services (for example, general water and waste disposal charges).

Many of these overhead costs are not in any way special to open, flexible and distance learning, and so this book does not consider the nature of these costs in detail. However, it is necessary to know how such costs may be 'attached' to products and services so that the 'full cost' of a particular product or service can be established. The way in which this problem is approached has been the subject of very considerable changes in recent years with the development of activity-based costing systems in place of traditional management accounting systems.

7.2 Traditional management accounting

Under traditional management accounting systems, the process of 'attaching' overhead costs to products or customer services is by *cost apportionment* and *cost absorption*. Cost apportionment involves the division of costs between two or more cost centres, products or customers in proportion to the estimated benefit received where direct measurement of the benefit is not possible or is not worth while. Cost absorption is the final step in this process, in which overhead costs are assigned to the products. Figure 7.1 illustrates the steps taken in the allocation and apportionment of costs.

The first step in the process illustrated in Figure 7.1 is to identify and allocate (process 1) the direct costs (Box A) to the product (Box E). This is relatively easy and will take care of many of the costs incurred in departments primarily responsible for production.

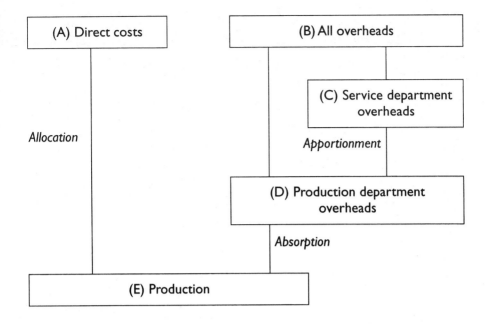

Figure 7.1   *Overhead apportionment and absorption*

This leaves the overheads to be dealt with (Box B). Some of these will be attributable to particular production departments (for example, depreciation of equipment used by the department). Others (such as personnel, finance etc) will be incurred by departments that provide internal services to production departments. The second step is therefore to divide overheads into two categories of production overheads and other, general, overheads.

The third step is to apportion the general overheads to production departments in some way that seems fair. There are a number of ways of doing this, and it may involve more than one step. For example, the costs of personnel administration may be allocated across all departments in proportion to the number of staff they have; and the cost of finance may be allocated across departments in proportion to the size of their budget or some other measure. Eventually, however, the point is reached at which all service department overheads have been apportioned to the production departments and become part of their overhead charge.

The fourth step is then to absorb all these overhead costs into the products. However general overheads were allocated to cost centres in the earlier steps, virtually all companies absorb the overheads of production departments to products on the basis of the proportion of total direct labour costs consumed by the product, although sometimes the calculation is performed on the proportion of direct material consumed by different products. Example 7.1 shows how this is done using direct labour costs as the basis of absorption.

Example 7.1: Absorption of overheads by conventional management accounting methods

A factory produces two products, A and B. The production run for each product is 100 units. Four direct labour hours are required to produce product A, whereas product B requires three direct labour hours. Both products are inspected. Each batch of 100 units of product A requires two inspection hours, and each batch of 100 units of product B, six inspection hours. The inspection overhead cost is £800 (or £100 per inspection hour). The direct labour cost per hour on both products is £150.

The direct labour costs of each product are:

Product A: 4 hours × £150 = £600 direct labour cost
Product B: 3 hours × £150 = £450 direct labour cost
Total direct labour cost: £ 1050

In a conventional costing system the overhead costs of inspection (£800) are likely to be apportioned in proportion to the cost of direct labour hours, so that the apportioned cost of inspection for these two products are likely to be:

Product A: £800 × 600/1050 = £457.14 ÷ 100 units = £4.57 per unit
Product B: £800 × 450/1050 = £342.86 ÷ 100 units = £3.43 per unit

7.3 Criticism of traditional management accounting

It is now widely recognized that the traditional management accounting approach fails to provide good costing information, and can, indeed, be positively misleading. The major factors affecting the reliability of traditional management accounting approaches to product costing include the following.

- For many products, direct costs (including the costs of direct labour) have become a small fraction of the total cost of producing and delivering the product or service, while overhead costs (the costs of design, development, marketing, selling, distribution and service) have become a more significant proportion of the total cost. Indeed, overheads are the major source of cost in most manufacturing companies.

- The use in traditional costing systems of direct labour to allocate overhead costs to cost centres and products (see Example 7.1) focuses attention on the costs of direct labour – and hides the fact that the vast majority of costs are in fact driven by other factors. In such a situation rational managers, asked to reduce their costs, will tend to focus on direct labour since it is this cost to which all overheads are 'attached'. This has the disbenefit that it moves attention away from the escalating costs of overheads. To avoid incurring direct labour costs (with all the attached overheads), there is a great temptation to subcontract work, because this is apparently cheaper. But in fact overhead costs tend to rise with increased subcontracting, because this imposes more demands on the purchasing department and on receiving and inspection departments (Johnson and Kaplan, 1987: 189).

- Overheads are themselves driven by management: for example, decisions to develop accounting systems, or decisions to have the grounds around a factory managed on environmentally friendly lines. They are often driven by factors that have nothing to do with the volume of production and services delivered. However, when in traditional costing systems overhead costs get lumped in as a direct labour variable cost, it is not surprising that there is a resulting failure to understand the true dynamics of the cost structure.

7.4 Activity-based costing

Whereas the underlying assumption of a conventional costing system is that products cause costs, an activity-based costing system assumes that cost objects create the demand for activities, which in turn cause costs. Figure 7.2 captures the relationship between activities, cost and cost objects.

Figure 7.2   *Assumption underpinning activity-based costing systems*

Cost objects are the reasons for performing activities. They include products, services and customers. Activities are the processes or procedures that cause work. Related activities are usually grouped in an activity centre. An activity centre is a cluster of activities – usually clustered by function or process. For example, in the UK Open University, many of the student advisory activities are clustered in an advisory section within regional offices of the University. Activity centres may be responsible for several activities.

Activities involved in administering a student's progress through the year might typically include the following:

- recording an application from a student on the computer system;
- changing a student's record;
- asking students about their choice of course;
- advising students about their choice of course;
- receiving students' course options;

- vetting students' course choice;
- enrolling students on a particular course;
- allocating students to tutors;
- informing students of their tutor's name;
- informing tutors of their students' names;
- timetabling a tutorial;
- booking a room for a tutorial;
- receiving queries about non-receipt of materials;
- following up queries on non-receipt of materials;
- receiving notification of the student's intention to withdraw from a course;
- following up on a student's withdrawal;
- actioning a fee refund to a student who has withdrawn;
- receiving notification of a student's change of address;
- actioning the change of address so as to change the student's record;
- organizing a special home examination for students unable to go to an examination centre;
- sending a letter or materials to a student or tutor.

In the absence of an activity-based costing system (and unlike activities such as marking an assignment or teaching a tutorial where the fees and expenses paid to a tutor accurately reflect the direct cost of the activity), none of these transactions is likely to have an accurate cost attached to it. Each will be treated as a broad student services overhead, divided across the number of students to give an overhead student services cost per student. The result is as follows.

- The institution has no knowledge of the unit cost of each type of transaction.
- The value that each transaction adds to the overall progress of each student cannot be computed.
- There is no way of judging where efforts should be concentrated to seek more efficient ways of carrying out the transactions.
- Transaction costs cannot be attached to individual students or to different kinds of students. Since students study courses within academic programmes that may have different requirements, it is likely that the cost per student on different academic programmes will vary. For example, teacher training programmes may require detailed vetting of an application including establishing that a student does not have a criminal record, while other programmes may not require such checks. Similarly, there may be particular classes of students who consume more or less resources. For example, disabled students may require detailed assessment of their needs and the provision of special services such as home examinations.
- There is no way of knowing what the effect any efforts made to reduce costs actually has.
- There is no way of knowing where savings can be made as a result of a fall in the number of students, or where additional provision needs to be made in response to growth.

In order to attach costs to cost objects, the activities must be costed. Figure 7.3 shows how this is done. The first step is to determine who is doing the work (academics, secretaries, editors, tutors, clerks) and how much of their time (in time-based systems) or how many units of input (in performance-based systems) goes into the activity. The costs of accommodation, depreciated cost of equipment and furnishing, supplies, expenses etc will also need to be assigned to the activity.

Figure 7.3   *Process in an activity-based costing system*

Each category of resource traced to an activity (eg the salary costs of processing applications, the depreciated cost of equipment) becomes a *cost element* in an *activity cost pool*. The activity cost pool constitutes the total cost associated with an activity. Activities may be performed at three levels.

1. At the level of each individual unit of product. An example would be the time spent assembling a home experiment kit. Determining the cost of unit activities accurately requires measurement of the inputs to the activity: for example, the time taken to pack the box and seal it, the cost of the packing materials etc.
2. At a level that benefits two or more products at the same time. Examples are the time spent copying cassettes using an audio tape copying machine.
3. At a level that benefits all units of a particular product. Examples are the recording of errors in texts, so that future editions of the text can be corrected, or clearing the copyrights for a course.

Hence different activity cost pools may have a different relationship to the products or services offered.

The second stage is to assign the costs of the activity to the cost objects. Each activity cost pool is traced to the cost object (eg customer) through an activity driver; this measures the demand for the activity instituted by the cost objects. Each activity has a *unique* activity driver that accurately measures the cost object's consumption of the activity: for example, the cost of advising students is traced to the volume of letters and telephone calls received in which students seek advice. Figure 7.4 shows the cost drivers likely to be involved in some of the activities listed above.

Example 7.2 is based on exactly the same scenario as that given in Example 7.1, but shows how inspection costs might be allocated in an activity-based costing system. Traditionally, as Example 7.1 shows, the costs of inspection would have been regarded as an overhead, and as such would have been absorbed into the product cost on the basis of the proportion of direct labour hours used in manufacturing each product. In an activity-based costing system one would seek to identify the real driver of the inspection activity.

Activity	Activity driver
Asking students about their choice of course	Number of forms generated and sent out
Advising students by telephone	Number of telephone enquiries received
Advising students by letter	Number of letters sent out
Receiving students' course options	Number of forms received
Vetting students' course choice	Number of forms to be vetted
Enrolling students on a particular course	Number of course choices to be keyed in
Allocating students to tutors	Number of students to be allocated
Informing students of their tutor's name	Number of letters to be sent out
Informing tutors of their students' names	Number of tutorial group lists to be produced and sent out

Figure 7.4 *Cost drivers in a distance learning system*

Example 7.2: Absorption of overheads by activity-based costing methods

A factory produces two products, A and B. The production run for each product is 100 units. Four direct labour hours are required to produce product A, whereas product B requires three direct labour hours. Both products are inspected. Each batch of 100 units of product A requires two inspection hours, and each batch of 100 units of product B, six inspection hours. The inspection overhead cost is £800 (or £100 per inspection hour). The direct labour cost per hour on both products is £150.

The direct labour costs of each product are:

Product A: 4 hours × £150 = £600 direct labour cost
Product B: 3 hours × £150 = £450 direct labour cost
Total direct labour cost: £ 1050

An activity-based costing system measures the cost of activities and attaches these to the products. On this basis, the allocated costs of inspection would be:

Product A: 2 inspection hours × £100 = £200 ÷ 100 units = £2.00 per unit
Product B: 6 inspection hours × £100 = £600 ÷ 100 units = £6.00 per unit

Comparison of Examples 7.1 and 7.2 show that the two approaches to costing can make a very considerable difference to the apparent cost of a product. The example, although very simplistic, usefully illustrates the principles involved.

There are always some activities that are not associated directly with products or customers: for example, the costs of maintaining the grounds around a college or the cost of providing security guards. However, security and grounds maintenance are proper cost pools in their own right, to which costs can be allocated. There is then a choice as to whether or not such costs should be assigned to products or customers. It is possible not to assign the cost of such activities to products – thus recognizing that assigning such costs to products and customers is fairly meaningless; or, alternatively, they can be assigned using some non-matching activity drivers. The costs of landscaping could, for example, be allocated evenly across each student. However, it is questionable whether this has any meaning.

7.5 Identification of cost objects

Some plants manufacture one product or a limited number of similar products where the costs of each of the products are the same. In such circumstances, it is possible to count the number of products coming out of the plant and then divide this into the total cost of running the plant over the period of the count. Such an approach to costing is called *backflush costing*. The Ford Motor Company's Rouge Plant, which in the 1920s produced the Model T, essentially used this kind of approach: it counted the number of cars coming off the assembly line over a given period of time, and then divided this figure into the total running costs of the plant for that period to give a cost per car.

Another example of this approach would be to count the number of graduates being produced each year by a single product distance teaching university such as the Universidad Nacional Pedagógica in Mexico (which only produces Bachelor of Education graduates), and divide the total costs of the institution by this number to obtain a cost per graduate. This assumes that the annual institutional costs are supporting an unchanging mix of first-, second-, third-, etc year students (ie there is no expansion or contraction going on). Interestingly, some of the early estimates of the cost per graduate at the UK Open University were derived using this kind of approach (see Section 13.1).

For most purposes, backflush costing is unrealistic because it only works where there is a single uniform product. Most manufacturing plants produce a range of products – sometimes many hundreds or thousands – as do educational institutions. What constitutes a graduate varies considerably from one course of study to another, both in terms of the length of time the graduates have studied and the demands that they have made on the facilities of an institution (eg varying use of laboratories, libraries, computing facilities, intensity of tuition etc) during their study. In a distance teaching institution, the products of the system may include, for example:

- the various technological products of the system (eg texts, videos, CAI software etc);
- courses;
- academic programmes related to awards (for example, programmes leading to a higher secondary school certificate, bachelor's degree in subject Y, master's degree in subject X);
- different types of students (secondary, undergraduate, postgraduate etc);
- services for students with different needs (eg students in prisons, students with disabilities);
- research reports;
- academic publications;
- consultancy reports.

Higher education institutions are particularly difficult to analyse because they may have multiple objectives and functions including teaching, research and community service. The latter may embrace a wide range of activities including extramural teaching, occupational services (careers advice, remedial training, on-the-job training), projects, counselling, research and development work for local industry and the provision of sports, catering and library services (see Crosson, 1983, for an exhaustive taxonomy of such services within the context of higher education in the United States). Deakin University, when it embarked on an activity costing exercise, identified three major segments in its activities: teaching, research, and professional and community services. Rumble (1986b:15), in the work that informed Deakin's definition of outputs, identified a simple taxonomy (by no means exhaustive) of outputs in a mixed-mode higher education institution (Figure 7.5). In such circumstances, there is a need to apportion costs adequately across the various outputs.

Use of such a taxonomy allows managers to identify more clearly the different segments of the business. Each segment has cost objects (products, services and customers) which result in activities that consume resources. Within each segment there may well be a hierarchy of cost objects for both products and customers (Figure 7.6). ,

At the bottom of the products hierarchy is the individual part or component, and the individual customer. Parts and components make up particular products. Within the teaching function, the product is normally a course, which is what is sold to a customer. Product families might then be all the courses that go to make up a particular academic programme (eg an MBA).

Services may be grouped into broad categories (those related to enrolment, assessment etc), and then progressively broken down into particular tasks that make up the overall service.

Customer costing will include all the costs of meeting the customer's needs, including the cost of products supplied to the customer and the cost of support activities provided to the customer. At the bottom of the customer hierarchy is the individual customer. Groups of customers may be identified. For example, institutions may use different modes to reach students including traditional, face-

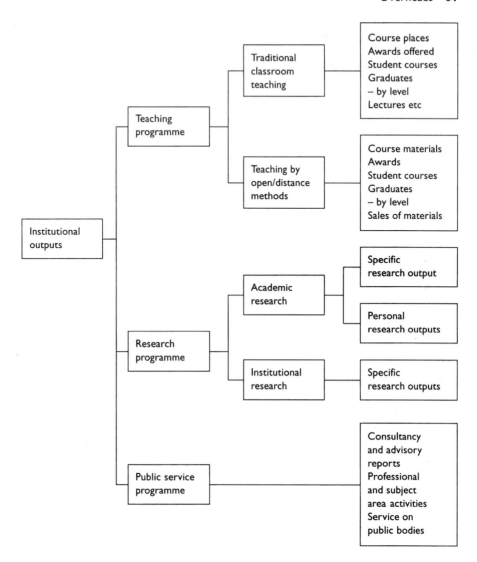

Figure 7.5 *Taxonomy of segments in higher education*
Source: Based on Rumble, 1986b:15

to-face methods of education; multi-media distance learning methods; and the newly emerging electronic delivery systems sometimes referred to as 'third generation distance education' (first generation being correspondence education and second generation being multi-media systems) (Nipper, 1989: 63). Other groups might include students with special needs and students in prisons. At the highest level, there may be different market segments (secondary, tertiary, undergraduate, postgraduate) and territories (students in different jurisdictions or regions).

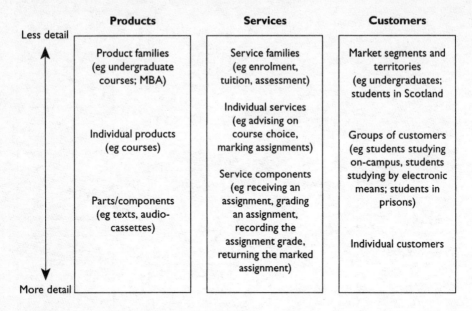

Figure 7.6 *Hierarchy of cost objects*

7.6 Conclusion

Earlier chapters in this book have tended to take a traditional approach to management accounting and the analysis of cost, not least because most of the literature on the costs and economics of open and distance learning is embedded in that framework.

One of the benefits of activity based costing is that it explicitly brings overhead costs under scrutiny. In traditional costing systems, there is a tendency to see overheads as divorced from the real work of the institution. Activity based costing makes it clear that overhead costs are the result of activities, some of which are related to the products, services and customers (the cost objects), and others of which (for example, grounds maintenance) are self-standing. In the process, the distinction between direct and indirect (overhead) costs becomes far less clear cut, requiring reassessment of the framework offered in Chapter 4, and in particular the often quoted statement that what distinguishes distance education from traditional education is the high level of fixed costs involved in such systems. The fact is that most of these costs are *not* fixed; they too are variable, driven by factors other than students. Seen in this light, the whole nature of the economics of distance and open learning becomes more complex. Further, with pressure to reduce costs, it becomes more urgent to see overheads not as indirect costs that are largely fixed, but as *burdens* that need to be decreased.

It is fairly easy to cut costs indiscriminately by shedding staff and activities. It is rather harder to do this sensibly. For example, in traditional cost systems, the cost of human resources is packaged into jobs or posts. Pressure to cut costs has therefore led to job shedding and 'down-sizing', with the result that, in general, fewer people do the same amount of work, working longer hours, under greater stress, with lower morale. Outsourcing and the employment of part timers and piece-workers (for example, part-time tutors and contract authors in the place of full-time teachers and academics) may be seen as a further solution to the reduction of costs, since it leads to a reduction in core staffing. But these decisions rarely take account of the additional costs incurred in hiring, contracting and managing contract labour. Indeed, traditional accounting systems do not identify these costs because they fail to pick up the costs of overhead activities. It is necessary to look at the activities and determine which ones add value, and which do not.

Activity-based costing systems provide help in identifying the relative value of the work being undertaken. The questions that need to be asked are these.

- Does the work (activity) add value for the customer?
- If not, why is it being done at all?
- If it is not adding value to the customer, what causes it to be done?
- Can it be eliminated?

Activity-based costing systems help managers to identify:

- activities that provide value for the customers (primary, value-adding activities): for example, delivering a tutorial;
- activities that are partially relevant to adding value for the customer (secondary, partially relevant activities): for example, travelling to a tutorial;
- activities that are non-value-adding (wholly irrelevant activities): for example, correcting a tutorial timetable that was issued with a mistake in it – after all, the customer would rather not pay for mistakes that should never have occurred.

This does not mean that all non-value-adding activity can be eliminated: some of it (for example, compliance with legislation) may be necessary. But the aim should be to seek ways that will eliminate as much of this activity as possible, and in particular all of that activity (checking, reworking etc) that arises from a failure to deliver quality first time.

A small example will perhaps suggest what might be done: when a student withdraws before having consumed the full range of services paid for, it seems reasonable to offer a refund. Such a practice is consistent with maintaining good relations with one's customers. From the point of view of the student, what is important is the receipt of a fee refund. Refund policies often say that a percentage of the fee will be refunded up to a certain date in the course. Where there is a staggered start to the courses on offer, with some courses starting in the first week of October, some the second and some the third, it would be possible to articulate the refund policy so that there is a refund either a set number of weeks after the start of the course (say six), or on a fixed date (say 1 December). The advantage of the fixed date over the variable date is that student services staff actioning refunds will have a single date to remember, and students will have a single date by which they will know they need to withdraw if they want a refund. The variable date causes much more work since it requires the start and refund dates of every course to be listed. For large numbers of courses, staff will have to refer to lists giving the refund dates of each course. These lists have to be prepared and distributed to staff and students may also need to be informed of the dates. Whereas a fixed date might operate from year to year, a variable start date is likely to have to be recalculated every year. None of this additional work actually adds value for the customer. The costs of this work are not identified in conventional accounts. The work also detracts from the more productive work that student services staff might be doing.

An activity-based costing system that allows for both the identification of the cost of work done (in this case, the refunding of fees) and the examination of the processes involved is more likely to enable managers to focus on the issues concerning costs than a conventional costing system.

Chapter 8

Attribution of costs to joint products

The previous chapter introduced activity based costing (Section 7.4) and the concept of cost objects (Section 7.5). Although a great deal of attention has been paid to those institutions that teach only by distance means, historically *dual-mode institutions* that teach by both traditional and distance means have been far more common than pure distance teaching institutions. Such institutions offer a choice of learning modes to their customers, and in the process have diversified to serve two, often quite distinct, markets – on-campus and off-campus students. Recently, however, faced by increasingly acute pressures to reduce their unit costs, they have seen the utilization of materials originally developed to teach distant students as a way of reducing their costs of teaching traditional campus-based students, by substituting resource-based learning (see Section 1.2) for face-to-face teaching – to the extent that, with the development of open and flexible learning, the distinction between traditional and distance forms of education is increasingly questionable (Rumble, 1994a: 15).

Figure 7.6 proposed a hierarchy of products. With the development of open and flexible learning on campus, learning materials (that is, products at the parts/component level) are being used to teach both students studying on campus within an open learning framework and those studying off campus at a distance. Here, the traditional and distance versions of the course are joint products developed using some common components. A joint product is one of two or more products which takes a single stream of inputs until a 'separation point' is reached, after which the products are acted on separately. Products are called joint products if they are of roughly equal significance (see Figure 8.1). If one of the joint products is of less significance than the others, it may be referred to as a by-product.

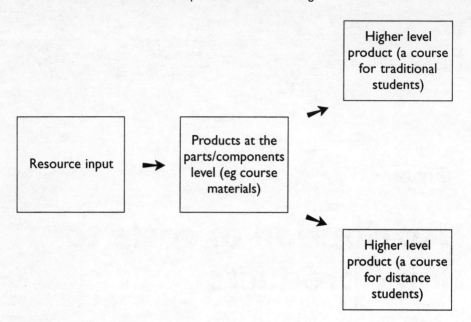

Figure 8.1 *Joint products*

How should the costs of the components be split between the joint products, for costing purposes? And how should pricing decisions reflect these costs? Although activity based costing strictly requires costs that are shared across more than one product to be apportioned across those products more or less objectively, this is not necessarily what happens. Under conditions of joint production, decision-makers may allocate the common costs to different products in a variety of ways that satisfy market and/or political considerations.

8.1 Approaches to the attribution of costs to joint products

In 1985/86 Rumble surveyed a number of dual-mode universities in Australia, Canada and the United States, to see if there was any pattern in the way in which they allocated course costs to on- and off-campus programmes. The results showed considerable variation in practice, and some surprise that the question had been asked at all. Rumble (1986b: 23–7) identified six approaches to the allocation of development costs in situations of joint production where a distance education course was developed alongside a traditional course, and two approaches to the allocation of presentation costs.

8.1.1 Development costs

To help understand these different approaches to the allocation of development costs, imagine a fairly typical situation in which a small team of academics developed a short face-to-face course at a cost of £11,000. Subsequently, it is decided to offer the course at a distance and the team undertakes further work (£4000) to do this. The total cost of all their work is therefore £15,000. Policy requires that the costs of developing a course are allocated against the students taking the course, to derive a per capita cost per student. There are 15 students taking the traditional course, and 50 taking the distance version. For the sake of this example, it is assumed that the course will only run for one year so all the development costs are allocated to the students in the first (and only) year the course is going to run. The question is: How should the development cost of £15,000 be shared between the two groups of students? The six approaches give widely varying results.

(a) Shared attribution of the original cost equally across modes, coupled with full additional costs of distance version going to the distance programme

Utilizing the general principles of activity based costing suggests that while £4000 of the total cost can be clearly identified as a cost properly allocated to the distance education mode, the original £11,000 is a true joint cost, attributable to both the distance and the traditional versions of the course, and hence properly shared between the two modes. Various possibilities are available: in the example below, 50 per cent of the original £11,000 cost is charged to each programme.

	Traditional programme	Distance taught programme
Development costs (£)	5500	9500
Number of students	15	50
Cost per student (£)	366.66	190

(b) Shared attribution of the original cost across modes, proportionate to student load, coupled with the full additional costs of distance version going to the distance programme

A variant of approach (a) would split the original cost between the two programmes on the basis of student numbers, so that the original cost of £11,000 is shared 15/65ths to the traditional programme, and 50/65ths to the distance programme, but the full cost of the adaptation is charged to the distance programme.

	Traditional programme	Distance taught programme
Development costs (£)	2538	12,462
Number of students	15	50
Cost per student (£)	169.23	249.24

This approach tends to subsidize the programme with the lower number of students.

(c) Joint production costs treated as one and all costs shared equally across all students

Under this approach no distinction is made between the two modes of study. All students are treated as students of a single programme, and all the costs that went into developing the materials are treated as common costs, notwithstanding the fact that the two groups of students study in very different ways. The average cost per student is therefore the same, irrespective of the mode of study. This approach seems to be common in Australian dual-mode institutions where integration is the norm.

	Common programme
Development costs (£)	15,000
Number of students	65
Cost per student (£)	230.77

The same result would, of course, be obtained by apportioning the development costs between the two methods in direct proportion to the number of students studying in each mode (see approach (b) above). In other words, 15/65ths of the total development cost would be apportioned to the traditional course, and 50/65ths to the distance mode version.

(d) Development costs shared across both products equally, but average student costs worked out on the basis that the two products are distinct

Another approach divides the development costs equally between the traditional and the distance programme, but then works out separate average student costs for each programme. Where the number of students in each mode differs, the cost per student on the two programmes reflects this. The greater the difference in the volume of students, the greater the difference in unit costs.

	Traditional programme	Distance taught programme
Development costs (£)	7500	7500
Number of students	15	50
Cost per student (£)	500	150

(e) Distance education treated as a by-product

Here, the original development costs (£11,000) are allocated to the traditional programme to be shared out across its 15 students, and only the additional costs of making a distance version of the course (£4000) are charged to the distance students. This approach was the one commonly found by Rumble to apply in Canadian dual-mode institutions. This approach tends to underplay the cost of the distance version.

	Traditional programme	Distance taught programme
Development costs (£)	11,000	4000
Number of students	15	50
Cost per student (£)	733.33	80

(f) Development costs allocated wholly to one or other programme

Under the final scenario, the development costs might be treated as a whole, and allocated to either programme in their entirety. Two possibilities exist: the full sum is charged to the traditional programme:

	Traditional programme	Distance taught programme
Development costs (£)	15,000	0
Number of students	15	50
Cost per student (£)	1,000	0

or, alternatively, it is charged to the distance programme:

	Traditional programme	Distance taught programme
Development costs (£)	0	15,000
Number of students	15	50
Cost per student (£)	0	300

All these models have been framed in terms of 'student heads': that is, each individual studying the course has been assumed to count as one student. Many funding models argue that part-time students cost less than full-time students because they are studying less hours. To cope with this, many models cost the student load in terms of full-time equivalent students (FTES). Variants of these models based on the assumption that a distance student studies part time and therefore costs less than an FTES are possible.

8.1.2 Direct student costs of delivery

As well as the shared costs of development, there are the costs of delivering the course. Here Rumble (1986b: 27) identified two possible approaches.

1. An attempt to work out the real direct costs of delivering courses in each mode (the campus-based, traditional mode, and the open and distance mode), and charge these different levels of cost to the two different kinds of students.
2. No distinction was made between the two modes. The direct costs of delivery in each mode was aggregated, and charged across all students, irrespective of the mode in which they were studying.

8.1.3 Overhead costs of student support and general overheads

By and large there was no attempt to identify the overhead costs of student services and allocate these across the different modes, despite the fact that some institutions felt that the administration of student services in support of distance students was more costly than that of on-campus students. It was clear that where institutions had set up separate administrative wings to support on- and off-campus students, there was a possibility of identifying the different support costs simply because these were organizationally located in separate cost centres. However, this was not apparently being done at the time of the study. Many institutions had also integrated their administrative services, and where this was the case it would have been much harder for them to separate the costs out.

Rumble found no attempts to allocate general overheads across programmes.

8.2 An example of joint product costing: part-time provision in the UK, 1989

It is obvious from these examples that not only are there several ways of allocating costs to joint products, but that these can have a marked affect on average costs. In circumstances where there is no required approach, institutions feel able to choose the method that best meets their internal and external interests. What might such interests be? An insight can be obtained by looking at the way in which British higher education approached the costing of part-time provision in 1989

(Smith and Saunders, 1989; 1991). The example does not quite equate with the concerns addressed above since what is being explicitly apportioned is overheads (the subject of Chapter 7) and not the joint costs of developing two parallel products. However, the case study involves the apportionment of joint (overhead) costs, and the way in which these were apportioned usefully illuminates the problem of apportioning joint product costs.

In 1989 the British higher education system was still divided between a polytechnic and a university sector. In June 1989 the polytechnic sector received guidance on the funding of part-time students from the Polytechnic and Colleges Funding Council in the form of a document entitled *Recurrent Funding Methodology 1990–1991: Guidance for Institutions*. The document proposed the separation of full-time, sandwich and part-time studies, with institutions being required to state precisely how many students in each category they proposed to enrol. The Council proposed to give each institution some core funding, based on a proportion of their last year's enrolments, coupled with a component for which they could bid competitively – the institutions proposing a price to the Council at which they would enrol students. The overall approach was designed to clarify the relative costs of full- and part-time students. The document also proposed an incentive scheme whereby moneys might accrue to institutions recruiting above their part-time student targets. At the time polytechnic sector public funding was based in large measure on the number of full-time equivalent students (FTES) in each polytechnic, with day time part-time students being weighted as 0.4 FTES, and evening part-time students weighted at 0.2 FTES (though this was being changed to 0.4 FTES). In other words, for funding purposes, each part-time student was worth two-fifths of a full-time student. In the university sector the University Funding Council had inherited a policy from its precursor body, the University Grants Committee, that urged universities not to distinguish between full- and part-time students. In the British system at this time most part-time students paid their own fees, while full timers received grants.

When Smith and Saunders carried out a survey of the costs of part-time higher education in the United Kingdom, in both the university and polytechnic sectors, they found the vast majority of course leaders involved in teaching part-time students had no idea of the cost per student per year. Further, where course leaders did claim to know the cost per student, there were very wide variations in the costs of degrees cited by different institutions. For example, they found that two virtually identical degrees (in subject and structure) in different institutions were costed at £335 and £995 per student (Smith and Saunders, 1991: 44). Initially, they thought that their questionnaire must have been badly constructed because of the very different results they were getting from different course leaders, but subsequent investigation showed that these differences arose from the different costing practices employed by institutions.

Smith and Saunders (1991: 47) identified three approaches to the costing of part-time students.

1. The first approach was a full-cost model, in which part-time provision was charged its proportion of all costs. This tends to make part-time provision look relatively expensive.

2. The second approach was effectively a marginal cost calculation: it was argued that since the part time students used facilities at times when full timers were not, they incur minimal additional costs and should therefore be costed on the marginal cost of the provision. In addition to the direct costs of providing teaching, the part-time provision should also be charged the marginal additional overhead costs incurred (eg postage, portering, library, heating etc). (Technically, the *marginal cost* is the cost of producing one additional unit of output, but it is used here in the wider sense of the additional costs involved in doing something more, having chosen to ignore for the purposes of costing the output of this activity, all costs incurred in the production of other joint products.) This makes part-time provision appear very cost efficient.

3. The third approach argued that the part-time provision is in addition to the standard provision, and that the latter should cover all the institutional overhead costs. The part-time provision should only be charged for the additional costs of teaching and administration. This makes part-time provision appear very cost effective indeed.

The information provided does not enable the technical approach to apportioning joint costs to be pinpointed accurately within the terms of Rumble's models in Section 8.1, but it is clear that joint costs and overheads were apportioned in different ways. What should be noted is that the way in which costs are apportioned can affect the apparent costs of the products, making them appear more or less expensive, and that the reasons for doing this may stem from different *technical* approaches to the problem of costing, from differing perceptions of the political/funding environment, or from different perceptions of the market and justifications of pricing policy.

8.3 Conclusion

Many of these methods of allocating joint costs do not meet the requirements of activity based costing. Joint product costing raises technical questions that analysts need to confront. The approach adopted should apportion costs in ways that reflect the cost of the activities underpinning the products and services offered to customers. Product and service costs should accordingly be apportioned in ways that take account of the relationship of the parts to higher level products and services (see Figure 7.6), hence development costs are best allocated across joint products on a shared basis, with the specific costs attributable to different products being attributed to them and them alone.

On the other hand, when setting fees, the issue may be one of overt or covert subsidy, as illustrated by Smith and Saunders's study (Section 8.2). In cases where joint product costing applies, the political or market context within which the costing is being carried out is of considerable importance. Does one want to underplay the costs of the programme – to make a product appear cheaper, either for funding purposes, or for the purpose of setting fees? If so, one should take a marginal costing approach. Does one want to 'share' the costs more equitably? In that case, some kind of apportionment should be made, and the question is then, what is the most appropriate balance? Whatever the technically correct approach, the answers are not necessarily straightforward.

Chapter 9

The activity of costing

How costing is done and which elements within a system are costed will be determined very largely by the reasons for which the costing exercise is being undertaken. It is absolutely crucial that those undertaking the exercise identify their audience and the questions to which they need to provide answers. This will affect the technical cost content, the format and the presentation of the study.

There are various helpful frameworks around which costing exercises can be structured:

- the distinction (see Section 2.1 and Chapter 3) drawn between the costs of human resources, premises and accommodation, furniture and equipment, and stocks, supplies, consumables and expenses;
- the systems framework set out in Section 1.3;
- the cost objects of the system (products, services and customers) (see Section 7.5).

Almost all cost studies will be interested in separating out revenue costs from capital costs (Section 2.3) and recurrent costs from non-recurrent costs (Section 2.2). The proper identification of furniture, equipment and the capital costs of premises and accommodation, is crucial. It must be established whether capital costs need to be discounted, and whether the social discount rate (see Section 6.2) needs to be applied. Much will depend upon the nature of the decision the cost study is seeking to support.

The ability to understand and apply the concepts of direct and overhead costs (Section 4.2), and variable, semi-variable and fixed costs (Section 4.3) is necessary to understand the behaviour of costs, to carry out cost projections and to an understanding of the economics of open and distance education. However, as Chapter 7 indicates, there is considerable danger in treating overheads as an aggregated, fixed cost: in this connection, it is very important to identify the factors that drive costs, including overheads (Section 4.4). Indeed, modern thinking plays down the significance of fixed costs within cost structures, preferring to argue that all costs are variable.

Up to now this book has focused on the basic technical tools required to undertake costing. Readers should now be in a position to understand the concepts, use them to cost projects and recognize problems as they arise.

There is no absolutely right way of carrying out a costing exercise, but analysts are more likely to be successful if they are methodical in their thinking. It helps to break down any costing exercise into three phases, each of which involves two stages.

Phase 1: Preparation

1. Identify the scope of the study

- Obtain a broad understanding of the project and its scope. What kinds of costs are involved (premises, equipment, human resources, consumables etc)? What is driving the costs?
- What is the project seeking to do? What outputs does it have?
- Who has asked for the cost study to be done? What do they want the study to achieve? What questions are they asking? How much detail are they expecting? Are they commissioning the report for presentation to another audience, and if so, what will that audience be looking for?
- Who might be able to help with the analysis? Where will the data come from?

2. Decide on the basic format of the analysis

- Decide in greater detail exactly what it is that is being costed or measured. Nothing can be more frustrating than having to backtrack to disaggregate data that one thought unnecessary to analyse in detail. Rough out the approach that is being taken. It is a good idea in all but the simplest costing exercises to check back with the study's sponsors that they have been understood correctly and that the planned study will give them the information they need.
- Decide on which cost ingredients are going to be included in the study and which excluded. For example:
  - (a) should the costs paid by other agencies be included or excluded? This might include student costs and the costs of the time people give freely in order to develop the system or be trained to use it.
  - (b) if a system developed elsewhere is replicated, should one include or exclude the costs of development? This could be a crucial consideration when it comes to pricing the product.
  - (c) where a change in practice is being costed, have the additional, supplementary costs and the costs that were incurred in the old system but will no longer be incurred in the new, both been identified?

- Are the prices correct? Prices change all the time. Is a current price being used, or the price paid for an 'earlier generation' technology? Was the original equipment bought as a 'special deal', and should the 'special deal' price be used, or the market price? Have changes in exchange rates affected the costs of foreign equipment?

Phase 2: Execution

1. Collection of data and information

- Collect the data and information on inputs, their costs and the outputs.
- Check the meaning of the data. Are the salary costs inclusive or exclusive of on-costs? Is this cost, which your informant tells you is a fixed cost actually a semi-variable one – fixed given the range of output he considers on a day-to-day basis, but likely to increase or decrease given the changes under consideration? Is the information built into the organization's budget fully understood? Has one been given a budget cost, or historical expenditure? How reliable is the coding of expenditure underpinning the management accounts?
- In dealing with capital, what assumptions are being made about the depreciation period of an item? Is the assumption realistic?
- Understand the limitation of the data. Is this an estimate, or an actual cost? If it is a notional cost, is it a sensible one or not?
- Remember, it is much better to record the data in ways that will enable it to be aggregated later, if necessary. It is a nuisance to those who are providing the data to be asked to disaggregate figures that may have been specially prepared.

2. Analysis

- Be clear as to the purpose of the costing exercise, and decide how this will affect the analysis. What needs to be included in the analysis, and what can be excluded? Is the exercise concerned only with the budgetary cost, or with the whole system cost – including the costs that are carried by others (such as students) whose costs do not normally appear on the budget at all?
- How accurate are the findings? What assumptions have been built in? If the assumptions are wrong, or have to be changed, what affect will this have on the findings? How optimistic or pessimistic are the assumptions?

Phase 3: Delivery

1. Presentation

- What are the aims of the study? What questions were being asked? How can these be best met and answered?
- How public are the findings?
- In the light of this, what needs to be described? What information needs to be presented?
- Does the accuracy of the information need to be qualified?
- Is there an explanation of the methodology used, and its limitations?
- What are the findings? How reliable are they?

2. Evaluation

- How successful was the study? Did the sponsors of the study feel that their questions were answered? Did they accept the methodology? Could one have done better? What criticisms have been made by others (eg academic researchers), and how valid are these?

Costing, like statistics, can be used and abused. Although there are conventions and standards, there is a great deal of scope for the creative interpretation of data and presentation of information. The next chapters will show how it has been used to analyse the costs of distance and open education.

Chapter 10

Designing courses

Teachers in open and distance learning systems have to develop or buy in materials within the context of a series of courses leading to the awards that the institution offers. The design phase involves:

- defining the aims and objectives of the curriculum, in relation to what the students will be asked to do, and what awards (if any) they will work towards;
- agreeing the content of courses;
- deciding on the method of teaching (in open, flexible and distance learning, this involves choice of media and technologies);
- designing the assessment strategies;
- designing the support systems.

Once this is done, work can begin on the development of the course materials. Texts have to be written; scripts need to be prepared for audio and video programmes; assignments and tests developed; associated textbooks evaluated and chosen; computer-based teaching/learning systems designed; illustrations and technical drawings produced; photographs obtained; practical activities designed (and the equipment needed to carry out experiments specified and designed). And all of this activity needs to be co-ordinated so that the end product – a course – fits together.

10.1 Production rates

The various processes involved in designing and creating a course take time. In any distance learning system, a range of specialist staff will be involved in addition to the subject teachers. Audio and video producers, computing staff, graphic artists and technical designers, photographers, technicians and editors. Even then, the work may not be over. In countries where there are a number of official or dominant languages, materials may need to be translated (as in Sri Lanka). In some countries, texts have to be prepared by professional calligraphers (as in Pakistan, where the Allama Iqbal Open University pays its calligraphers on the same scale as university lecturers). Behind the main production staff, there may be significant numbers of support staff (production assistants, research assistants, scenery makers and so on). Consultants and contributors may be required.

How much staff time is needed is difficult to quantify. Sparkes (1984: 219) suggested that, depending on the different media employed, it would require the following number of hours of academic work to produce a product that would take a student one hour of work:

Table 10.1 *Academic work to produce one hour of student learning*

Media	Hours of academic effort
Lecturing	2–10
Small group teaching	1–10
Teaching by telephone	2–10
Video-tape lectures (for tutored video instruction)	3–10
Audiovision	10–20
Teaching text	50–100★
Broadcast television	100★
Computer-aided learning	200★
Interactive video	300★

Source: from Sparkes, 1984: 219

★ Requires additional support staff as well

These figures need to be treated with care. Many would regard them on the high side. Even within a single technology, there can be a range of options affecting the resources and time needed to produce teaching materials. The choice and mix of technology, and the way in which people work, can have a real impact on course costs, as Case Study 10.1 illustrates.

Case Study 10.1: Academic productivity at the Open University

The Open University studied academic production rates in the mid-1970s (Open University, 1975). The purpose of the exercise was to establish an objective basis for the allocation of academic staff posts to the faculties.

The exercise, which was conducted annually over a number of years, sought to establish what the output of each faculty had been in terms of the materials designed to keep an average learner studying 10–12 hours a week (referred to as a 'unit'). It also looked at the number of units currently presented in the University's profile of courses. It recognized that academic staff spent some of their time maintaining these, writing new assignments, checking on feedback from students and tutors and logging changes that should be incorporated into the next edition. Without undertaking a diary exercise, it was impossible to judge how much time was spent developing new materials and redeveloping existing ones, but the consensus was that an academic could maintain ten units of existing materials in the time taken to develop a new unit from scratch. Thus the exercise assumed that a 'maintenance unit' was worth 0.1 'new units'.

Additionally, it was known that a number of units were developed by consultant authors and contributors. To identify the central staff time, these units had to be discounted. Staff nevertheless argued that they had to oversee and sometimes rework the units prepared by consultants, so another arbitrary decision was taken to discount consultants' units at half their weight.

This output was then compared with the input of staff time. In order to derive the input, the exercise sought to establish the total amount of staff months employed, less time taken for research, holidays, University closure and public holidays, and the time spent teaching face to face at residential school. All staff were thought to spend some time on administration and an allowance of ten days per year was set aside for this, but a few (such as the Dean) had heavy administrative loads, and were taken out of the equation entirely. This gave the University a measure of the time its central academic staff had spent developing courses and maintaining existing courses. On average, the remaining staff seemed to have about 120 days per year which they were spending on course development.

The overall result suggested that staff in the faculties of Technology and Science were producing 1.4 'units' of student study time per year; those in the faculties of Mathematics and Education were producing 1.6 units per year; those in Social Sciences 2.4 units per year; and those in Arts 2.6 units per year (Rumble, 1976: 22–5).

These results were then used, in conjunction with assumptions about the number of years a course should remain in the profile (four years), and the extent to which replacement courses might need the same level of staff input as wholly new ones (deemed to be 50 per cent of the effort)*, to inform internal decision-making about the relative allocation of new academic posts to the faculties, and overall funding decisions about the size of the academic faculty and the number of courses that the University should produce. Since an implication of the findings was that, for the same level of output of courses, Science and Technology needed many more staff than Arts, the findings were both controversial and required some explanation.

One explanation was almost certainly the different media mix between the faculties: thus Arts and Social Sciences had roughly twice as many radio programmes as Mathematics, Science and Technology, but half as many television programmes. Equally, Science, Technology and Maths had more week-long residential courses than Arts and Social Sciences, each of which required considerable planning and development work. The study did not attempt to quantify the differences in output with variations in the mix of media used, but there was widespread acceptance that this was part of the explanation, and Sparkes's figures (Table 10.1) would seem to bear this out. One other reason for the differences was advanced: it was argued that the development of subject matter in the Sciences and Mathematics required more careful planning as students had to build up their knowledge, unit by unit. The greater coherence required meant that the Sciences had to spend much more time checking the relationship between the content of one unit and that in earlier and later units of the course – and this had an affect on academic productivity. None of this could be proved, but everyone agreed that it was likely.

One final point needs to be made. The overall assumption was that staff worked reasonable hours. In fact, many were not taking time off for research, and the study accommodated this by looking at the actual research leave taken. However, many staff claimed that they were working excessively long hours and often working at weekends, during vacations and over public holidays. The study made no attempt to adjust productivity for these factors.

* Later studies suggested that most replacement courses took as long to develop as new courses, and the University therefore revised its productivity rate for replacement courses to be equal to that of new courses, but compensated for this by assuming that course lives would extend to eight years.

It would be foolish to try to extrapolate from the Open University's early experience to the situation in other institutions, but Case Study 10.1 does throw up some of the general problems involved, and suggests ways in which studies of academic productivity in open, flexible and distance learning might be approached. What the Open University did was to establish a production rate (p), by dividing the total units of output of courses of a standard type (X), by the amount of staff time, measured in standard units such as staff months or staff years, involved in production (N):

$$p = X/N \qquad\qquad \text{[Eq. 10.1]}$$

It then used this production rate, multiplied by the planned future output of courses (X_f), to determine future staffing needs (N_f):

$$N_f = pX_f \qquad\qquad \text{[Eq. 10.2]}$$

Clearly, these are extremely simple formulae, and would need to be extended to take account of variations in the mix of components (texts, video programmes etc) and staff involved (academics, educational technologists, editors etc).

10.2 Implications of production rates for institutions teaching by traditional and open/distance learning means

In distance teaching systems, the relationship between the input of staff time and output of materials is straightforward. In dual mode institutions, where staff have both to develop open and distance learning materials and teach traditional campus-based students, some kind of equivalency needs to be established between the workloads involved in teaching in class and in teaching students at a distance. In the early 1980s, for example, Bynner (1985: 527) found that in many Australian dual-mode universities there was no attempt to make allowances for the additional work undertaken by lecturers involved in developing materials for external students: 'The tradition of the typed lecture notes supplemented later, as in Macquarie [University], by the taped lecture, does not acknowledge the need for teaching time to design and develop external courses.' Similarly, the universities of Queensland and New England did not recognize the staff effort put into course development. At Murdoch University, on the other hand, Bynner (1985: 528) reported that lecturers were allowed a remission of 16 teaching hours per week to enable them to design course materials.

Looking at the development of open learning in British further education, Birch and Cuthbert (1981, 53–5; 1982: 103–6) modified the instructional workload model to take account of the need for staff to be allocated time to develop open learning materials. The instructional workload model takes account of the fundamental variables (class size, average number of taught hours or contact hours and average number of teaching-hours per lecturer) that affect the teaching load, such that:

$$T = [S \times ASH] \div [ACS \times ALH] \qquad \text{[Eq. 10.3]}$$

where:

T   = the number of full-time equivalent (FTE) lecturers determined by dividing the total class contact hours of staff by the average class contact hours of full-time staff

S   = the number of full-time equivalent students (FTES) determined by dividing the total student taught hours by the average student taught hours (ASH) of full-time students in the same subject area

ASH = the average taught hours of a FTE student which is obtained by dividing the total student hours by the number of FTES

ACS = the average class size determined by dividing the total student contact hours by the total lecturer hours

ALH = the average lecturer hours taught by a FTE lecturer, determined by dividing the total lecturer hours by the number of FTE lecturers.

Birch and Cuthbert started by noting that further education college lecturers in the UK were required to spend a minimum number of hours per week in college (30 hours), of which a proportion (20 hours) was spent in front of a class. The balance (ten hours) was available for preparation, marking, administration etc. Where teaching patterns are developed that require lecturers to spend more than the normal time on preparation and marking (as in open learning situations), there has to be a way of negotiating a reduction in class contact hours. However, they warned that 'any agreement which gave the teacher one hour's class remission for less than six [open learning] students in his case load would lead to a unit cost for the open learning programme which was higher than for equivalent conventional work' (Birch and Cuthbert, 1982: 105).

Clearly, releasing staff from their face-to-face teaching duties so that they can develop materials is problematic in situations where staff are heavily committed – and hence a potential barrier to conversion from a traditional to an open/distance learning based institution. Still, there are a number of institutions that do this: thus Jennings and Ottewill (1996: 16) report that within the University of Sheffield's Business School, the preparation of materials for open learning students is funded in part from 'top slicing' some of the individual member of staff's personal workload hours allocated for teaching, and redirecting it to materials preparation.

10.3 Working practices

Models of the kind described in Section 10.1 can be used to project staffing requirements into the future, but their use is based on the assumption that the working and employment practices embedded within them remain in being. Clearly, it is possible to change the level of staffing needed not only by changing the mix of media, but also by changing the processes involved in developing materials, or by making greater use of temporary staff paid on a piece-work basis.

Changing the media mix may increase or decrease labour costs, as Sparkes's work suggests (see Table 10.1). Another factor affecting labour costs is the extent to which the curriculum has been broken down into modular courses. Broadly, the smaller the modules (ie the fewer student study hours each module requires), the more likely it is that they can be written by one or two academics, thus reducing the costs of interaction and hence of labour. The longer the course, the more likely it is that it will need to be written by a team of people, thus increasing the transactional costs of the process as consultation has to take place to ensure that each individual contribution fits with the others.

The course team approach was developed at the Open University and subsequently adopted by other institutions. No one person could produce a course of the length (at least 450 hours of student workload) initially envisaged by the University's planners within the time set aside for development (about 18 months). It had to be a team effort. The working practices that evolved required team members to read and comment on each other's draft contributions to the course, reflecting the need to ensure that each person's contribution fitted into the course as a whole. The University's first Vice-Chancellor, Walter Perry, believes that 'the concept of the course team is the single most important contribution of the Open University to teaching practice' (Perry, 1976: 91), and that 'a course produced by this method will inevitably tend to be superior in quality to any course produced by an individual'. However, he admitted that it is an expensive way of developing materials and could only be justified where the materials were going to be used by large numbers of students.

Although the course team has had a very high profile as a result of the Open University's experience, it is not the only possibility for developing materials. A range of different approaches have been described and various authors (eg Stone, 1975; Lockwood, 1993) have attempted to provide typologies. Most course development processes involve a range of staff with different specialisms. The differences in approach tend to focus on the way in which the teams are managed and the work progressed.

(a) Multi-specialist team approaches

Team approaches include the following.

- Interdisciplinary team approach, in which persons from different specialisms (subject matter authors, educational technologists, editors, secretaries, designers, audio-visual producers, broadcasters, programmers etc) are brought together to work on the design of a course. Teams may have autonomy under a project manager, or be required to work within a matrix structure in which the head of the various specialist functional areas retain responsibility for the quality of the work done by the specialists assigned to the project from that area (Stone, 1975). The latter arrangement tends to add to the work because it involves additional transactional and control costs. Teams may be of varying sizes, from a few to many persons. Team members who are unused to working in this kind of structure may need considerable training. This may be given prior to starting work on developing materials. However, Lockwood (1993: 147–8) describes a personalized training model in which a group of subject experts is assembled to work with an educational technologist who co-ordinates and administers the task group, and briefs and trains the writers so that they are equipped with those skills and techniques they need to prepare self-instructional training materials, giving training at the time the authors need it, and not at the outset of the task. Regular meetings of the task group take place, and writers are kept to schedule between meetings. Lockwood argues that this kind of approach reduces costs.

- Transformer models, in which one person (the transformer) works on materials prepared by other people to create structured open learning materials. Macdonald-Ross and Waller (1969) describe what appears to be a labour-intensive and therefore expensive transformer model in which a team of subject experts, supported by an educational technologist who decides on the subject matter of the course, produces course outlines and possibly draft texts. The products of their work are then handed over to a second team of transformers who consist of subject specialists, educational technologists, broadcast producers, editors, graphic designers and course managers, some of whom will have been members of the first team. The subject experts in the second team are teacher oriented, whereas those in the first team are research oriented. The second team converts the outline materials and drafts produced by the first team into a complex, multi-media course designed to teach effectively. Lockwood's (1993: 148) workshop model, which involves a group of specialists working together over a limited period of time with a clear objective to generate a set of teaching materials that would be beyond the scope of a single person, is a much more cost-efficient transformer model. The members of the group retain collective responsibility for the end result, but the task of preparing the material on the basis of the information that has been pooled during the workshop is delegated to a writer/editor. What distinguishes the approach is the speed with which a final product can be produced. The planning of the workshop, selection of experts, briefing of experts, co-ordination of their inputs and following up of suggestions and sources may take the writer/editor several weeks – but the actual workshop may take only a few days. As an example, the National Council for Educational Technology convened a workshop of four experts who worked with a co-ordinator and editor to develop a handbook on *Costing Open and Flexible Learning* (Crabb, 1990). The team had three two-day meetings over a five or six month period, during which they discussed structure and content. In the interim periods the editor and co-ordinator worked on preparing draft materials for the team's consideration.

- Shears (1992: 53-4) describes a two-person educational adviser model in which a distance education expert works in an iterative way with an academic to determine an appropriate format and mode of delivery for a course leading to a workable course design. The expert adviser introduces the academic to the advantages and drawbacks of distance education methods and the range of technologies available. Once the design is agreed, the academic works on the materials. Shears refers to the economical development of a *Bioethics* course in the School of Physiotherapy at Dalhousie University using this approach, in which the academic recorded a series of audio-cassettes to supplement the material in a prescribed textbook, and the adviser then developed a student guide.

(b) Multi-specialist assembly line models

Stone (1975) describes two models in which materials are produced by different specialists in what is in effect an assembly line.

1. The specialized approach, in which the various tasks are allocated to different professional staff. In the first stage, educators plan the curriculum and define the contents; then, in a subsequent phase, 'communicators' including authors and script writers execute the plan by developing texts; and, finally, studio and production staff create the finished product. Each specialist works on his or her own tasks in isolation from the others. The main problems with this approach are discontinuity of work, poor communication between specialists, and a failure to integrate development on a project basis.

2. The chain approach, which seeks to ameliorate some of the discontinuities and lack of integration of the specialist approach by ensuring that each specialist participates in both the stage immediately prior to and that immediately after his or her own.

(c) One person models

Shears (1992: 52) describes a solo author model of course development under which a single academic works alone, often revising a traditional course so that it can be delivered at a distance. Individual academics make their own decisions on the methodologies and media. This model is, of course, the way in which many classroom delivered courses are developed, and it was used at Dalhousie University to develop undergraduate nursing and physiotherapy courses. While inexpensive, the model involved considerable duplication of effort and resulted in a lack of consistency in the quality of the courses.

In general the more interaction required between individuals involved in designing a course, the greater the time spent and the higher the cost of labour. Thus Stone's specialist and chain approaches, and Shear's educational adviser and solo author models, are much cheaper than the transformer and large team approaches. Case Study 10.2 shows how Deakin University in Australia consciously tried to develop different models.

Case Study 10.2: How working practices affect costs

At Deakin University in Australia, in the late 1980s, courses were notionally divided into two types – Type A and Type B (though many courses did not fall neatly into the two different categories). Type A courses were complex undergraduate-level courses developed by five-member course teams, in which the text was reviewed by course team members and instructional designers, and was fully edited, designed and typeset, and either externally paperback bound or sent out in four-ring binders. The text was accompanied by one 30 minute video-cassette and six 60-minute audio-cassettes.

Type B courses at honours and postgraduate level were developed by one or two members of staff, received no team planning or review, and no instructional design input. There was no audio-visual material. Wordprocessing was to a standard format with typed texts being laser printed. The text master went straight to the printer for printing and binding.

Deakin University reported that the fixed costs of Type A courses averaged out at A$54,750, against A$27,740 for Type B courses (Deakin University, 1988: 25).

10.4 Reducing the cost of labour

As well as considering the design of working practices, there are four other approaches that can be used to reduce the cost of the labour input to the design and development phase.

1.   Using external consultants paid on a performance-basis.
2.   The practice of commodifying traditional lectures.
3.   Transforming existing materials to create courses.
4.   Buying in material to use as it stands.

(a) Using consultants

Using consultants can significantly reduce the cost of developing materials. Institutions such as the National Extension College, Cambridge, UK, and the Universidad Estatal a Distancia in Costa Rica, which contract authors to write their courses, pay a flat-rate fee per text. The consultants are contracted by a commissioning editor, who briefs them on curriculum, content, style, level etc. The contract specifies that the text must be acceptable to the commissioning editor.

Editors, copy editors, graphic designers and artists, and a range of other people involved in the development of materials, may also be hired as required. Using consultants obviously reduces costs: eg the costs of training, equipping and accommodating staff, and the costs of paying for staff time when they are not actively engaged in developing materials. The savings have, of course, to be weighed up against possible additional costs – for example, the costs of contracting, briefing and managing consultants, and of checking and editing their work into final form.

(b) Commodifying traditional lectures

Many institutions teaching by traditional means have begun offering their courses to a wider off-campus audience through the simple expedient of video-taping the normal lectures given to on-campus students, and preparing simple lecture notes and low-cost materials (eg slides) to accompany the video-tapes. Once lecture theatres have been equipped with video cameras and recording equipment, the additional per capita costs of preparing videos and lecture notes for use by off-campus students is very little, as Wagner (1975) showed in an early study of the system used in the off-campus engineering programme at Colorado State University. This basic approach, pioneered in the 1960s in the United States, later became the basis for the National Technological University in the United States (Case Study 10.3). In reading this case study, note that the costs of satellite delivery are a significant proportion of the total costs. In small-scale systems with *very* few students, video materials may be put on video-cassettes and distributed through the post. The additional costs of such systems are very small.

Case Study 10.3: The National Technological University
(cost data from Fwu *et al.*, 1992: 122–4)

The National Technological University (NTU) was set up in 1984. Basically it co-ordinates a networked system joining universities offering off-campus engineering courses to firms wishing to enrol employees on courses. Member universities of NTU (and NTU selects from the best graduate engineering schools in the United States) supply the same courses that they offer on campus. Lectures are delivered in television-equipped lecture theatres on campus, and the great majority are recorded live for transmission through an uplink to a satellite, from which they are beamed through downlinks into reception sites at the firms, where the students watch the lectures. No special preparation is required beyond sending advance course notes to the students. Tests may be taken at the university, or under supervision at other colleges or at the workplace.

NTU's headquarters cost US$4,694,000 in 1989/90, of which just over 50 per cent represented the cost of telecommunications, including the rental of two satellite transponders, and the maintenance of the various uplinks at the participating universities. About $3,200,000 of the headquarters cost is fixed; the rest is variable, at a unit cost of $80 per enrolment.

The principal costs to the participating universities are the cost of setting up an ITV (Instructional Television) classroom and paying the studio running costs, the hourly uplink charge and the professor's time. The overall cost per 45-hour course is estimated to be $20,150. In addition, there is a cost of about $90 per enrolment, to cover the cost of assignment marking and examinations.

Firms joining the scheme pay a one-off access fee which reflects the size of the firm, but has averaged out at $10,000. They must set up a reception site (involving an up-front minimum cost of $40,800), but the annualized costs of the buildings and equipment plus the recurrent cost of running the system (involving a site coordinator and maintenance) comes to $17,500. There are also variable costs of textbooks and photocopying, estimated at $50 per course.

The basic elements in NTU's costs are therefore as follows:

Headquarters:

- Fixed costs (F) $3,200,000
- Variable cost per enrolment (δ_1) $80
- Number of enrolments (N)   3639

Participating universities:

- Variable cost per course (α) $20,000
- Number of courses (C)   200
- Variable cost per enrolment (assessment) (δ_2) $90

Participating firms:

- Number of reception sites (R)   145
- Variable cost per reception site (β) $17,500
- Variable cost per enrolment (textbooks, photocopies) (δ_3) $50

The total costs are held to be affected by three cost drivers: the number of enrolments, the number of courses and the number of reception sites. The total cost (TC) function is therefore:

$$TC = F + \alpha C + \beta R + N(\delta_1 + \delta_2 + \delta_3) \qquad \text{[Eq. 10.6]}$$
$$= \$3,200,000 + (\$20,000 \times 200) + (\$17,500 \times 145) + [\$(80 + 90 + 50) \times N]$$
$$= \$9,737,500 + (\$220 \times 3639)$$

The average cost (AC) per enrolment can be calculated using Equation 5.3:

$$AC = V + (FC/N) \qquad\qquad [Eq. 5.3]$$

where, in this case:

V = the variable cost per enrolment = $(\delta_1 + \delta_2 + \delta_3)$ = \$220
FC = the fixed cost = $F + \alpha C + \beta R$ = \$9,737,500

such that:

$$
\begin{aligned}
AC &= \$220 + (\$9{,}737{,}500 \div 3639) \\
&= \$2896
\end{aligned}
$$

Expansion of enrolments would of course bring the average cost down, other things being equal (ie no increase in the number of courses or reception sites, and no quantum changes in costs).

(c) Transforming existing materials

In some cases materials already exist that might be used to teach students at a distance, but which are unsuitable in their present form. There are two possible strategies that can be adopted:

- text transformation;
- development of wrap-around texts.

Text transformation, the process by which existing materials are transformed into high quality self-instructional materials (Lockwood, 1993: 148), may involve the adaptation of all the existing material in some way. Lockwood (1993: 148) describes how an existing Computer Assisted Learning package (POPTRAN) on population statistics and dynamics developed by Cardiff University's Population Centre was transformed through minor changes (removal of textual duplication, reduction in the number of examples etc), moderate changes (redesign of certain computer graphics) and major changes (involving a complete reconceptualization of how POPTRAN could be used as a self-instructional package rather than a tutor-led package).

In contrast, the development of wrap-around materials involves a new self-instructional package being 'wrapped around' a pre-existing text that is itself left untouched. Lockwood (1993: 149) cites as an example the development of the Open University's *Producing an Open Learning Package*, which involved the creation of an audio tape and a 100-page study guide that was wrapped around an existing book – Derek Rowntree's *Teaching Through Self-instruction* (Rowntree, 1991). The net result was that the package, which in other circumstances would have required a small team working over two years to produce it, was produced by a single author working over nine months. Those considering this approach should nevertheless note that the use of existing materials may involve copyright charges.

(d) Buying in material

The fourth approach is to buy them in from another institution. Many small distance teaching institutions do this, in order to avoid the relatively high fixed costs of developing courses. The Singapore Institute of Management, the Open College of the University of East Asia, Macau and the Open Learning Institute, Hong Kong, are all examples of institutions that import materials from other providers. Ekins (1993: 102–3) describes various models for doing this and provides examples of all these models (pp 103–4), based on the use by others of the Open University's undergraduate Foundation Course in Mathematics (known by its course code as M101).

- Purchase of teaching materials. This involves buying in teaching materials 'off the shelf'. The materials are then integrated into the purchasing institution's own course structure. The institution produces its own assessment materials and arranges its own validation. North Island College, Vancouver Island, purchased half of M101 for its own use from 1980. Ekins reckons that the staff input required had North Island College wished to use the *whole* of M101 would have involved two person years, as opposed to the 20 required to develop the course from scratch at the British Open University – a 90 per cent saving in staff time.
- Whole course user. The purchasing institution buys in the materials and the assessment structure. The Open College of the University of East Asia, Macau used the whole of M101 from 1982, and the Open Learning Institute, Hong Kong used it from 1989. In both cases the set-up costs in person years was equivalent to about one member of staff – a 95 per cent saving in staff time.
- Institution as tutor. The purchasing institution effectively runs the course on behalf of the institution that created it, but acts as its teaching agent, appointing tutors locally and arranging local student support facilities. Assessment remains the responsibility of the originating institution. M101 has been taught by the National Distance Education Centre, Ireland. The materials were identical to the course offered in the United Kingdom, but tutors were locally recruited by NDEC. The set-up cost was equivalent to about 0.25 person years.
- Collaboration with validation. Similar to the institution as tutor model, it allows the local institution the option of adapting course materials and possibly introducing local courses of its own, without losing the fall-back position of students being able to transfer credit back to the originating institution. M101 was tailored to meet the needs of students in Singapore by the Singapore Institute of Management. The course was, however, validated by the British Open University, which vets any modifications to the course. The overall input of staff time amounted to about 0.5 person years.

Buying in therefore represents a real saving in staff time. However, there are also additional costs. A variable cost, in the form of a cost per copy used (though sometimes institutions selling materials also charge a fixed 'license to use' fee), is substituted for the high fixed costs of developing materials coupled with the low variable costs of producing copies of one's own materials. Comparative costs suggest that this is not a particularly attractive option, unless:

- the number of students on each bought-in course is low; and
- the costs of investment in developing one's own materials is high.

The National Distance Education Centre at Dublin City University compared the costs of buying in a course to the costs of developing their own course, and concluded that the break-even point at which it became cheaper to develop their own material was 123 students (Curran, 1993: 21). Robertshaw (1993), reporting on the costs incurred by the Open Learning Institute (OLI) of Hong Kong when buying in courses from the UK Open University, indicated that the materials cost of the courses imported from the Open University (which covered their production and capital costs) was twice as expensive as the materials costs of locally developed courses. Buying in did, of course, enable OLI to avoid in-house development costs, though local practice, involving the use of consultant authors, tended to keep such costs down.

10.5 Conclusion

This chapter has sought to show that there are ways of reducing the cost of developing course materials: by adopting media that require less development effort; by adopting appropriate low cost processes for course development; and also by adopting practices that reduce the cost of the labour input into the development process. Interestingly, buying in materials is not necessarily a low-cost option.

Chapter 11

Media: text, audio, video and computing

This chapter and the next explore the factors affecting the costs of developing, producing and distributing open and distance learning materials.

11.1 Text

Sparkes's estimate (see Table 10.1) that it takes 50 to 100 hours of academic staff time to develop a text that will keep a student occupied for one hour suggests that the cost of developing text is a major part of the cost of most distance-taught text-based courses. However, Sharratt (1993: 118) makes the valid point that the time taken to develop textual material depends on a number of factors, including the level of the subject matter, the extent to which the author is writing from experience of previous text-based or lecture-delivered courses, the author's experience of writing open learning courses and the length of the course.

With the development of computing the process of producing text has undergone a rapid technological change that has had a marked effect on costs. Authorial processes involving the preparation of handwritten manuscripts, copy-typing, and laborious correction have been eliminated as authors word process their own material themselves, while the ability to edit and style text on screen (using style templates, spell checkers and grammar-checking tools), has made the job of proof-reading endless drafts as they progress through the production process less laborious. Diagrams can now be stored in digitized form, manipulated on screen through mouse and keyboard and pasted into text, while desk top electronic publishing systems have revolutionized text production.

Of course, the introduction of electronic publishing systems involving, at least in well-resourced institutions, the installation of computers and the associated software on virtually every academic's desk, costs money. Bates (1995: 129) estimated that the Vancouver-based Open Learning Agency invested about US$1.5 million in setting up an electronic publishing system, but reduced its print costs by around US$375,000 per year (including staff savings).

Bates (1995: 128) summarized the per student costs of text at the UK Open University in 1989 as follows, the fixed costs of developing text equating to 400 hours study being spread over the student population, and the variable costs reflecting the per capita cost of print for each student (Table 11.1); and Pillai and Naidu (1991: 19–25) analysed the cost of developing and producing texts at the Indira Gandhi National Open University (Table 11.2).

Table 11.1   *The cost of text at the UK Open University, 1989 (£s)*

Cost component	Cost type	Cost per student		
		1000 students (125 per year over 8 years)	5000 students (625 per year over 8 years)	10,000 students (1250 per year over 8 years)
Text development	Fixed	400.00	80.00	40.00
Printing (from bromides)	Variable	14.43	7.51	6.26
Storage	Variable	3.00	3.00	3.00
Packaging	Variable	6.00	6.00	6.00
Mailing	Variable	6.50	6.50	6.50
Total		**429.93**	**103.01**	**61.76**

Source: Bates, 1995: 128

Table 11.2   *Average costs of developing and producing texts for an eight-credit course at the Indira Gandhi National Open University (Rs)*

	Rs	%
Development		
Salary of academic staff	140,978	69.8
Course team/course writers meetings	25,752	12.7
Course writers fees	28,000	13.9
Editorial charges	7,384	3.7
Total development	202,114	100.0
Production		
Typing by outside agencies	3,849	3.3
Secretarial and word processing: salary costs	30,975	26.3
Illustration and design fees	5,405	4.6
Design charges	18,750	15.9
Composing charges	58,880	50.0
Total production	117,859	100.0

Source: Pillai and Naidu, 1991: 23, 25

Electronic storage of text and the use of on-demand printers has also changed the economics of textbook production. The economies of scale reaped by longer print runs always had to be balanced against the additional costs of warehousing texts and the problems of deterioration (particularly acute in the tropics) when stocks were kept for a long time. They were in any case only available where there were significant numbers of students on a course. On-demand printing eliminates the costs of storage. Open learning organizations such as the Open Learning Agency (Bates, 1995: 117) and the National Distance Education Centre, Dublin City University (Curran, 1993: 24) print texts on demand, thus avoiding the need to tie up capital in costly stocks and warehousing.

There are, however, some economies of scale in printing. Courses that attract relatively small numbers of students are significantly more expensive per student than those with large populations (see Table 11.1). Chambers (1993: 139) reports on efforts made by the UK Open University to spread the cost of print more widely through collaborative publishing deals with commercial publishers. Since 1986, the University has entered agreements with publishers to produce books. Two strategies are used.

1. In those cases where the publisher can produce the texts more cheaply than the University, it prepares the texts to film stage, for hand-over to the publisher. The latter then prints and binds the books, markets and stores them and distributes them through commercial outlets. The University buys back an agreed number of copies for distribution to its own students, at a cheaper price per copy than the commercial selling price, and more cheaply than in-house production would allow.
2. In those cases where the University can produce the texts more cheaply than the publisher, it produces the bound copies which it then sells on to the publisher, reserving for itself the number that it requires to meet students' needs. The publisher then markets the book commercially.

Both approaches increase (and typically double) the print run, thus reducing the unit costs of the books to both parties. In addition, the publisher pays the University a royalty on every book sold (see Table 11.3).

While changes in technology have reduced the costs of developing text significantly, this is not true of the costs of distributing print. The distribution costs, including the cost of packing and distributing texts to students (either through outlets such as bookstores and local resource centres, or direct to the students' homes by post or courier), have been less affected by technology. However, increasing access to networked personal computers within the home may well change the way at least some printed material is distributed to students.

Other approaches to the provision of text were discussed in Section 10.4, in the context of buying in texts or wrapping materials around pre-existing texts. Yet another approach is to rely more heavily on loaning books. While this may work well in an open learning context where students have access to a well-stocked campus library with multiple copies of the books on the shelves, distance students often have great difficulty in accessing books from local, non-academic libraries,

Table 11.3 *Comparison of costs of co-publishing against internal text production, UK Open University, 1992 (£s)*

Product	Description	Total cost	Print run	Unit cost	Total cost to student	Royalties
Internally produced text	A4, 10 bindings, 500,000 words	32,667	1483	2.20	22.00	—
Co-published book	Demi-octavo, 4 books, 390,000 words*	17,430	5000	1.90† 2.30‡	8.40	5% of UK published price; 7% on export sales

Source: Chambers, 1993: 140
* An additional study guide is prepared, for internal use only, at low cost
† Two books at this price
‡ Two books at this price

and it is not always feasible to require them to buy the books themselves. One way round this is to provide a postal library loan service. Cavanagh and Tucker (1993: 63–5) analysed the costs of Deakin University's loan service to its off-campus students. They found that 3836 first degree and 2287 postgraduate off-campus students made 49,126 requests for loans of books and audio-visual materials, of which 32,145 were supplied at a cost of A\$206,383 or A\$6.42 per item. In addition, the library provided 13,790 free photocopies and microfilms of journal articles to external students at an average cost per item supplied of A\$4.43.

11.2 Audio

Audio embraces a range of technologies, some of which only allow one-way communication from the teacher to the learner, and some of which allow for two-way communication (discussed in the next chapter).

(a) Radio

Bates (1995: 142–6) reported on the costs of broadcast radio at the UK Open University in 1982, at a time when the University still used radio extensively, with an annual production of 280 20-minute programmes. He calculates the cost of producing and transmitting a 20-minute programme, including the input of staff time, the direct costs of each production (including travel, fees to contributors and copyright clearance) and the overhead costs of production (studio staff, administration, rent, heating etc). The cost of transmission allowed for two transmissions, a first broadcast and a repeat.

The Open University made its programmes on the assumption that they would be broadcast every year, over an eight-year period. Over the eight-year period,

Table 11.4   *Broadcast radio costs at the UK Open University, 1982 (£s)*

	Cost per 20-minute programme	Cost per student of one hour radio programming		
		1000 students (125 per year over 8 years)	5000 students (625 per year over 8 years)	10,000 students (1250 per year over 8 years)
Development/production				
Academic time	200			
Production overheads	1592			
Direct production	315			
Subtotal	2107	6.32	1.26	0.63
Delivery				
Transmission (two per year)	150	3.60	0.72	0.36
Total		**9.92**	**1.98**	**0.99**

Source: Bates, 1995: 143, 145

courses usually had fluctuating numbers of students, with a few courses averaging 4000 to 5000 students each year, but with many having under 200 students per year. Table 11.4 shows the cost per student for one hour of radio programming, assuming varying numbers of students taking the courses.

While academic time and direct production costs are variable with programme output, the production overheads were regarded as fixed within a range of programme output, and so the overhead charged to each course would come down if the number of programmes being produced went up. Given the studio capacity at that time (1982), programmes production might have been increased from 280 to 350, thus bringing the production overhead charge per programme down from £1592 to £1211.

Bates's analysis has, however, to be seen within context. Programming for the Open University was to the BBC's very high public service broadcasting standard, and the University was able to use the national transmission networks of the BBC at marginal cost. In other scenarios, other costs would apply. Jamison, Klees and Wells (1978: 240) reported on the costs of four different instructional radio projects (Table 11.5).

Table 11.5   *Costs of four instructional radio projects, 1972 (US$)*

Project	Year of study	Number of hours	Number of students	Annualized fixed cost	Variable cost/ student	Average cost per student per year
Radio Mathematics, Nicaragua	1975	450	250,000	73,400	3.06	3.86
Radioprimaria, Mexico	1972	280	2800	0	0.15	13.12
Radio Schools of Tarahumara, Mexico	1972	640	1081	33,424	0.40	42.20
Thailand	1967	165	800,000	100,400	0.22	0.35

Source: Jamison *et al.*, 1978: 240

These figures show considerable ranges in the fixed, variable and average costs of instructional radio. There are several reasons for this.

- Jamison and McAnany (1978: 98) reported that the costs of programme production is highly variable: in the Nicaraguan Radio Mathematics Project, the cost of production was around US$2000 for an hour of programming, whereas the Mexican Radioprimaria spent about US$115 per hour.
- Some systems have to set up their own studios and transmission networks; others can use existing facilities at marginal or even no cost. There are trade-offs between setting up a transmission network and leasing time on public or commercial broadcasting stations, and variations in the price of airtime. The Nicaraguan Radio Mathematics Project leased time at a rate varying from US$11.50 to $14.50 per 26-minute slot, depending on the time of day (Jamison and McAnany, 1978: 99).
- The costs of setting up a transmitter and relay stations may be part of the project. The more powerful the transmitter, the more costly it is. There are cost and quality trade-offs between transmitter power and receiver sensitivity which may need to be considered.
- An important element in the costs of using radio, often neglected in systems in which students own or have easy access to radios, is the cost of the receiver. Where penetration of a particular technology is high, such costs can be ignored, but they are of real importance in cases where either the system has to provide users with the technology or learners have to purchase the technology in order to take part.
- Where receivers are powered by batteries, the cost of replacement batteries may be very significant to the target audience.

There are also technical differences in the way cost studies are carried out. When Jamison *et al.* (1975) reported on the cost of instructional radio in Nepal, they took account of the capital costs of buildings and equipment, as well as the recurrent costs of production and transmission. Studies such as those done by Bates on the Open University take no account of the cost of capital.

(b) Audio-cassettes

Like radio, audio-cassettes involve both a production and a distribution cost. In the UK Open University the BBC argued during the 1970s and 1980s that the cost of audio-cassette production was the same as that of radio, hence the only cost difference between audio-cassettes and radio was in the cost of distribution. Given the wide range in radio production costs, this probably has little real validity as a statement, and reflected working practices in the BBC's Open University Production Unit at that time.

In the case of audio-cassettes, distribution involves the capital costs of the equipment used to copy cassettes from a master tape, the recurrent costs of the copying service and the direct costs of getting the cassette to each student (including the cost of blank tapes, labels, covers, packaging and postage, and handling costs). These costs are variable or, in the case of the copying service, semi-variable with the number of students. The presence of variable and semi-variable costs is an important difference from the cost of radio broadcasts, where the cost of transmission is fixed, unrelated to the number of students on the course. Although low (the Open University calculated in the early 1980s that the cost of supplying a single C60 tape with the equivalent of three Open University radio broadcasts on the tape was just under £0.50), the presence of a student-variable element to the cost means that the total cost of delivery rises with every student. Assuming that the cost of transmitting one hour's worth of programming would be £225, if the cost of sending a cassette is £0.50, it follows that cassettes would have to be sent to 450 students before the distribution cost matched the cost of a single broadcast of each programme. In the University's case, they compared cassette distribution with a transmission pattern that allowed for repeats. The break-even point in the number of students (S) at which the cost of transmission is equivalent to the cost of sending cassettes out to students can be calculated easily where:

F = fixed cost of transmitting one hour's worth of radio programming, with repeats = £450
V = variable cost of supplying one C60 audio-cassette, to a student = £0.50p.
S = the number of students.

such that:

$$F = VS = £450$$

and

$$S = F \div V = 450 \div 0.5 = 900$$

So the break-even point (S) where the cost of cassette distribution equals the cost of transmission (including one repeat) is 900 students. Below this level it is cheaper to distribute the programmes on audio-cassette; above this level, it is cheaper to broadcast the programmes. Of course, cassette-based distribution has certain pedagogic advantages over broadcasts (the programme can be designed to be started, stopped and replayed and the student can listen to the material again and again). Also, it is virtually certain that every student will be in a position to listen to the cassette. With radio broadcasts, there is a high chance that students will miss the broadcast. Hence there may well be quality-related arguments in favour of audio-cassettes.

11.3 Video

Like audio, video embraces a range of technologies including:

- film (an expensive medium, now generally replaced by video);
- television;

- video-cassettes;
- video-discs.

Television itself is a complex medium that can be delivered in analogue or digital formats, in various ways, each of which involves different costs.

- Terrestrial transmission, involving the sending of the signal from a ground transmitter, either direct to a receiver or to one or more additional transmitters that relay the signal. Terrestrial transmission works well in compact, densely populated countries, where it is economical, but not in large countries with sparsely populated areas, where it proves very expensive per receiver.
- Satellite transmission, involving the beaming up of the television signal to a satellite which may have various transmitters (known as transponders), each of which can carry either one analogue television channel and several radio channels, or many voice channels, or very large amounts of digitized information, or equivalent mixes of these. Digital compression allows each transponder to carry several television channels simultaneously. Satellites beam their signals down to earth within a given area (known as the footprint), where they can be picked up by dishes, or by a cable head end, for ongoing distribution by cable. Digitized television signals have to be converted into analogue signals before they can be received on an analogue receiver.
- Cable services involve the distribution of the television signal along a cable, which may be coaxial (using copper wires carrying a limited number of channels) or fibre optic, which has a larger capacity. Cable systems are best used in urban areas or large, multi-occupancy buildings. They may receive their signal from a satellite.

(a) Broadcast television

The costs of producing video vary considerably depending on the form and style of medium. The form varies from public service standard television through to educational broadcasting, interactive television and tutored video instruction; the variations in style cover relayed lectures, studio discussions, magazine format programmes, case studies, documentaries, animation etc. The range of costs involved is indicated in a study published by the National Board of Employment, Education and Training in Australia (1994: 36–7), which found that the cost of preparing a 30-minute video in Australian distance-based higher education ranged from as low as A$2500 for 'low-cost' video (though there were cases where costs were even lower) to around A$15,000 for broadcast quality video, with one particular series prepared by Griffith University in association with the Australian Broadcasting Corporation costing A$39,400 per 30-minute programme.

At the broadcast quality end of production, Bates (1995: 79–82) reports on the production costs of the UK Open University's television programmes in 1983/ 84, when the University, in partnership with the BBC, was operating close to its optimum output (Table 11.6). At this time the BBC/OU partnership was producing 230 25-minute programmes each year. The style of the programmes

Table 11.6 *Broadcast television costs at the UK Open University, 1983/84 (£s)*

	Cost per 25-minute programme	Cost per 60-minute programme	Cost per student of one hour of television programming		
			1000 students (125 per year over 8 years)	5000 students (625 per year over 8 years)	10,000 students (1250 per year over 8 years)
Development/production					
Academic time	1200	2880			
Production overheads	17,947	43,073			
Direct production	6000	14,400			
Subtotal	25,147	60,353	60.35	12.07	6.04
Delivery					
Transmission (two per year)	550	1320	10.56	2.11	1.06
Total			70.91	14.18	7.10

Source: Based on Bates, 1995: 81–2

varied enormously, from straight lectures to location filming and the use of animations. Some 85 per cent of the production expenditure in the BBC Open University Production Centre was fixed and 15 per cent variable with the output of programmes (Open University, 1988: 15). The BBC estimated that it could have increased production to 300 programmes per year without affecting its fixed costs.

Programming may, of course, be much less sophisticated than that produced by the BBC for the Open University. Jamison (1977: 30) provides information on the range of costs involved in video production. Stanford University's Instructional Television system used one teacher, one camera operator and two cameras in the studio. The system also included an audio-link back to the studio so that students could question the lecturer and make comments. The format involved direct lecturing to camera, with notes and graphs, by the teacher. The costs per hour for production were approximately US$91. This compared with production costs of approximately US$490 per hour in the case of the Mexican Telesecundaria, which involved a teacher, a director, a camera operator, a technician and materials produced by a graphics department; and with those at the British Open University, using the professional services of the BBC, which cost US$9600 per hour.

The National Technological University video-tapes university lectures for satellite transmission (see Case Study 10.3). The overall production costs per hour are US $178 for the professor's time, $150 studio charges and $120 uplink charges, or $448 per course hour at 1989/90 price levels (Fwu *et al.*, 1992: 122). These are the direct costs, and do not include the costs of reception and of using the satellite. NTU videos live lectures, so these costs are very economical. Other systems set out to record a lecture in a studio. Bates (1995: 103–6) has calculated that it probably takes two days to prepare a one-hour instructional televised programme broadcast live; to this must be added the costs of the studio and its crew, the programme budget, the costs of distribution and the costs of the telephone link back to the studio that enables students to interact with their lecturer. The organization and structure of instructional television systems varies considerably, affecting both the cost structure and the actual costs.

Bates suggests that academic preparation and delivery of a one-hour programme would cost $300, to which would be added a programme budget of $500, giving a variable production cost of $800. Annual studio costs including staff ($100,000) and equipment replacement and maintenance ($150,000) would be spread across all productions. Assuming an output of 117 programmes (as Bates does), this would give a fixed production cost of $2137, to which one would have to add variable production costs of $800 to arrive at a production cost per hour of $2937. Generally, interactive instructional television systems enable institutions to reach out to a dispersed but still group-based student population. Bates suggests that each lecture reaches a not untypical audience of 50 students spread across ten reception sites. The cost per hour of transmission by satellite would be $350. The cost of a telephone link back to the instructor in the studio, using leased lines, for a system of this size, would be $75 per hour. The delivery cost is therefore $425 per hour. A system producing 117 hours of instructional television per year for classes of 50 students would incur a cost of $67.24 per hour per student; if the production level rose to 195 programmes, the cost per hour per student would come down $50.14. However, because each lecture is a new production, and is not reused in subsequent years, the cost of interactive instructional television systems is surprisingly high.

Systems that record lectures and reuse them from one year to the next would incur the same production costs but these would be spread over the number of years the programmes are used. Satellite transmission costs would be unchanged, as would the cost of any interactive telephone link back to the studio. Table 11.7 adapts Bates's data to show the difference between the costs of interactive instructional television where the lecture is filmed each year, and the cost of such a system where the same lecture is used each year, over a four-year period. It is perhaps worth noting that US satellite costs, which rose 300 to 400 per cent during 1996, were historically low because capacity exceeded demand.

Table 11.7   *Interactive instructional television: typical costs*

	Cost per hour ($)			
	Programme used only once		Programme reused over 4 years	
Production level per annum	117 progs	195 progs	117 progs	195 progs
Programmes used	Once	Once	4 times	4 times
Students per course	50	50	50	50
Total students over life	50	50	200	200
Development/production				
Production costs per programme	2137	1282	2137	1282
Development costs per programme	800	800	800	800
Subtotal	2937	2082	2937	2082
Delivery costs				
Per programme, over life of course	425	425	1700	1700
Total cost per programme over life	**3362**	**2507**	**4637**	**3782**
Cost per student hour ($)	**67.24**	**50.14**	**23.19**	**18.91**

Source: Bates, 1995: 104–5; and derived from Bates, 1995: 107–9

(b) Video-cassettes

Video material can be recorded on tape and distributed in the form of video-cassettes. While video-cassettes may be used to capture and copy high quality video material for distribution to students, they have also been used to deliver illustrated lectures to groups of students and individuals in 'tutored video instruction' (TVI) format. TVI normally entails group viewing and discussion of the lecture, in the presence of a tutor who facilitates the discussion. The use of video-cassettes impacts most on the costs of distribution. Cost comparisons between broadcast transmission and distribution on video-cassette in 1988 (Open University, 1988) suggested that the cost of a single 25-minute broadcast transmission was £290. Broadcasts were repeated, so the total cost of transmitting a programme was £580. At this level of cost, it was cheaper to loan students a video-cassette wherever there were under 350 students taking the course. Over this number, broadcast transmission was apparently a more economical option, but this assumed that every student managed to watch the programme – and viewing figures indicated that this was not the case.

11.4 Computing

The development of the personal computer (PC) and associated technologies such as the video-disc and CD-ROM which can be controlled by computer has revolutionized open, flexible and distance education. PCs may stand alone or be networked either locally on local area networks (LANS) or globally (via the Internet) so that electronic communications such as e-mail can be passed between them. Current trends include greatly increasing storage capacity, the integration of video, audio and text, the development of more flexible interfaces between the human user and the computer (including voice recognition, pointing and gestures in the place of keyboards, roller ball and mouse controls), and the fall in the price of hardware.

There is a wide variety of applications of computers in open, flexible and distance education.

- Computer-based tutoring systems, generally called computer-assisted instruction (CAI) that support learner-directed learning. These may cover fairly low-level multiple choice objective tests with feedback to the student on their performance, but also embrace more sophisticated presentations using the presentation capabilities of CD-ROMs and video-discs (Van den Brande, 1993: 20).
- Intelligent tutoring systems (ITS) in which the 'tutor' is embedded in the computer and adapted to the learner's individual needs. Such systems incorporate knowledge about tutoring techniques, the course, the learner (what can the learner do, what does the learner know, what kind of learner is being examined and what has the learner done so far?), and the learner/tutor dialogue. The most important feature of ITS is the ability to individualize the instruction. Systems may be user driven (learning environments, systems for learning by discovery and systems for learning by doing), or tutor driven (programmes in which the system has complete control over each step of the interaction). ITS uses various didactic strategies including (1) Socratic dialogue where the system poses questions and presents situations through which the learner is driven to recognize inconsistencies in his or her own reasoning; (2) reactive environments, which allow learners to solve problems

without intervention from the programme, only when the learner asks for help is it given; (3) rote learning, where the tutoring system actively intervenes to facilitate the learning process; and (4) learning while doing, where the tutoring system is incorporated into the operating system, and intervenes at appropriate points when the learner gets stuck or makes a mistake (Van den Brande, 1993: 20–22).

● Explorative learning environments. Explorative learning scenarios do not try to guide the learner towards some predefined end, but offer a stimulating environment that the learner can explore. They include computer-based simulations (Van den Brande, 1993: 27).

Computer-based learning systems are difficult to cost, and generalizations about current costs have dubious future utility as the costs of hardware come down and as software tools help bring down the labour costs of developing and producing systems. At the same time, individual systems may span an enormous range of complexity, from the relatively simple to the very complex. The costs to an institution also vary depending on whether the system has been specially designed in-house, developed for the institution under contract, or bought in off the shelf. Bates (1995: 197) suggests that development costs can range from Canadian $2600 per hour to $21,170 per hour. The range of cost per student study hour reflects the wide variation in development costs, as well as the number of learners using the system.

Computers can also be used to facilitate communication between students and tutors, and among students, and these applications are considered in the next chapter.

11.5 The relative costs of the different media

Clearly, different technologies have very different cost structures: that is, the relative balance between fixed and variable costs varies, and therefore the behaviour of the costs relative to the volume of learners in the system also varies. For a given number of students, each technology will be more or less cost efficient relative to another (ie have a higher or lower unit cost per student). The key issues are as follows.

● Are the fixed costs high or low?
● Are the variable costs per learner high or low?
● How many students are there using the technology?

Over the years, various writers on the economics of educational media and distance education have drawn generalized conclusions from the studies available. By the late 1970s and early 1980s, these writers (Eicher, 1978, 1980: 14; Jamison and Orivel, 1978: 174–5; Perraton, 1982: 15) felt able to draw some broad conclusions based on the various studies on the economics of new educational media undertaken during the 1970s.

- The cost structure of distance education systems differs considerably from that of traditional systems. Investment and fixed costs are higher and operating costs are generally lower.
- The proportion of fixed costs within the total cost is often high, frequently exceeding 50 per cent. This cost structure means that enrolment levels are of particular importance.
- Design and production costs for audio-visual educational programmes are generally much higher than the costs of transmission and reception.
- Production costs are particularly high for film.
- Production costs are high for television but economies of scale can be rapidly achieved as audience sizes move from 2000 to 200,000.
- Production costs are low for radio.
- Fixed costs of transmission are much higher for television than for radio (of the order of 10:1), although they vary considerably depending on the geographical coverage and the number of broadcasting hours involved.
- The transmission costs of audio-visual educational programmes can be lowered significantly where existing broadcasting installations are used, as opposed to building new transmission networks.
- Transmission and duplication costs are very high for video systems.
- Unit costs for open-circuit television transmission are high for audience sizes below 200,000 but thereafter drop rapidly before rising slightly for audiences of one million or more.
- Unit costs for radio transmission are moderate for audience sizes below 100,000 and very low above that number.
- The media giving the greatest potential economies of scale are television, radio and computers (excluding interactivity).
- The media giving the least or no economies of scale are language laboratories and film.
- The media for which unit cost increases with the magnitude of the project are films (once a certain level of population dispersal is reached) and video systems, the costs of which rapidly become prohibitive because of duplication problems.
- As a rule, the 'little media' (that is, those requiring inexpensive equipment such as slide projectors and tape recorders) offer far greater cost advantages than the 'big media' (such as television and computer-based instruction) where small audiences are concerned, but their relative advantage diminishes subsequently.
- Radio, however, keeps its relative advantage over the 'big media' whatever the audience size. Further, where radio reaches large audiences, it is much cheaper than any other medium.
- Audio-cassettes are likely to be cheaper than radio where the audience size is restricted.
- Radio is cheaper than television except where television reaches very large audiences.
- Projects using television seem to have higher unit costs.

More recently Bates (1995: 4–6) has summarized the position on the basis of his own studies. He concludes that print, audio-cassettes, and prerecorded Instructional Television are the only media that are relatively low cost for:

1. courses with small (under 250 students a year) populations – where the cost is likely to be less that US$2 per student contact hour;
2. courses with populations of from 250–625 students a year – where the cost is likely to be less than $1.50 per student contact hour; and
3. large population courses (over 1000 students a year) – where the cost is likely to be less than $1.50 per student contact hour.

In addition, radio is also likely to be low cost (under $1.50 per student hour) on courses with populations of 1000 or more students. Of the various media:

- audio cassettes and radio have low fixed and low variable costs;
- good quality broadcast television has high fixed costs but zero variable costs;
- pre-programmed computer-based learning and multimedia have high fixed and high variable costs.

While these findings have some general validity, they need to be treated with care. The actual costs of any particular system are affected by many factors – the quality of the output, the exact specification of the technology employed, the working practices used, local factors affecting costs etc – and hence the range of costs reported may be very wide. Bates's findings are very largely based on his studies of media costs at the UK Open University – and these are not necessarily transferable to other settings. Nevertheless, the absolute (total) cost of any media can be established within any particular system, and this data can be used to establish whether, for a given number of students, the unit costs are high or low, relative to alternative media. This is important information for management to have.

However, while cost is clearly an important consideration, it is not the only one: other criteria such as the accessibility of the technology, the extent to which it can be supported within a particular organizational environment, the extent to which it meets the needs of teachers as a vehicle to deliver the course and the extent to which it does or does not provide for two-way communication, either synchronous or asynchronous, are also important. The relative pedagogic effectiveness of each medium is also important. After all, if students learn as well or better using cheaper technologies, there is no real pedagogic or economic case for using more expensive ones. The rational choice should be to maximize cost effectiveness. However, media are rarely used on their own. Disentangling cause and effect to reach a judgement about the relative cost effectiveness of one medium as against another is probably impossible, given the number of other influences on the teaching-learning process. The most that can be done is to say that students studying in such and such an institution with such and such a combination of media have a certain success rate. Section 14.3 addresses this complex area.

Chapter 12

Student support

This chapter examines the costs of supporting students. It is divided into two parts, the first dealing with pedagogic interaction with individual students and groups of students, and the second with the administration of students.

12.1 Interaction with students

The technologies that enable teachers and students to interact with each other, and students to interact with other students include:

- correspondence tuition;
- face-to-face tuition;
- two-way radio, using short-wave receive and transmit sets;
- telephone tuition;
- audio-conferencing;
- narrow-band satellite transmission, allowing two-way audio communication;
- video-conferencing;
- computer conferencing;
- electronic mail (e-mail) systems.

(a) Correspondence tuition

Correspondence tuition involves the submission of written assignments by the student to a tutor for marking and assessment. The marked assignment is returned to the student with the tutor's comments, so that the student can learn from the comments. The main cost of correspondence tuition is the fee paid to the tutor, and normally a fee is paid for every script marked. Additional costs include the cost of postage from the student to the tutor (usually paid by the student) and back to the student, the costs of any stationery and the handling costs. In projecting the costs of correspondence tuition, account needs to be taken of the proportion of students likely to return an assignment.

(b) Face-to-face tuition

Many open, flexible and distance learning systems offer their students some face-to-face tuition. These may be tutorials of from one to three hours duration, or longer periods of study, possibly involving a residential element. In the latter case, a distinction needs to be made between the teaching cost and the cost of residence. The teaching cost may involve several elements.

- The costs of tutoring students. In systems where the tutor is employed by the institution on a salaried basis, the cost of tutoring a particular course is likely to be calculated on the basis of the hourly cost of tutoring (related in an appropriate way to the tutor's total salary cost) times the number of hours tutored. Many institutions, however, will employ casual staff as tutors and pay them a flat rate fee per hour. In such cases, the total cost of tutoring will be the number of hours tuition times the fee per hour for tutoring. Some systems may pay tutors a flat rate fee for preparation which should also be taken into account.
- The costs of tutor's expenses (eg travel).
- The costs of equipment required to teach students.
- The costs of any consumables used during teaching.
- The costs of accommodation hired for teaching purposes.

The overall costs of tutoring will be affected greatly by the staff:student ratio. Basically, the higher the ratio, the fewer tutors there will be for a given number of students, and hence the more economical the system.

However, there is another factor, and that is the geographical spread of the students. In urban areas there may well be large numbers of students taking a course, making it possible to set up a number of tutor groups of, say, 25 students each, in the knowledge that the students will be able to travel easily to tutorials. In less populous areas, or where there are relatively few students taking a course, establishing a tutor group based on the rigid application of the standard tutor:student ratio of, say, 1:25, would result in students having to travel excessively far to attend tutorials. In such circumstances one of the following decisions might be taken.

- Appoint more tutors than the ratio would formally allow, so that more, smaller groups can be established, and students do not have to travel so far for a tutorial.
- Change the teaching strategy so that while some students may still have to travel a long way, it is made more worthwhile by concentrating tutorials into a given day. Students then travel to attend a 'day school' or 'weekend school' providing them with six, 12 or 15 hours of tuition in return for one journey – rather than offering lots of one- or two-hour tutorials on different days throughout their course. Of course, this may not be as desirable in terms of pacing students through their course with regular tutorials.

- Change the teaching strategy by scrapping face-to-face tutorials and putting the money into other forms of support (for example, telephone tuition and various forms of conferencing).
- Make tutorials optional, providing them only for those students who live in areas where it is viable to have tutorial groups.

(c) Telephone tuition and audio-conferencing

Telephone tuition is the process of linking one telephone used by a tutor to another used by a learner. In many cases, there will be a single learner at the learner's end of the conversation, but sometimes there may be several students grouped around a loud-speaking telephone. Audio-conferencing in which several lines are connected at the same time through a special switchboard (called a bridge) allows one or more tutors to speak with several students or groups of students, all at different locations.

Technological change in telecommunications, and particularly the development of Integrated Services Digital Networking (ISDN), coupled with other developments in satellite and fibre optic technologies, is bringing the cost of telephone services down. However, an important factor in the costs of these services to both the providing institution and the user is the pricing structure adopted by telecommunication providers, and the extent to which institutions use public networks or have access to their own private networks. The enormous variation in telephone costs makes it difficult to provide guidelines on costs.

The advantage of conferencing is that it reduces travel costs. Robinson (1990) has argued that audio-conferencing is always cheaper than the costs of face-to-face travel when the travel costs of all the participants (students and tutors) are taken into account. Budget holders, however, usually think about their own budgets – and not necessarily about the costs of all the contributors.

(d) Video-conferencing

Video-conferencing can be of two kinds: from a central point, via satellite, to a number of reception sites; or point-to-point, linking two or more sites through telephone lines. Satellite-borne video-conferencing involves the cost of a central studio and the requisite staff, both presentation and technical; the cost of reception sites, usually including a local facilitator; the cost of transmission and, for any sizeable system, the costs of project management. Some studies suggest that costs compare well with the alternative of bringing staff together, but it is not always clear whether the full costs of the system have been taken into account. Nettleton's study of the Telecom/Telematique project (see Case Study 12.1) suggests that the costs of video-conferencing were a large part of the overall project costs.

Case Study 12.1: The Telecom/Telematique International Course in Project Management
(derived from Nettleton, 1992)

Nettleton (1992) reports on an international course designed and implemented by Telecom/Telematique Inc for the International Telecommunications Union to train telecommunications administrators in advanced management skills. The course was designed to meet the needs of small groups of managers (from five to ten per group) in countries in Asia, Africa, Latin America and the Middle East. In the event, students enrolled from ten countries: Barbados, Curacao, Brazil, Chile, and Colombia in the Americas; Cameroon and Kenya in sub-Saharan Africa; Egypt and Malta in the Mediterranean; and Malaysia. The course was taught by a professor from the George Washington University. The 16-week course, which was based on a pre-existing one offered by the professor, involved the development of a detailed workbook and exercises, and the use of relevant readings. Each group received a copy of the course's 22 video-taped lectures, together with the printed narratives and overheads from these lectures. They also received the participant's manual containing readings, case studies, class notes, problems and exercises. The syllabus set out weekly activities, assigned readings and homework, and requested discussion summaries and group activities to be submitted to the faculty.

Students met in groups each week to view the lectures, prepare the assignments, and receive and transmit materials to the course headquarters. They also spent considerable time working on their own. In Washington, course staff received and graded the students' assignments and quizzes, and responded to participants' queries. Assignments and queries were delivered electronically by e-mail supplemented by fax when graphs and diagrams were involved, and the professors' comments and grades were sent back in the same way. In the event the storage costs of long text messages sent to numerous mailboxes in each country proved to be higher than the project's designers had expected, and as a result the number of electronic mailboxes was reduced. Instead, a microcomputer was purchased and installed in George Washington University which could be accessed by participants. This reduced the storage costs, but greatly added to participants' costs because they had to pay long-distance call tariffs to obtain and exchange text required for reading and assignments.

Audio conferences were held once a month for each region, simulating classroom seminars, and four video-conferences were held. The format of the latter involved the delivery of a lecture by a guest lecturer, who then joined the Telecom/Telematique faculty in discussion of presubmitted, written questions from the participants.

Nettleton (1992: 143–4) provides details of the costs of the course (in 1990 US$) (see Table 12.1 below). She makes the point (p. 144) that $201,432 of the delivery costs was the video-conferencing element, and that without this element the ratio of course development to delivery costs would have changed from 18:82 to 39:61. Similarly, without the video-conferencing element, the cost per participant would have come down to $2587.

> Without the video-conferencing element, the course cost compares well with the cost of delivering a comparable course in-country ($4286 per student) or of bringing a participant to Washington for a ten-day seminar ($4000) that would inevitably have lost a lot by compressing a 16-week course into 10 days.

Table 12.1   *The Telecom/Telematique International Course in Project Management*

Cost component	Total ($)	Per student ($)	Per cent (%)
Course development	69,978	1000	18.3
Course delivery			
– staff and overheads	41,729	596	10.9
– courseware	32,724	467	8.5
– telecommunications	238,130	3402	62.3
Subtotal	312,583	4465	81.7
Total	**382,561**	**5465**	**100.0**

Source: Nettleton, 1992: 143

Point-to-point video-conferencing systems can be bought off-the-shelf from a range of manufacturers, and can vary from desk-top systems linking one person sitting at a particular desk to another, to self-operated studios where several people can join in the conference at the same time. Charbonneau and Cunningham (1993: 99) report that at Athabasca University video-conferencing with a video-out, audio-back link to sites at Edmonton and Calgary resulted in three kinds of savings: the elimination of travel costs, a 50 per cent reduction in instructional time and costs (given that instructors could teach two groups simultaneously from one location) and an increase in faculty productivity owing to the elimination of travel stress and downtime. Against this, they rightly point to the capital requirements involved if the providing institution decides to buy the facilities. Each site requires a minimum Canadian $50,000 investment in hardware – and this can only be justified economically if a substantial number of courses and students are involved at each site. The alternative to buying facilities is to rent them. In Athabasca's case, Alberta Government Telephones rented studios at the then (late 1992) commercial rate of Canadian $275 per hour. The cost of leasing exceeded the savings identified above.

(e) Computer conferencing and e-mail systems

Electronic mail provides one-to-one or one-to-many written communication over telephone lines. Computer conferencing provides a more sophisticated environment in which participants can, as well as exchanging e-mail with each other on an individual basis, join conferences on particular topics in which written messages can be read as they are added to the conference. Participants may have read-only rights to the conference, or they may be able to add their own written comments to the conference in the form of messages. One or more participants (usually the conference moderator who, in distance education systems, tends to be a tutor) have the right to remove messages. The conference provides a structure in which messages can be grouped by topic, and one of the key functions of the moderator will be to do this.

Students may also be able to access bulletin boards (giving them the option of reading any messages or articles posted on the board) and databases.

E-mail and computer conferencing systems rely on networks. Most educational institutions are linked to the Internet, paying a flat rate fee for the privilege that varies depending on the bandwidth used by the institution.

Muzio (1992: 75) reports on the communications costs of the Certificate Programme in Computer Based Information Systems offered by the University of Victoria, Canada. This system went through a process of transformation. In the first phase (January 1988 to September 1990) students connected to the University of Victoria's mainframe computer from their own PC, via a modem, using Kermit communications software and BC Telephone's DATAPAC packet switched network. On the mainframe, students were able to use electronic mail to communicate with instructors, transfer data files to and from their own PCs and participate in computer conferences. Students were charged Canadian $50 for this service. However, the average cost per student including DATAPAC and mainframe charges was $128 (1989 price levels). The programme was therefore subsidizing students by about $78 each. In the second phase, students used their PCs, modems and Kermit communications software to link directly to an IBM PC in the course office, which ran a bulletin board. It cost the course $350 to have the bulletin board. The students paid their own telephone charges to access the system.

Rumble (1989b) undertook a study of the costs of using computer conferencing on the Open University's DT200 course, *An Introduction to Information Technology*. Case Study 12.2 reports on his findings.

Case Study 12.2: Computer conferencing in an Open University course
Based on Rumble, 1989b: 146–65

DT200 *An Introduction to Information Technology: Social and Technological Issues* was first offered to Open University students in 1988. At the time of writing (1996), the course has been withdrawn and replaced with a new course. What made the course interesting from the Open University's point of view was that it was the first to use computer conferencing extensively. The University was therefore very interested in the costs of its computer-mediated communications element. The course required students to work through texts, watch television programmes, listen to radio programmes and audio-cassettes and undertake assignments. However, 20 per cent of the estimated 420 hours of student study time was allocated to working on a microcomputer system, developing practical skills in the use of various IT systems, including computer conferencing and electronic mail. Students were given a technical specification for an IBM PC compatible, and it was assumed that some students would already have a machine that satisfied this specification. Arrangements were made for other students to buy an approved machine (an Amstrad PC1512). Finally, some students were to be allowed to rent a machine from the University. Of the 1403 students who enrolled on the course, 537 (38.3 per cent) rented a machine, 382 (27.2 per cent) purchased one and 484 (34.5 per cent) made their own arrangements for access. Students needed a telephone with a standard socket to use the modem that was loaned to them, together with a lead, by the University. Some students with older telephones needed to have a suitable telephone socket installed. The University decided to adopt the CoSy Conferencing System that had been developed by the University of Guelph, but, to make the system more user-friendly, it developed its own front-end system to CoSy.

(a) Development and fixed production costs

The development costs could be annualized over the life of the course. The introduction of computer-mediated communication required the acquisition of considerable technical expertise, and staff developing the course spent some time in learning about e-mail and computer conferencing. This had a significant cost (£37,370). The front-end development of CoSy cost £39,730. Although this human and system capital would have a utility beyond the life of DT200 (ie DT200 might have been regarded as a joint product which along with other courses would derive benefit from the investment in human capital), the cost study charged all of this cost to DT200. The development of associated course text and an audio-cassette involved a fixed cost of £2622. Equipment purchased at this stage involved the expenditure of £3600 on micros, for course team use. The space cost was estimated at £2126. These were legitimate charges to the course alone.

In addition to these costs, the team developed supplementary textual material which it expected would require annual replacement. The annually recurring fixed development cost of this was £2780.

(b) Distribution costs

These effectively covered the costs of storage and despatch of course materials, and the handling costs of servicing the modem which was loaned to students on a returnable basis. Apart from some of the packaging, which was reusable, the costs were all recurrent.

(c) Reception costs

Members of the University's academic staff taught the course on-line at an estimated cost of £20,720. The University's other significant costs were the network and central computer costs associated with the course (£74,736), the purchase of a pool of microcomputers for loan to students (£360,000), and the purchase of modems for loan to students (£159,505). The tuition costs associated with this element of the course cost £38,722 in total.

The students' most significant costs involved purchase of a microcomputer. The estimated costs incurred by all the students registered on the course were:

- £521,010 spent on the purchase of a microcomputer. An assumption was made that all students who owned their own micro bought it for the course, even though some already owned one. Another assumption was that they bought a standard course micro. Some of course bought more expensive machines;
- micro hire (for those who did not purchase) at a total of £80,550;
- line charges (£24,357);
- the cost of installing a modern telephone socket to take a modem (£18,270).

The tutors' most significant costs included purchase of a microcomputer (£10,710) and line charges (£2827). The University also paid out £7200 renting micros for some tutors.

Table 12.2 below provides information on the costs of the system.

Table 12.2   *Costs of computer-mediated communication in a UK Open University course*

Who pays for what	Category of cost	Item of expenditure	Non-recurrent (£)	Recurrent (£)
UNIVERSITY				
Development	Human resource	Course materials	37,370	
		CoSy front-end	39,730	
	Stocks	Fixed print and audio	2,622	
		Fixed supplementary print		2,780
	Expenses	CoSy license	1,359	
	Equipment	Microcomputers	3,600	
	Space	Recharge	2,126	
Distribution	Human resource	Modem servicing		4,600
	Stocks	Variable print, audio and discs		2,781
	Expenses	CoSy licence		567
		Postage		658
		Packaging	3,000	600
		Storage/despatch recharge		7,000
Reception and delivery	Human resource	Central academic teaching		20,720
		Help desk (marginal additional cost)		1,000
	Expenses	Network running costs		74,736
		Help towards tutor purchase of microcomputer	1,050	
		Hire of micros for tutors		7,300
		Tutor costs (insurance/line charges)		853
		Fee for tutoring on CoSy		9,012
		Tutor marked assignment fees		29,710

Table 12.2 *Costs of computer-mediated communication in a UK Open University course (continued)*

Who pays for what	Category of cost	Item of expenditure	Non-recurrent (£)	Recurrent (£)
	Equipment	Microcomputers bought for student loan	360,000	
		Modems for loan to students/tutors	159,505	
	Space	Recharge		535
Subtotal			**610,362**	**162,852**
STUDENTS Reception and delivery	Expenses	Hire of microcomputers		80,550
		Micro carriage (mail order purchased machines)		1,930
		Insurance		4,092
		Maintenance contract option		2,000
		BT line charges		24,357
		Telephone calls to help desk		100
		Installation of modern BT socket	18,270	
	Consumables	Paper and discs		13,700
	Equipment	Microcomputers (already) owned	280,350	
		Microcomputers (purchased)	240,660	
		GEM software	3,038	
Subtotal			**542,318**	**126,729**
TUTORS Reception and delivery	Equipment	Microcomputers (already owned)	6,300	
		Microcomputers (purchased)	4,410	
	Expenses	Installation of modern BT socket	580	
		Line charges		2,827
Subtotal			**11,290**	**2,827**
TOTAL			**1,163,970**	**292,408**

Source: Based on Rumble, 1989b: 154–5

Case Study 12.2 provides an indication of the costs that could be incurred in setting up a computer conferencing system to support student learning. It also shows clearly why one should be wary about drawing conclusions from the costs of one system, and applying them to another. For example:

• It is unlikely that many organizations would build a front-end support system for a commercial computer conferencing system.

- The University wanted to keep the costs of the system down so as not to penalize students. The provision of a pool of computers that students could hire (rather than commit themselves to the purchase of a machine), and the practice of providing some items of equipment (in this case a modem) on loan to the students, reflects this objective.
- When the system was developed, very few students had access to a personal computer. Now, seven years later, ownership of PCs is more commonplace, and it is arguable that the University could now have assumed student ownership of a PC, just as it assumes that students have a radio and a television set. Assuming student ownership of a PC, the overall cost would have looked very different indeed.

The case study also illustrates the importance of costing the full computer conferencing system – including the contributions from the University as provider, the students and the tutors. It is arguable that the costs of computers which tutors and students had already bought might have been treated as sunk costs, but on the other hand this would be an important consideration in cases where student ownership could not be assumed. In this connection, it is worth noting that the Open University project included a mix of people who already owned a computer, those who bought one and those who hired one. The figures would have to be recast to find out what the relative costs of buying against hiring microcomputers might be. Also, some of the users chose to, or had to, incur costs which others did not: for example, only some students bought the GEM software, only a few took out maintenance contracts and only some of them had to install a modern telephone socket. Again, these are context-specific issues. Finally, the original costing made no attempt to identify the overhead administrative costs of the scheme, nor, as Bates (1995: 220) points out, did it include the cost of tutor training.

Phelps *et al.* (1991: 12–14) compared the costs of a two-week, traditional classroom-based residential engineering course for US Army reservists with a computer-mediated communications (CMC) version of the same course. Both versions of the course involved some start-up costs. The CMC course involved modifying the materials written for the residential course, so that they could be delivered on-line. Their calculations are not wholly clear but the data they provide suggests that the CMC version of the course involved three cost elements:

1. conversion costs (staff time in redesigning the course) of US$152,300;
2. start-up costs (equipment and training) of $73,100, which they amortized over five presentations (ie $14,600);
3. recurrent presentation costs of $121,300.

so that the total cost of the CMC version of the course after one presentation was $152,300 + 14,600 + 121,300 = $288,200. It is unclear why the start-up costs were amortized but not the costs of conversion, particularly as the intention was to show that the CMC course became progressively cheaper. The start-up costs are not amortized in the table below. The residential version of the course cost $5793 per student, so that after one presentation the total cost was $289,600 for 50 students. Phelps *et al.* then projected the total costs of the residential and CMC courses over five and then ten presentations, comparing the cumulative costs of the CMC and residential versions of the course to show how the CMC course becomes progressively cheaper:

Table 12.3   *Comparative costs of residential and computer-mediated communications courses*

	Total cost (US$)		
	1 presentation	**5 presentations**	**10 presentations**
CMC course			
Fixed cost	225,400	225,400	225,400
Variable costs per student	121,300	606,500	1,213,000
Total CMC course costs	346,700	831,900	1,438,400
Residential course	289,650	1,441,000	2,882,000
CMC course costs as % of residential course costs	119.7%	57.7%	49.9%

Source: Derived from data in Phelps *et al.*, 1991: 12–14

(f) Third generation distance education systems

Third generation distance education systems combining electronic access to multi-media materials held on CD-ROMs and in tele-libraries, computer conferencing, and the electronic interchange of assignments between tutors and students, provide exciting opportunities which educationalists are beginning to exploit. Such systems have cost structures that are different to those found in either traditional education or in first and second generation distance education systems.

It seems likely that the development costs may come down provided that designers only use pre-existing materials. If the materials are purpose built, then the development costs may well be high, particularly if full advantage is taken of the opportunities to develop multi-media. Production costs may be much less, especially where students access materials from a central tele-library. Delivery costs will vary, depending on the bandwidth required to transfer the materials electronically from the tele-library to the student. Most systems seem to put these costs onto the student. Support costs may also change. There could be 'just in time' (JIT) and 'only when required' tutoring systems in which tutors are paid for the time they spend helping a student, with students able to choose whether they put in an assignment for formative marking, or whether they exchange messages with the tutor, seeking advice. The costs of the administrative infra-structure are also likely to be different, with students registering on line and paying by electronic transfer of funds. Associated with these changes, there is likely to be a significant reduction in buildings and accommodation costs as organizations shift from physical to virtual locations. On the other hand, virtual organizations can only operate where course developers, tutors, students and administrators have access to interface devices through which they can communicate. The costs of the hardware, software and courseware used in virtual systems is volume dependent, and while it seems likely that unit costs will drop as more and more people use the systems, it is by no means clear what the cost structure is likely to be, relative to volume of participants in the system. Most of the systems for which economies of scale are being claimed appear to be quite small.

Some of the present systems in existence are experimental, run by small groups of idealists who are not interested in making money. For example, Hall (1994: xii) reported that the Globewide Network Academy, an on-line university incorporated in Texas, has been established by a group of academics with a shared vision of 'a non-profit-making higher education establishment available to all, free of the hierarchy and bureaucracy... [that]... bedevils traditional academia'. Whether such a structure can be sustained remains to be seen. Hall reports that a 'variety of administrative and financial platforms' (ibid: xii) are emerging to support virtual schools and universities. What is certain is that the cost structures and funding mechanisms of new organizational forms is likely to be very different from existing systems, and may well eventually be funded on a utility-like pay-as-you-consume basis.

12.2 Administration of students

In addition to the costs of teaching, there are the costs of administering students. Functional analysis can provide a way into the costing of such services by ensuring that every element of the services offered is identified. The main approach is to break down the functions through a process of 'functional decomposition'. This process can go through a number of levels: for example, the function of student administration may be broken down into a number of subsidiary functions:

- promoting and marketing courses;
- providing advice about the services offered;
- enrolling students;
- assigning students to services (tutors, tutorial centres, examination centres etc);
- managing students' fee accounts;
- setting up and maintaining a student's record;
- examining students.

The actual process of planning and developing student services to support distance learners can itself be a major financial commitment (for example, the most recent full-scale redevelopment of the student record system at the UK Open University was estimated in 1993 to have a cost in excess of £10 million over a five-year redevelopment period). No specific guidance can be given about the costs of the student administrative system, but in general the following holds true.

- The more standardized the system, and the fewer exceptions requiring individual attention, the cheaper the system is likely to be. Any system that sets up academic rules and regulations, and then allows individual students to plead special circumstances that require clerical, administrative or academic vetting, will see the costs of handling students increase.

- Modern IT systems have enormous advantages. They enable data and systems to be shared between the various functions of the business. There are considerable savings to be made in handling data and information on students in ways that enable decisions about a student's case to be made rapidly, on the basis of data available on screen.
- It pays to invest in electronic interchange of information, not only between the various functions of an organization, but also between the organization and its customers and suppliers. It is extremely inefficient to produce an order (or a course application) on paper, send it to the institution, and then key in the information. Electronic information exchange will help reduce costs by having students key in their own data.
- The designs of processes can have a major effect on the costs.

12.3 Conclusion

In her book on three telecommunications technologies (computer conferencing, audiographics, and video-conferencing), Mason (1994: 9) decided not to include any costings because 'having been involved myself in a cost study of each of these media, I feel that generalizations about costs are not very useful, and specifics are too dependent on context'. I agree: I would hope that anyone reading this book would treat the examples and case studies in this chapter and Chapters 10 and 11 with care. The fact is that costs are context specific. Salary levels, prices, even the structure of costs, can vary from one situation to another. There is no substitute for costing your own project.

Having said that, there are some generalizations that can be made.

- Correspondence tuition, face-to-face teaching, telephone teaching, e-mail used for teaching purposes and moderated computer-conferencing, have low fixed costs but high variable costs.
- Because these costs are variable with student numbers, total costs escalate rapidly with increases in student numbers.
- The costs of delivering face-to-face tuition may involve the costs of building or hiring and equipping local centres. The more centres there are, the greater the costs.
- If it is important to keep total costs down, then audio- and video-conferencing are best used only on courses with low student numbers.
- Any system that provides equipment for student use (for example, computers and home experiment kits) will see costs increase rapidly. Computer-conferencing and e-mail systems must ultimately rely on student-owned equipment. This raises questions about affordability and access.

Chapter 13

Cost-efficiency

Efficiency is the ratio of output to input. A system is *cost efficient* if, relative to another system, its outputs cost less per unit of input. A system increases its cost efficiency when it maintains output with a less than proportionate increase in inputs. Efficiency can conveniently be divided into two components: *allocative efficiency* is concerned with the allocation of given resources between alternative uses in ways that maximize social welfare; *x-efficiency* is concerned with producing more output without any change in the allocation of inputs. It therefore focuses on inefficiencies such as overstaffing and managerial waste.

Given the desire to reduce educational costs, it is not surprising that considerable amounts of academic research have been generated on the determinants of educational costs and the relative costs of different media and technologies (see Chapters 11 and 12). In the late 1960s and early 1970s there was considerable interest in the cost and effectiveness of new educational media. By 1975, UNESCO was drawing various researchers and agencies together to see if a common approach to the costing of new educational technology initiatives could be agreed. The result of this work was summarized in three volumes (UNESCO, 1977, 1980; and Eicher *et al.*, 1982). This was the period, too, when research undertaken in the United States (cf Jamison *et al.*, 1975, 1978; Schramm, 1977) was indicating that the big educational television and radio instructional systems in countries such as El Salvador, Mexico, Nicaragua and elsewhere, could be efficient and effective ways of delivering primary and particularly secondary education. Finally, the publication of early cost studies of the UK Open University (Wagner, 1972, 1977; Laidlaw and Layard, 1974) led higher education planners elsewhere to think that open universities might prove to be cheaper than traditional forms of higher education. Thus the planners of the Andhra Pradesh Open University, India (now the Dr B R Ambedkar Open University) cited Wagner's studies on the cost efficiency of the UK Open University to support their view that the development of an open university in the state would be the most cost-efficient means of expanding higher education (Committee on the Establishment of an Open University, 1982: 55–6).

The nature of the cost structure of distance education explains why this belief took hold. The costs of traditional education are driven by the labour costs of classroom teachers, and hence are directly related to the number of students. They rise inexorably with increases in student numbers. Distance education changes the production function of education by substituting a range of media for classroom teachers, offering to educationalists what Wagner (1982: ix) described as 'a mass production alternative to the traditional craft approach'. Planners facing massive population growth were pleased to think that there might be an alternative and cheaper way of meeting the rising demand for education.

On the face of it, it should not be too difficult to establish whether one system is more cost efficient than another. However, there are a number of method-ological problems that need to be addressed, and the next section looks in detail at the particular case of the Open University in the United Kingdom because the numerous studies undertaken exhibit some of the problems of comparing the cost efficiency of distance education with that of traditional education.

13.1 The Open University: A case study in methodology

In 1972 Wagner published a paper in which he compared the costs of the British Open University, using 1973 *budget* data, with the costs of traditional universities in the United Kingdom, using information on their *actual* recurrent expenditure in the academic year 1968/69. He *assumed* that there had been no change in the productivity of traditional universities between 1969 and 1973. This enabled him to compare the *recurrent* annual costs of undergraduates in the Open University and in the other universities. On this basis he argued that the recurrent cost per 'equivalent' student in the Open University was about a quarter (26.7 per cent) than in a traditional UK university (£251 against £940) (pp 168, 181). In a footnote to the paper, Wagner made an *adjustment* for the very different volume of research done in the Open University and in traditional universities. This brought the recurrent cost per 'equivalent' student down to £226 in the Open University, and £611 in traditional universities (40 per cent). Surprisingly, having accepted the principle that universities were multi-product enterprises and that the paper was concerned with comparing the costs of teaching in the Open University and in traditional universities (p 161), Wagner chose to provide the unadjusted figures in the summary of his findings on p 181.

The concept of an 'equivalent student' mentioned above needs explanation. Recognizing that the traditional universities taught both undergraduates and postgraduates, while the Open University at that time was teaching very few postgraduates, Wagner used a weighted student load designed to equate post-graduates to undergraduates to give an undergraduate equivalent student. He also pointed out that Open University students were part-time students, while those at traditional UK universities were (almost exclusively at the time) full time, and that if one weighted Open University students as 0.5 of a full-time equivalent student (a weighting that the Open University would broadly have agreed with), the recurrent cost per Open University full-time equivalent student doubled to £502, compared with £940 in traditional universities (53.4 per cent) (p 168). If research were taken into account, the comparison was £453 against £656 (69.1 per cent) (p 170). This was a much more realistic figure. However, Wagner himself chose to compare the lower Open University 'equivalent student' cost with traditional university costs in support of the contention that the Open University was extremely cost efficient, thus ignoring the difference between full- and part-time student costs. He also chose to ignore the effect of research on the comparative costs.

Wagner then looked at the likely comparison between the costs of a 'standard weighted' graduate produced by the Open University and the traditional universities. In the latter this was at least £4000 at 1971 prices, and possibly nearer £4500 (p 176). To do this, he had to project future Open University costs per graduate, anticipating likely graduation rates given likely drop-out rates, which, it was acknowledged, were almost certainly going to be higher in the Open University than in traditional British universities. He concluded that the drop-out rate at the Open University would need to be at least 85 per cent for the cost per graduate at the Open University to rise to the level of cost in traditional universities. Since the drop-out level was likely to be less, the Open University would be more cost efficient than traditional universities (p 177).

Wagner also looked at the *capital* cost per student place which was about £3000 (excluding student residences) in traditional universities, and about £165 in the Open University (pp 173–4). Finally he looked at the total resource cost of two systems, taking account of the opportunity costs involved, including the cost of output foregone through students not being in employment, and the benefits accruing to the Open University system given that Open University students were either in employment or not seeking employment. This enabled him to conclude that the resource cost per equivalent undergraduate in the Open University was about one-sixth that in the traditional universities (£268 against £1577). While he warned against concluding too much from the figures, 'the gap between the Open University and the conventional universities' figures is too large to be ignored... The Open University would seem to have a substantial cost advantage over conventional universities, particularly when capital costs are taken into account' (Wagner, 1972: 181).

Wagner's paper elicited some comments from Carter (1973) who argued it was wrong to make a direct comparison between the costs of teaching in the Open University and in traditional UK universities. The other universities taught expensive subjects such as medicine, which the Open University did not (p 69). In a reply, Wagner (1973: 71) acknowledged that making such an adjustment would reduce the conventional university per equivalent undergraduate by about £40. Carter also argued that the allowance for research should be made, and should not be relegated to the footnote. Making such an allowance would in

Carter's view have a greater impact than Wagner suggested since many costs – for example, library expenditure – would be lower if traditional universities only taught undergraduates. Making allowances for the research output of universities would also change the capital cost comparison significantly (Carter, 1973: 69–70). Surprisingly, perhaps, Carter did not comment that in his conclusions Wagner compared the costs of part-time Open University students with full-time undergraduates, rather than the adjusted comparison for full-time equivalents. However, he did comment that the Open University benefited from the use of public libraries at no cost to its system, whereas traditional universities had to provide their own libraries. The cost of such *free facilities* needed to be taken into account (p 70) – but then, as Wagner (1973: 71–2) replied, conventional students also make use of public libraries in their vacations. In a later comment, Lumsden and Ritchie (1975: 244) pointed out that the Open University did not always bear the real marginal costs of using study facilities in universities, polytechnics, colleges and schools.

Subsequently, Wagner (1977) compared Open University and conventional university costs based on *actual* 1973 expenditure, and projected Open University costs from 1975 to the end of the decade. He revised his original 1973 calculations to show:

- an average recurrent cost per 'equivalent' undergraduate (not, note, per full-time weighted equivalent undergraduate) of £258 in the Open University and £960 in the traditional universities (Open University at 26.9 per cent of traditional universities);
- an average recurrent cost including imputed rental cost of capital at £272 in the Open University and £1111 in traditional universities (Open University at 24.5 per cent of traditional universities);
- an average recurrent cost per graduate of £2719 in the Open University in 1973, with a long-run projection of £1842, compared to a recurrent cost per graduate in traditional universities of from £4049 to £4801;
- a resource cost per 'equivalent' undergraduate of at least £272 in the Open University compared to £1647 to £1947 in traditional universities (Wagner, 1977: 365).

Interestingly, since Wagner's calculation for the cost per graduate took account of the average time it would take an Open University 'equivalent' student to graduate, his comparison with conventional university graduate costs was a reasonable one.

Wagner then went on to look at the changes since 1973. Analysis showed that as the Open University expanded its student numbers, so it reaped economies of scale (Table 13.1).

As Wagner (1977: 366) comments, while the average cost per student indicates that costs are dropping, short-term factors (in Table 13.1, the very small rise in student numbers in 1976 compared to 1975) can limit the value of the year-on-year comparison. This was particularly so because the University was expanding its curriculum, from 43 full-credit equivalent courses in 1975 to 55.16 such courses in 1976, with consequential implications for its non-student-related 'fixed' costs.

Table 13.1 *Average costs at the Open University at 1971 price levels*

Year	Recurrent expenditure £m (current prices)	Student numbers	Average recurrent cost per student at current prices (£)	Average recurrent cost per students at 1971 prices (£)
1973	9.9	38,424	258	258
1974	14.6	42,636	342	255
1975	19.6	49,358	397	240
1976	26.1	50,994	512	249

Source: Wagner, 1977: 374–5, 366

A more detailed analysis of costs, reflecting both student numbers and course numbers as cost drivers, is therefore needed (p 367).

The costs of the Open University were also attracting the attention of other researchers. Lumsden and Ritchie (1975) pointed to *possible adjustments* required in calculating the cost of producing Open University graduates. The University operated a credit transfer scheme under which students who had previous educational qualifications were exempted from the requirement to take some courses towards an Open University degree. Any calculation of the costs of an Open University graduate would need to make adjustments for the fact that some of the work counted towards some students' degrees had not been done within the Open University system (pp 251, 264). They also pointed out that Open University graduates, while they could graduate with a degree after three years equivalent full-time study, had at that time (in the mid-1970s) to take more courses (equivalent to one additional year of full-time equivalent study) to gain an honours degree. An honours degree was the normal qualification gained by traditional university students after three years of full-time study. If the value of an Open University honours degree was the same as the value of a traditional university honours degree, then the cost of the input to teaching had to reflect this by assuming that the honours degree was the normal product of the university system (p 265). As they put it, 'the assumption that the Open University ordinary degree is equal to the average degree of the conventional university is clearly weak' (p 266). The alternative of comparing the cost of an Open University honours graduate with the cost of a traditional university graduate would reduce the alleged cost advantage of the Open University significantly. On this basis, if the Open University's graduation rate dropped below 27 per cent, the Open University's cost per graduate would be higher than the average cost per graduate in traditional universities.

Rumble (1976) calculated that the average recurrent cost per Open University student was £505 in 1976, compared with an average recurrent cost per conventional student of £2446. The incremental cost of expanding the Open University was likely to be nearer £248 per student, with very small numbers of additional students being accommodated at a marginal cost of £116. These figures needed to be doubled (to £1010, £496 and £232) to provide the cost per full-time equivalent student (Rumble, 1976: 20–1, 29).

So far as the cost per graduate was concerned, Rumble argued that the simplest approach was to assume that the Open University was in a steady state, producing a fixed number of graduates per year (at the time, roughly 6000). One could then divide the total recurrent budget by the annual output of graduates to give a recurrent cost per graduate of £4358 (in 1976). However, while many students opted to take a Bachelor's degree following completion of six Open University credits (currently 360 credit accumulation and transfer (CATs) points), some opted to do a further two credits (120 CATs points), to gain an honours degree. If honours graduates had a weighting of 1.33 of a non-honours graduate, and if 50 per cent of ordinary graduates went on to take an honours degree, then the annual output of graduate equivalents was 6990 and the cost per graduate equivalent was £3740, with the cost per non-honours graduate being £3210 and the cost per honours graduate being £4270 (p 29). This backflush costing approach (see Section 7.5) would not work in situations where the University was producing a more varied range of 'products', or where it was expanding. Rumble therefore suggested that the cost per graduate could be derived by multiplying the annual average cost per student (£505 in 1976) by the average number of years a student would be in the system. Another approach was to calculate how long a student was likely to stay in the Open University system and what his or her chances of gaining a degree were. Whereas Wagner (1977: 365) had assumed that students progressed towards their six credit (360 CATs points) degree at the rate of one credit (60 CATs points) per year, and that about 25 per cent of students failed a particular course, Rumble (1976: 31) derived the following formula to measure the number of years a student would remain in the system, taking account of credit exemptions, student course loads and pass rates:

$$\{[C-X] \div [fp]\} \, R = D \qquad \text{[Eq. 13.1]}$$

where:

C = the number of credits required to obtained a degree (six for an ordinary degree, eight for an honours degree)
X = the number of credit exemptions awarded to the average student (0.94 credits)
f = the average number of credits taken by a student each year (1.03)
p = the pass rate per course (0.76)
R = the average cost per student per year (£505)
D = the average cost per graduate (in £s)

Using these figures to compute the average time Open University students would take to graduate gave comparable figures of £3264 for a non-honours graduate, and £4555 for an honours graduate (p 31). However, this credited the University with the value of credits awarded through the University's credit transfer policy. Had the University given no credit for previous study, the average cost per non-honours graduate would have risen to £3870, and the average cost per honours graduate to £5161 (p 31). This compared with the average cost per conventional graduate of £7338.

The importance of course costs had already been indicated in a study by Laidlaw and Layard (1974). They sought to look at the relative costs of individual courses in the Open University, compared with the costs of similar courses in traditional universities, in order to establish first, whether the Open University should expand, and second, whether it should add to its profile of courses. Their studies clearly showed the economies of scale to be reaped as the University expanded (p 440). Unlike Wagner's 1973 study, which was based on the Open University's budget for 1973, their study was based on Open University expenditure in 1971 and 1972. They distinguished between (a) course costs, including costs that are fixed in the sense that they are inescapable if a course is put on, and those that are variable with student numbers on a course; and (b) central University costs, including those that are fixed in the sense that they are inescapable if the University is to exist, and those that are variable with the number of students in the system. Having identified the costs of developing courses, they chose to spread them (ie depreciated them) over the life of the course, such that 'the annual mortgage … if paid over the life of the course, repays the total costs of development' (pp 448–9). They also identified the University's capital costs, which they amortized on an annual basis (p 449). Academic staff time and hence the cost of course production was determined using a formula-approach that assumed staff spent 60 per cent of their time on course development, 10 per cent on central University administration, and 30 per cent on research and other activities. They admitted that the amount allowed for research might be on the high side (p 449). Most other cost elements could be determined or approximated reasonably easily. From this information and from other research into the costs of campus-based courses (see Layard and Verry, 1973), they were able to compare Open University and campus-based course costs at 1971 price levels. Table 13.2 reproduces their data for some courses.

Laidlaw and Layard followed Wagner (1972) in assuming that an Open University student studied half the load of a full-time traditional student, but they counted the actual course load of Open University students (1.2 'full-credit courses' each), and then assumed the load for full-time students was 2.4 full-credit courses, whereas Wagner used student heads as a count, thus underestimating the Open University student load. Laidlaw and Layard acknowledged that this approach might well be seen to underestimate the comparative output of the Open University (Laidlaw and Layard, 1974: 455–6).

Laidlaw and Layard concluded that the real strength of the Open University's system lay in 'the potential economies of scale which can be reaped by substituting capital for labour' (pp 456–7). However, as their detailed figures showed, some courses had not attained sufficient numbers of students to pass the break-even point at which the Open University's system became more cost efficient than campus-based universities, and in at least one case (that of the early geography course, D281) the variable cost per student of the Open University course was such that it would never be more cost efficient than a comparable campus-based course. On this basis they concluded that some of the higher level courses with fewer students could only ever be justified 'on the ground that they are an integral

Table 13.2   *Open University and campus-based university course costs, £ (1971 prices)*

OU courses			Campus courses			Breakeven number of students per annum	Actual OU students 1972
OU courses	Overhead per full-credit course	Variable cost per student per full-credit course	Campus-based university department	Overhead per full-credit course	Variable cost per student per full-credit course		
A100	162,558	56	Arts	401	117	2658	5399
S100	181,158	89	Physics/ Biology	666	218	1398	3596
M201	108,442	56	Maths	671	88	3367	1448
D281	73,702	109	Social Science	671	87		283
E283	78,016	32	Social Science	671	87	1406	3030
SDT286	109,314	70	Physics/ Biology	666	218	734	1634
TS282	115,786	158	Engineering	673	223	1770	1232

Source: Laidlaw and Layard, 1974: 454

part of a system providing wider access to complete degree courses rather than on the ground that they are a cheap way of doing this' (p 458). Laidlaw and Layard (1974: 455) also looked at the central costs of the Open University and campus-based universities, where the fixed costs were £1.584 million and £130,935 respectively, and the variable costs per student were £44 and £111 respectively.

On this basis, the Open University would 'break-even' with 21,691 students. With 31,383 students enrolled in 1972, the Open University was already cost efficient in its second year of teaching. Their figures showed that the ratio of fixed to variable costs at the Open University was 2000:1, compared with about 8:1 in campus-based universities.

Costs which are fixed per course become variable costs if the number of courses are increased. Wagner, building on work done by Smith (1975) and Rumble (1976), used a simple formula:

$$C = a + bx + cy \qquad \text{[Eq. 13.2]}$$

where:

C = the total expenditure
a = fixed costs
b = the variable cost per course (per year)
x = number of courses
c = the variable cost per student
y = the number of students

to analyse and project Open University expenditure (Wagner, 1977: 367). Determining the values of a, b and c for the level of activity in 1976 (Wagner's base year) involved the use of various assumptions about the attribution of costs to output-related activities, but led Wagner to conclude that the value of the cost elements of his formula was:

$$C = £6,967,000 + £100,000x + £248y$$

He went on to point out that although costs could be projected forward by inputting different values for x and y, there were difficulties in doing this. For example, while the average variable cost per student was £248, for small increases the marginal cost per student might be as low as £116, as Rumble (1976: 21) showed. Equally, the average variable cost per course might change depending on the average number of years courses were kept in presentation, and the balance between totally remaking and partially revising them at the end of their life. To allow for this, he adjusted his formula

$$C = a + b_n X_n + b_m X_m + cy \qquad \text{[Eq.13.3]}$$

where:

C   =   the total expenditure
a   =   fixed costs
b_n =   the annual annualized variable development and production cost per new course
X_n =   number of new courses
b_m =   the annual variable cost per course in presentation
X_m =   number of new courses
c   =   the variable cost per student
y   =   the number of students

and input as cost values:

$$C = 19{,}824{,}000 + 436{,}000X_n + 44{,}000X_m + 200y$$

By inputting values for X_n, X_m and y, Wagner was able to project the Open University's costs forward to show continuing economies of scale as the University expanded. However, with the curriculum growing, he concluded that there were unlikely to be further significant falls in the average cost per student, at least in the next few years, suggesting that most of the economies of scale of the Open University had been achieved in its first few years (Wagner, 1977: 370–1). The main reason for this was that the University was using the economies of scale produced by rising student numbers to increase the number of courses it presented (p 371). He then went on to ask how the University might further lower its average cost per student. His answer included changing the components of the University's teaching system by, for example, eliminating costly elements such as broadcasting, by reducing the face-to-face teaching element, by changing the balance between cheaper (arts) courses and more expensive (science) courses or by amortizing courses over a longer period following an extension to their life (pp 372–4).

In 1978 Mace questioned the prevailing view that the Open University was cost efficient: the view that it was producing graduates more cheaply than traditional universities was 'a dangerous myth because it may well inhibit further attempts at economic evaluation of the OU' (Mace, 1978: 295). He argued that there is a general requirement in situations of scarce resource to use the least-cost method to produce a given product (p 303). Could the University, Mace asks, produce graduates at a lower cost by improving its internal efficiency? Mace had no final answers, but he questioned, for example, whether the relatively expensive broadcasting component was essential to the effectiveness of the Open University's teaching system, and he pointed out that by eliminating or reducing dependence on broadcasting, the University might improve its efficiency.

13.2 Technical issues in drawing comparisons

Drawing comparisons between the costs of one institution and another is never easy. The case study on the methodology of the Open University presented in 13.1 shows how difficult comparisons can be. What follows is a check-list of issues that need to be considered when making comparisons.

(a) Comparing like with like in multi-product ventures

Educational institutions are very often multi-product ventures, particularly at the higher education level where staff are involved in teaching, research and development, consultancy and community service, and in the general storage of knowledge and transmission of cultural values. When comparing the costs of different institutions, it is important to separate out the costs of teaching from non-teaching activities, in order to ensure a fair comparison.

(b) Comparing student loads

Some common measure of student load needs to be established if comparisons are to be valid. The unit costs of teaching primary, secondary and tertiary students are normally different; and at tertiary level, the unit costs of undergraduate, taught postgraduate and research postgraduate studies are also different. Some subjects are much more expensive to teach than others – for example, medicine is more expensive than sociology – and account needs to be taken of these differences. Equally, different courses impose different teaching loads on institutions: some degree courses may last three years, others five years. Some kind of adjustment needs to be made for these differences. Also, students may study full or part time, and again, a standard measure of student load needs to be established. Frequently used loads are the full-time equivalent student, however this is defined, and the credit hour.

(c) Comparing outputs

Schools, colleges and universities produce graduates of different kinds. Comparing the relative value of graduates can be problematic. For example, how can we be assured that a graduate in biotechnology from one university is the same as a graduate with a similarly titled degree from another university? Notwithstanding differentiation by degree level (Bachelor's, Master's), subject and class (first, second, third, ordinary), there is no uniform graduate. While this may not in itself be a problem, how do we determine the relative worth of a UK graduate from London, Leicester, Lancaster and Luton universities, let alone graduates from different jurisdictions (UK, India, Japan, United States)? For the purposes of this chapter, and in common with most cost-efficiency studies, one can work on the assumption that, within any jurisdiction, one degree is very much like another of the same level and class and subject. However, cost benefit studies (see Chapter 15) may rightly seek to establish that the degrees of different universities have a different value.

(d) Using common price levels

Inflation is a recurring but intermittent historical phenomenon. During periods of inflation, prices tend to rise, with the result that a unit of currency (say, the pound) buys less and less. The opposite of inflation is deflation, when prices drop over a sustained period of time. In either case, comparisons of actual expenditure from one year to the next become meaningless. Any comparison of data from one year with that from another has to be made using a common price level. This is done through the use of a price index that measures real changes in expenditure having allowed for general inflationary or deflationary pressures. Common indices measure changes in the general cost of living or in retail prices. Such indices take a standard 'basket' of goods and services, and price it. If the price goes up, then this is a measure of inflation. If it goes down, then this is a measure of deflation. The problem with such indices is that the inflationary movement in prices in the goods used to determine a cost of living or retail price index may not apply to education: for example, steep rises in food prices would not be immediately reflected in rises in teaching costs (though ultimately they might affect the salaries of teaching staff). For a while, and to get round this problem, a separate index of university costs was used in the United Kingdom (The Tress-Brown Index), but such purpose-built indices may not exist.

(e) Are the costs realistic, and are all the costs taken into account?

One of the issues raised in the studies of the Open University was whether the University was paying the true market price for some of the facilities it used. The extent to which the costs in a particular system represent the true market costs will affect judgements about its relative cost efficiency.

Generally speaking, when analysing the costs of projects, the market price of resource inputs is used as a measure of their value. Market prices, however, do not always reflect the true economic cost of a resource. Where this is so, economists use a *shadow price* that better reflects the opportunity cost of engaging in some economic activity. For example, many technology-intensive projects, particularly in developing countries, rely on foreign exchange to purchase the technology inputs. Normally the 'price' of foreign currency is reflected in its market exchange rate, and this is therefore the appropriate means for translating the imported technology into local currency values. However, the market for foreign exchange may be imperfect. If a country's currency is overvalued on the world market, a 'black market' may emerge in which one can obtain a higher rate of exchange than the official one. In such circumstances a technology-intensive project will appear less expensive than it really is to the local economy. An artificially low exchange rate in effect means that the local government is subsidizing the importers of technology. While evaluative studies do not depart from the market rate, project planners may need to take account of such features when evaluating alternative options.

Equally, some of the costs may be incurred outside the institutional budget – for example, paid for by students. These costs also need to be reflected in an economic analysis of the system. On the whole, cost studies based on the providing institution's budget and expenditure will take account of fees paid by students, but not those costs that students and others may bear which do not pass through the institutional accounts.

(f) The need to project costs with care

Projecting costs forward is fraught with difficulties, and great care must be taken to ensure that the assumptions used are reasonable. In particular, current unit costs per measure of output may not be a guide to future unit costs. Also, many of the models used to project costs forward assume that the overhead costs of the institution are fixed. This is a dangerously wrong assumption, as Chapter 7 makes clear.

13.3 The development of a common methodology for economic studies of distance education

The desire to compare the relative costs of projects led researchers in the mid-1970s to develop a common, agreed methodology for cost studies. This methodology, developed under the auspices of UNESCO (see UNESCO, 1977, 1980; Eicher *et al.*, 1982) was eventually summarized by Orivel (1987). In summary Orivel pressed for cost analyses that:

- recognize that there are no free resources – the total costs from all contributors (government, local communities and students) need to be included; shadow prices should be used for inputs that do not appear in the accounts;
- separate recurrent costs from capital;
- separate recurrent costs into salary costs (divided between professional staff, and administrative and support staff) and non-staff expenses;
- separate capital costs into equipment and building costs;
- annualize capital costs using three main life-expectancy categories (a) two to five years, (b) six to ten years, and (c) above ten years;
- use a social discount rate of between 0 per cent ('which even satisfies those who disagree with the concept of opportunity costs applied in this context') and 15 per cent ('considered by most specialists as a ceiling rarely achieved on the financial markets');
- separate variable and fixed costs;
- analyse the costs of any system into the following heads: production, diffusion, reception and administration (Orivel's framework is derived from cost studies of educational broadcasting systems, and differs marginally from the systems view put forward in Section 1.3 of this book);
- analyse the costs of each medium separately.

One of the issues that those working in this field face is the question of making comparisons across different jurisdictions. Some researchers choose to convert costs into US dollars in order to give an idea of the relative cost of different systems in a currency that most people in the world understand. This gives a common currency against which one can evaluate the relative cost of, say, a teacher training project in Malaysia with one in Madagascar. But this is in fact a potential source of distortion because the value of the dollar moves against other currencies all the time, and because the cost of inputs (salaries, equipment, paper etc) vary significantly from one country to another. In 1980, for example, Rumble undertook a cost study of the Universidad Estatal a Distancia in Costa Rica (Rumble, 1981). At the time the study began, early in 1980, the value of the colon against the dollar had been fixed for many years at 8.5 colones to the US dollar. In the next few months the colon fell to something like 24 colones to the dollar. Almost instantly, the *local* cost of the project quoted in dollars had been cut to a third of its former cost, though within the country nothing had changed, while the cost of *imported* goods bought with foreign exchange had risen greatly. Further, because the cost of inputs (salaries, paper etc) varies so much from one jurisdiction to another, given the impact of local supply and demand and local taxes on prices, monetary comparison is only really possible within a jurisdiction. Analysing costs in dollars provides a misleading sense of comparative value that does not exist in reality. For these reasons the costs of projects are cited in this book in local currency except where the researchers have converted costs to US dollars and not given the original local currency value in their study.

However, some kind of measure is still needed to enable comparisons to be made across jurisdictions. In any system where the average cost of a student/graduate in the distance mode has been compared with the average cost in the traditional mode, it is possible to establish the ratio of these costs by dividing the average cost in the distance mode by the average cost in the traditional mode. Thus in the case of the Institut de Radio-Educative de Bahia (IRDEB) in Brazil (see Table 13.3) the average cost per student-semester in IRDEB (Cr$2200) can be divided by the average cost per student-semester in private institutions (Cr$505) to give a ratio of 4.36. This ratio is referred to as the *efficiency ratio*.

The efficiency ratio has the value that it can compare the relative efficiency of any distance teaching system with traditional systems in the same jurisdiction, and allow comparisons to be drawn across jurisdictions. A ratio:

- of 1.0 would mean that the distance system is as efficient as the comparator system;
- of less than 1.0 means that the distance system is more efficient than the comparator;
- greater than 1.0 means that the distance system is less efficient than the comparator.

13.4 Evidence of cost efficiency in institutions or departments teaching by distance means alone

This section looks at the evidence of those distance education systems whose efficiency has been compared with the cost per student in a traditional system. Usually, the comparison is based on the cost per student or graduate, with some attempt to ensure similarity between the student in the distance and comparator system through the use of some kind of student equivalent weighting. Tables 13.3 and 13.4 provide information on the cost efficiency per student and per graduate, respectively, of a number of projects, compared with traditional institutions in the same country.

(a) Schools education
Use of educational media in schools has been of three kinds.

1. To supplement the work of the teacher, in the expectation that its use will improve the quality of provision. Where this happens, it tends to add to the costs of provision (though in some cases there are savings where the technology replaces existing methods).
2. In in-school equivalency programmes to replace the work of teachers or to enable schools to operate with less well-qualified teachers. Teachers have, not surprisingly, been resistant to the idea that the number of teaching jobs might be reduced, their status as professionals undermined and their work deskilled. Insensitive handling of the change evoked precisely these feelings during the introduction of educational television in American Samoa in the 1960s. However, in some countries where there is a shortage of trained teachers, distance teaching methods have been used successfully in schools to provide alternative in-class education. Materials have substituted for the teacher to a greater or lesser extent (with the teacher often being 'replaced' by monitors who are less well educated and less well paid).
3. To meet the needs of relatively small numbers of children on isolated rural farms and in isolated communities, as in Australia, or to meet the needs of large numbers of people who are unable to attend a regular school, as in Korea, but who can study at home. Here the materials have effectively been used to provide a correspondence-based education.

There have been a number of studies of in-school equivalency programmes, the results of which are summarized in Table 13.3.

● IRDEB offered the *madureza* (secondary school equivalency certificate for adults) programme to adult students. Oliveira and Orivel (1982a: 79, 84) indicated that with only 8000 student-semester enrolments, and with students studying less intensively than in other systems, the efficiency ratio of IRDEB's distance teaching system was 4.36 compared to conventional private institutions (ie much more expensive). To compete with them on cost grounds, IRDEB's student numbers would have to expand significantly in order to spread its fixed costs over a wider student base.

- With 17,700 students the Minerva project in Brazil provided a cost-efficient route to the madurez (efficiency ratio 0.65) (Oliveira and Orivel, 1982b).

- The Malawi Correspondence College, with 2884 students, provided an efficient correspondence/radio-based alternative route to secondary education (efficiency ratio of between 0.23 and 0.62, depending on the costs in the comparator institutions) (Wolff and Futagami, 1982; 96).

- The Mexican Telesecundaria provides classroom delivered televised lessons supported by monitors and study guides. An early cost study by Mayo et al. (1975a) suggested that the system was efficient (efficiency ratio of 0.76 with 33,840 students), but later cost studies (Molina, 1981; Arena, 1989: 59–60) indicated efficiency ratios of 1.09 (with 170,000 students) and 1.32 or greater (with 400,000 students). Arena (ibid.: 60, 49) may provide one of the clues for this loss of efficiency, even though the number of students in the Tele-secundaria has risen: the school has been so successful that it has expanded into smaller and smaller communities, with the result that the average group size has fallen from 29 in 1975, to 27 in 1981, to 20 in 1989. However, there may be other factors at work as well: for example, the traditional school system may have become more efficient.

- The Centros APEC de Educación a Distancia in the Dominican Republic had an efficiency ratio <1.0 compared with day, afternoon and evening secondary school (Muñiz Aquino, 1988: 36, 39).

- The Korean Air Correspondence High School (ACHS) was set up to reach some of the 1.4 million school-age population who in 1977 could not attend traditional high schools, as well as some of those who had been unable to attend traditional schools in the past. ACHS teaches basically the same curriculum as traditional high schools, using textbooks, self-marked and teacher-marked assignments and radio and television broadcasts. Students can attend at educational centres for face-to-face teaching (with the option of substituting correspondence support if they can not get to a centre). In 1976 the ACHS had 18,782 enrolled students. Lee et al. (1982: 151) indicated that some 90 per cent of the total cost was variable, driven by the number of students, student-hours in classroom teaching, broadcast-hours, production-hours, or student-hours involved in evaluation. The average cost per enrolled student at ACHS (US$41) compared very favourably with that of traditional public high schools (efficiency ratio 0.18) (Lee at al., 1982: 157).

Another way of measuring the efficiency of distance education is to measure the cost per graduate of a system. The drop-out rate in distance education is generally higher than in face-to-face education. This being so, the cost advantage of distance education may be eclipsed by the higher drop-out rate of distance students. Table 13.4 shows the cost per graduate in schools teaching at a distance, and compares this with the cost per graduate in conventional systems, using a *graduate efficiency ratio* (the cost per graduate in a distance system divided by the

Table 13.3 *Comparative costs per student of distance and traditional education systems*

Sector	Institution country*	Measure of cost	Number of students	Unit cost (given currency) (1) Distance	(2) Conventional	Efficiency ratio	Notes	Source study
Schools	IRDEB, Brazil	Average cost per student-semester preparing for three topics, 1977 at 1976 prices	8000	Cr$2200	Cr$505	4.36	1	Oliveira and Orivel, 1982a
	Minerva project, Brazil	Unit cost per student per year	17,700	Cr$258	Cr$400	0.65	2	Oliveira and Orivel, 1982b
	Malawi Correspondence College, Malawi	Average cost per student enrolment (junior secondary level), 1977/78	2884	K133	K216	0.62	3	Wolff and Futagami, 1982
				K133	K580	0.23	4	
	Telesecundaria, Mexico	Average cost per student, 1975 at US$1972	33,840	US$151	US$200	0.76		Mayo et al., 1975a
		Average cost per student, 1981	170,000	Pesos 12,928	Pesos 11,811	1.09		Molina, 1981
		Average cost per student, 1988	400,000 +	US$312.4	US$237	1.32	5	Arena, 1989
				US$327.8	US$237	1.38	6	
		Average cost per group, 1988		US$6239	US$12,318	0.51	7	Arena, 1989
				US$6546	US$12,318	0.53	8	
	Centros APEC de Educación a Distancia, Dominican Republic	Average recurrent cost per student	11,217	RD$180	RD$390	0.46	9	Muñiz Aquino, 1988
				RD$180	RD$325	0.55	10	
				RD$180	RD$300	0.60	11	
	Air Correspondence High School, Korea	Average cost per enrolment, 1976, compared with the public school system	20,000	US$41	US$233	0.18		Lee et al., 1982

(Table 13.3 *continued*)

Sector	Institution country*	Measure of cost	Number of students	Unit cost (given currency) (1) Distance	(2) Conventional	Efficiency ratio	Notes	Source study
Teacher Training	Correspondence Course Unit, Kenya	Average cost per subject equivalent: (a) 1970; (b) 1977	(a) 790 (b) 3650	(a) K£60 (b) K£120	K£40 K£40	(a) 1.5 (b) 3.0		Hawkridge et al., 1982
	Teacher Training at a Distance, Tanzania	Overt cost per distance student over three-year programme	45,534	Tsch 13,095 Tsch 13,095	Tsch 56,610 Tsch 84,915	0.23 0.15	12 13	Chale, 1993
	Distance-education project, Sri Lanka	Total cost per student per year, 1988	approx. 5000	US$251 US$251	US$1401 US$878	0.18 0.29	14 15	Nielsen and Tatto, 1993
	Universitas Terbuka diploma programme, Indonesia	Total cost per student per year, 1988	approx. 5000	US$952	US$1578	0.60		Nielsen and Tatto, 1993
Teacher	Radio Education Teacher Training (one session per year), Nepal	Average cost per teacher	(a) 1000 (b) 3000 (c) 6000	(a) Rs 4979 (b) Rs 3158 (c) Rs 2706	(a) Rs 3628 (b) Rs 3534 (c) Rs 3511	(a) 1.37 (b) 0.89 (c) 0.77		Holnes et al., 1993
University	Open University, UK	Average recurrent cost per student (1973)	36,500	UK£251 UK£226	UK£940 UK£656	0.27 0.34	16	Wagner, 1972
		Average recurrent cost per full-time equivalent student (1973)	36,500	UK£502 UK£453	UK£940 UK£656	0.53 0.69	16	Wagner, 1972
		Average recurrent cost per student (1973) – revised figure	36,500	UK£258	UK£960	0.27		Wagner, 1977

(Table 13.3 *continued*)

Sector	Institution country*	Measure of cost	Number of students	Unit cost (given currency) (1) Distance	(2) Conventional	Efficiency ratio	Notes	Source study
		Average recurrent cost per full-time equivalent student (1976)	51,785	UK£1010	UK£2446	0.41		Rumble, 1976
		Unit teaching costs per full-time equivalent undergraduate student, 1983/84, across various subjects	37,200 FTE	UK£1800 UK£1800	UK£3260 UK£2740	0.55 0.66	17 18	Smith, 1986
	AIOU, Pakistan	Average cost/student (1988)	n/a	Rs 4585	Rs 20960	0.22		Lockheed et al., 1991
	RTVU, China	Average cost/student (1981)	n/a	Y 1000	Y 2000	0.50		Lockheed et al., 1991
	KACU, Korea	Total cost per student per year (1981)	n/a	US$125	US$1250	0.10		Lockheed et al., 1991
	UAJ, Japan	Current expenditure per student (1986): liberal arts	n/a	Y 449,300 Y 449,300 Y 449,300 Y 449,300 Y 449,300	Y 948,900 Y 819,800 Y 545,400 Y 350,900 Y 58,800	0.47 0.55 0.82 1.28 7.64	19 20 21 22 23	Muta and Sakamoto, 1989
		Total cost per student (direct, overheads, and annualized capital costs) (1990)	n/a	Y 456,900 Y 456,900 Y 456,900 Y 456,900 Y 456,900	Y 3,147,100 Y 3,026,900 Y 2,532,900 Y 1,434,000 Y 149,000	0.15 0.16 0.18 0.32 3.07	19 20 21 22 23	Muta and Saito, 1993
	IGNOU, India	Per student cost (1991/92)	n/a	Rs 2046	Rs 5000–25,000	0.41–0.08		Ansari, 1993

(Table 13.3 *continued*)

Sector	Institution country*	Measure of cost	Number of students	Unit cost (given currency) (1) Distance	(2) Conventional	Efficiency ratio	Notes	Source study
	YCMOU, India	Per student cost (1991/92)	n/a	Rs 2214	Rs 5000–25,000	0.44–0.09		Ansari, 1993
	BRAOU, India	Per student cost (1991/92)	n/a	Rs 947	Rs 5000–25,000	0.19–0.04		Ansari, 1993
	KOU, India	Per student cost (1991/92)	n/a	Rs 1824	Rs 5000–25,000	0.37–0.07		Ansari, 1993
	UNED, Costa Rica	Average cost per student (1980)	8148 FYE	US$795 US$795 US$795	US$1301 US$2233 US$4361	0.61 0.39 0.18	24 25 26	Rumble, 1981
Training	Abbey National, UK	Average cost of training per trainee	2700	UK£28	£67	0.42	27	Coopers and Lybrand, 1990
	Scottish and Universal, UK	Average cost per trainee	40	UK£1110	£2173	0.51	28	Coopers and Lybrand, 1990
	Shropshire Health Authority, UK	Average cost per trainee	15	UK£1003	£1368	0.73	29	Coopers and Lybrand, 1990
	The Citizen, Group of Newspapers, UK	Average cost per trainee	68	UK£627	£1263	0.50	30	Coopers and Lybrand, 1990
	Thistle Hotels, UK	Average cost per trainee	20	UK£264	£2699	0.10	31	Coopers and Lybrand, 1990
	British Gas North Western, UK	Average cost per trainee	28	UK£1552	£2691	0.58	32	Coopers and Lybrand, 1990
	Land Rover, UK	Average cost per trainee	13	UK£1867	£2527	0.74	33	Coopers and Lybrand, 1990

(Table 13.3 *continued*)

Sector	Institution country*	Measure of cost	Number of students	Unit cost (given currency) (1) Distance	(2) Conventional	Efficiency ratio	Notes	Source study
	Mathieson's, Bakers, UK	Average cost per trainee	80	UK£295	£435	0.68	34	Coopers and Lybrand, 1990
	Triplex Safety Glass, UK	Average cost per trainee	248	UK£96	£259	0.37	35	Coopers and Lybrand, 1990
	Delco Electronics, UK	Average cost per trainee	72	UK£453	£421	1.08	36	Coopers and Lybrand, 1990
	University of Victoria Extension, Canada	Certificate Programme in Computer Based Information Systems						
		– foundation course without computer-mediated communications	40	C$155	C$175	0.89		Muzio, 1992
			60	C$138	C$183	0.75		
			80	C$126				
		– other courses, with e-mail costs falling on the university	40	C$261–311	C$181–231	1.44–1.35		Muzio, 1992
			60	C$238–263	C$133–158	1.79–1.66		
			80	C$230–247				
		– other courses, with e-mail phone bills met by students	40	C$161–211	C$181–231	0.89–0.91		Muzio, 1992
			60	C$138–163	C$133–158	1.04–1.03		
			80	C$130–147				

Abbreviations

IRDEB = Institut de Radio-Educative de Bahia
AIOU = Allama Iqbal Open University
RTVU = Radio and Television University
KACU = Korea Air Correspondence University (now the Korea National Open University)
UAJ = University of the Air of Japan

(Table 13.3 *continued*)

IGNOU = Indira Gandhi National Open University
YCMOU = Yashwantrao Chavan Maharastra Open University
BRAOU = Dr B R Ambedkar Open University (formerly the Andhra Pradesh Open University)
KOU   = Kota Open University
UNED   = Universidad Estatal a Distancia

Notes

1 IRDEB, Brazil: Traditional provision based on the average cost across six private institutions
2 Minerva project, Brazil: Traditional provision based on the average cost in a private college
3 Malawi Correspondence College: Traditional provision based on the average cost in a conventional day secondary school
4 Malawi Correspondence College: Traditional provision based on the average cost in a boarding school
5 Telesecundaria, Mexico: Arena study: Comparison based on the lowest cost of television
6 Telesecundaria, Mexico: Arena study: Comparison based on the upper cost of television
7 Telesecundaria, Mexico: Arena study: Comparison based on the lowest cost of television. Average Telesecundaria group size of 20 compared to conventional group size of 45
8 Telesecundaria, Mexico: Arena study: Comparison based on the upper cost of television. Average Telesecundaria group size of 20 compared to conventional group size of 45
9 Centros APEC de Educación a Distancia, Dominican Republic: Traditional provision based on the average cost in a secondary level day school
10 Centros APEC de Educación a Distancia, Dominican Republic: Traditional provision based on the average cost in a secondary level afternoon school
11 Centros APEC de Educación a Distancia, Dominican Republic: Traditional provision based on the average cost in a secondary level night school
12 Teacher Training at a Distance, Tanzania: Comparison with a traditional two-year trained teacher
13 Teacher Training at a Distance, Tanzania: Comparison with a traditional three-year trained teacher
14 Distance-education project, Sri Lanka: Comparison with a traditional College of Education
15 Distance-education project, Sri Lanka: Comparison with a traditional Teachers' College
16 Open University, UK: Wagner studies, 1972 and 1977: Costs adjusted to take out costs of research
17 Open University, UK: Smith study: Comparison with Loughborough University
18 Open University, UK: Smith study: Comparison with Middlesex Polytechnic
19 UAJ, Japan: Comparison with liberal arts programmes at national universities
20 UAJ, Japan: Comparison with liberal arts programmes at public universities
21 UAJ, Japan: Comparison with liberal arts programmes in private universities' day programmes
22 UAJ, Japan: Comparison with liberal arts programmes in private universities' night programmes

(Table 13.3 *continued*)

23 UAJ, Japan: Comparison with a correspondence programme
24 UNED, Costa Rica: FYE = Full Year Equivalents: Comparison with costs at the University of Costa Rica
25 UNED, Costa Rica: FYE = Full Year Equivalents: Comparison with costs at the National University
26 UNED, Costa Rica: FYE = Full Year Equivalents: Comparison with costs at the Technological Institute of Costa Rica
27 Abbey National (Building Society): Compares CBT with day course alternative
28 Scottish and Universal (newspapers): Compares bought-in course from Henley Distance Learning + additional tutorial support with three-week course
29 Shropshire Health Authority: Compares course around pre-existing materials plus tutorials on weekly day release with block release alternative
30 Citizen Group: Compares intensive one-to-one training for one week followed by use of open learning packs and other support with in-house course
31 Thistle Hotels: Compares use of bought-in materials with block and day release
32 British Gas: Compares use of open learning materials plus six tuition days and a residential weekend course against a five-week block release course
33 Land Rover: use of bought-in Open University materials compared with tailor-made course
34 Mathieson's Bakers: Compares shop-based open learning with face-to-face training
35 Triplex Glass: Compares interactive video with face-to-face training
36 Delco Electronics: Compares bought-in materials and support of in-factory open learning centre with in-house training plus local college release

Table 13.4 *Comparative costs per graduate in distance and traditional systems*

| Sector | Institution country* | Measure of cost | Number of students | Unit cost (given currency) | | Graduate efficiency ratio | Efficiency ratio (per student) | Notes | Source study |
				(1) Distance	(2) Conventional				
Schools	Malawi Correspondence College, Malawi	Average cost per graduate (junior secondary level)	2884	K931 K931	K583 K1276	1.60 0.73	0.62 0.23	1 2	Wolff and Futagami, 1982
	Centros APEC de Educación a Distancia, Dominican Republic	Average recurrent cost per successful student	11,217	RD$306 RD$306 RD$306	RD$483 RD$455 RD$360	0.63 0.67 0.85	0.58 0.55 0.60	3 4 5	Muñiz Aquino, 1988
	Air Correspondence High School, Korea	Average recurrent cost per promoted enrolment, 1976	20,000	US$51	US$233	0.22	0.18	6	Lee *et al.*, 1982
Teacher education	LOGOS II, Brazil	Cost of completing course, 1980	24,400	Cr$10,560 Cr$15,125	Cr$200,000 Cr$200,000	0.05 0.08	n/a	7 8	Oliveira and Orivel, 1993
University	Open University, UK	Average recurrent cost per graduate	n/a	UK£1842	UK£4049–4801	0.38–0.45	0.26		Wagner, 1977
		Average recurrent cost per graduate 1976	51,785	UK£3264 UK£4555	UK£7338 UK£7338	0.44 0.62	0.41	9 10	Rumble, 1976
		Average recurrent cost per graduate 1976, allowing for credit transfer points	51,785	UK£3870 UK£5161	UK£7338 UK£7338	0.53 0.70	0.41	9 10	Rumble, 1976

144 The costs and economics of open and distance learning

(Table 13.4 continued)

Sector	Institution country*	Measure of cost	Number of students	Unit cost (given currency) (1) Distance	(2) Conventional	Graduate efficiency ratio	Efficiency ratio (per student)	Notes	Source study
University		Unit cost per student successful in examinations, 1983/84	37,200 FTE	UK£2500 UK£2500	UK£3360 UK£3190	0.74 0.78	0.55 0.66	11 12	Smith, 1986
	STOU, Thailand	Average cost/graduate	n/a	B 7023	B 49,957	0.14	n/a		Lockheed et al., 1991
	Korea Air Correspondence University, South Korea	Average cost per graduate at junior college level based on expenditure over the period 1972–81	n/a	US$300	US$675	0.44	n/a		Harwood and Kim, 1985
	EU, Israel	Cost of a first degree (forecast)	8000 students in 1978	US$5600	US$11,000 to $12,000	0.51 to 0.47	n/a		Melned et al., 1982

Abbreviations:
STOU = Sukhothai Thammathirat Open University
EU = Everyman's University (now Open University)

Notes
1 Malawi Correspondence College: Comparison with cost per graduate at a conventional day secondary school
2 Malawi Correspondence College: Comparison with cost per graduate at a boarding school
3 Centros APEC de Educación a Distancia, Dominican Republic: Comparison with cost per graduate at secondary level day schools
4 Centros APEC de Educación a Distancia, Dominican Republic: Comparison with cost per graduate at secondary level afternoon schools

(Table 13.4 *continued*)

5   Centros APEC de Educación a Distancia, Dominican Republic: Comparison with cost per graduate at secondary level night schools

6   Air Correspondence High School, Korea: Comparison with cost per graduate at a public regular high school

7   LOGOS II, Brazil: Comparison with cost per graduate completing the course in 2.5 years

8   LOGOS II, Brazil: Comparison with cost per graduate completing the course in four years

9   Open University: Rumble study: Comparison based on Open University students completing six OU credits [360 credit accumulation and transfer points]

10 Open University: Rumble study: Comparison based on Open University students completing eight OU credits [480 credit accumulation and transfer points]

11 Open University: Smith study: Comparison with Loughborough University

12 Open University: Smith study: Comparison with Middlesex Polytechnic

cost per graduate in the comparator traditional system). The effect of drop-out on the relative efficiency of systems can be seen by comparing the graduate efficiency ratio and the efficiency ratio per enrollee shown in Table 13.3. Thus, for example:

- while the efficiency ratio (per student) in the Malawi Correspondence College (MCC) in 1977/78 was only 0.62 compared with the cost of conventional day secondary schooling and 0.23 compared with the cost of boarding school, because MCC students took much longer to graduate (seven years as opposed to 2.7 in the day schools and 2.2 in the boarding schools), this cost advantage was eroded, so that measured in terms of cost per graduate, MCC was more expensive than day schools while still retaining a cost advantage over boarding schools (Wolff and Futagami, 1982: 98);
- although there is a higher failure rate at Air Correspondence High School, the average cost per student promoted between 1976 and 1977 compared with traditional schools (graduate efficiency ratio of 0.22 per successful student) still favours the ACHS, and demonstrates little loss in efficiency against the efficiency ratio per student of 0.18 (Lee *et al.*, 1982: 157).

(b) Teacher education
Distance education has long been recognized as an efficient way of providing in-service training to teachers.

- The Kenyan Correspondence Course Unit's in-service training programme for teachers used correspondence study guides, textbooks and other materials as appropriate, assignments and radio, together with limited face-to-face tuition and optional residential sessions. The average cost per subject-equivalent was about K£60 in 1970 when the system had 3650 subject-equivalents studied, rising to K£120 in 1977 when only 790 subject-equivalents were taken. This is more expensive than comparable traditional systems (Hawkridge *et al.*, 1982: 203–5).
- The cost per student per year of providing in-service initial training to teachers in Sri Lanka was considerably less than traditional methods (Nielsen and Tatto, 1993: 109).
- The cost per student per year of providing in-service initial training to teachers in Indonesia was considerably less than traditional methods (ibid: 119).
- The costs of teacher training by distance means in Tanzania is cheaper than traditional alternatives (Chale, 1993: 36, 39).
- The relative cost efficiency of a radio-based Basic Teacher Training course in Nepal compared with a similar course delivered by face-to-face means depends on student numbers (Holmes *et al.*, 1993: 176).

Turning to the cost per successful student or graduate (Oliveira and Orivel, 1993: 78, 84) found the LOGOS II programme to be very cost efficient at providing in-service initial training of teachers in Brazil.

(c) Higher education

Distance teaching universities are becoming an important part of the total provision of higher education in many countries: Daniel (1995: 22–44), reviewing what he calls the mega-universities, gives enrolment figures of 850,000 in the Chinese Television University system (1993); 350,000 in the Centre National d'Enseignement à Distance, France (1993); 242,000 in the Indira Gandhi National Open University, India; 380,000 in the Universitas Terbuka, Indonesia; 196,000 in the Korea Air and Correspondence University (1995); 130,000 in the University of South Africa (1995); 130,000 in the Universidad Nacional de Educación a Distancia, Spain (1993/94); 300,000 in the Sukhothai Thammathirat Open University, Thailand; 823,000 in the Open Education Faculty of Anadolu University, Turkey (1995); and 150,000 in the Open University, United Kingdom (1994).

Clearly, such large-scale enterprises provide potential for economies of scale provided that the initial cost structure is right and the curriculum is not expanded to levels where the numbers of students taking individual courses fall below the break-even point at which distance education is more cost efficient than traditional courses. However, the potential for economies of scale can be over-stressed: studies of the Open University (Wagner, 1977: 370–1), Athabasca University, Canada (Snowden and Daniel, 1980: 74–5), and the Indira Gandhi National Open University, India (Pillai and Naidu, 1991: 53) show that the gain in cost efficiency begins to fall off quite sharply (Tables 13.5 and 13.6). Once institutions have about 30,000 to 50,000 students, further gains in productivity are marginal rather than significant. Efficiency gains can also be affected by decisions to increase the size of the curriculum. Many studies of cost-efficiency gains resulting from expansion tend to be forward-looking projections holding out the promise of cost efficiencies in the wake of expansion (eg Rumble, 1981; Rumble, 1982) rather than historical studies of what has happened. The promise of future gains is easy to make: it can be more difficult to achieve them in practice.

There are numerous studies comparing the costs of distance teaching universities with those of traditional systems (Table 13.3 summarizes some of the data that is available).

- The efficiency ratio of the UK Open University varies depending on the study: Wagner's 1972 study indicated an efficiency ratio of 0.27 (recurrent cost per equivalent undergraduate student, including the cost of research) or 0.34 (excluding the cost of research). This fell to 0.53 and 0.69 respectively if the comparison was based on the average cost per full-time equivalent undergraduate student. Rumble (1976) calculated an efficiency ratio of 0.41; Smith (1986) an efficiency ratio of between 0.55 and 0.66 as against the average student cost at Loughborough University and Middlesex Polytechnic.
- Dudézert (1993: 22) reports that at the Centre National d'Enseignement à Distance in France the break-even cost at which fees meet the costs of preparing students by distance means for the *brevet de technicien* (BTS) is F20,000, which compares with an average cost in 1991 of preparing students for the BTS using face-to-face methods of F36,990.

Table 13.5 *Economies of scale in distance teaching universities*

Institution	Athabasca University		Open University, UK	
Study	Snowden and Daniel, 1980*		Wagner, 1977‡	
Measure	Average cost per course enrolment		Average cost per student	
Currency	Canadian $ (1979/80)		UK £ (1971)	
Base year	1975/76		1971	
	Enrolments	Unit cost	Enrolments	Unit cost
Base year	726	2255		
Year 2	1257	2023		
Year 3	1724	1704	38,424	258
Year 4	3169	1288	42,636	255
Year 5	4390	1073	49,358	240
Year 6	5925	963	50,994	249
Year 7	7325	894		
Year 8	8440	857		

* *Source*: Based on Snowden, B L and Daniel, J S (1980) 'The economics and management of small post-secondary distance education systems', 1 *Distance Education*, (1). Reprinted by permission of the Open and Distance Learning Association of Australia.
‡ *Source:* Wagner, 1977: 366

Table 13.6 *Economies of scale at the Indira Gandhi National Open University*

Number of students	Total costs (Rs/millions)	Average cost (Rs)	% rate of decline of average cost	Marginal cost per student
5,000	59.522	1,1904.47	–	597.07
10,000	62.508	6250.77	−113.07	597.07
20,000	68.478	3423.92	−28.27	597.07
30,000	74.449	2481.64	−9.42	597.07
40,000	80.420	2010.50	−4.71	597.07
50,000	87.520	1750.40	−1.89	869.82
60,000	96.218	1603.64	−1.45	869.82
70,000	104.916	1498.81	−1.05	869.82
80,000	113.615	1420.18	−0.79	869.82
90,000	122.313	1359.03	−0.61	869.82
100,000	131.011	1310.11	−0.49	869.82
200,000	217.993	1089.97	−0.22	869.82
300,000	304.975	1016.58	−0.07	869.82

Source: Based on Pillai and Naidu, 1991: 53

- Lockheed *et al.* (1991), in a study cited in the World Bank (1994: 34), found the Allama Iqbal Open University (AIOU), Pakistan, the Chinese Radio and Television University (RTVU), and the Korea Air and Correspondence University (KACU), now the Korea National Open University, to be more cost-efficient than traditional universities, with efficiency ratios of 0.22, 0.50, and 0.10 respectively.
- Wei and Tong (1994: 112–13) refer to a 1990 study on the quality and cost effectiveness of China's Radio and TV Universities that showed an efficiency ratio of between 0.43 and 0.51 compared with conventional colleges and universities, but they admit that 'this calculation is not especially reliable'. However, they say that the average cost per student is rising because student numbers have been falling as a result of a number of policy decisions (pp 113–15).
- Ding Xingfu (1993: 95) holds that in 1988/89 the per student cost including both revenue and capital costs in the Chinese Radio and TV Universities system is about one-quarter of the average revenue expenditure in the conventional universities, and about one-fifth if capital expenditure is excluded from the calculation altogether.
- Muta and Sakamoto (1989: 594–5) compared the costs of liberal arts programmes in national universities, public universities, the day and evening programmes of private universities, and the correspondence programmes of private universities, with the costs of the University of the Air of Japan (UAJ). The figures showed that UAJ was cheaper than day programmes (efficiency ratio between 0.47 and 0.82), but more expensive than night programmes at private universities (efficiency ratio, 1.28). UAJ was also considerably more expensive than other correspondence programmes (efficiency ratio, 7.64). Subsequently Muta and Saito (1993: 87) published further figures that took account of the capital as well as current costs of the UAJ, comparing this with the same groups of other universities in Japan. This showed that in 1990 UAJ was significantly more economical than other universities because of its low opportunity costs (efficiency ratio of between 0.15 and 0.32). However, it was still not as economical as the correspondence programmes of private universities (efficiency ratio 3.07). Overall, UAJ's cost advantage over national and public universities had increased even more in 1991.
- Ansari (1993: 114) gave figures comparing the unit costs of the Indira Gandhi National Open University (IGNOU), Yashwantrao Chavan Maharashtra Open University (YCMOU), Dr B R Ambedkar Open University (BRAOU) Hyderabad and Kota Open University (KOU), with the costs of conventional universities. He also compared their costs with those of eight selected distance education institutes in the traditional universities. Unit costs in the latter, at Rs 600 to Rs 2300, were not out of line with the costs of the open universities. The efficiency ratio is never worse that 0.45, and often under 0.10.
- Rumble (1981: 397–8) compared the costs of the Universidad Estatal a Distancia (UNED), Costa Rica with the costs of the three other state-funded

universities in Costa Rica, and showed that even at a very early stage in its development the University was cheaper per student than any of the campus-based ones.

So far as the cost per graduate is concerned (see Table 13.4 for details):

- Wagner's 1977 study of the costs of the Open University showed that the average recurrent cost per graduate in the Open University in 1973 was £2719, with a long-run projection of £1842, compared to a recurrent cost per graduate in traditional universities of from £4049 to £4801. Thus in 1973 the OU cost per graduate was somewhere between 56.6 and 67.1 per cent of the cost of a conventional UK graduate, though likely in the long term to fall to between 38.4 and 45.5 per cent (Wagner, 1977: 365). Wagner's figures might overestimate the relative cost advantage of the Open University if one accepts the methodological objections raised by Lumsden and Ritchie (1975), who argued (a) that any calculation of the costs of an Open University graduate would need to make adjustments for the fact that some of the work counted towards some students' degrees had not been done within the Open University system, but had been transferred in through credit transfer schemes (pp 251, 264), and (b) that most Open University graduates exited with a non-honours degree, and that to make a true comparison one would need to compare the costs of producing an honours degree graduate (p 265). As they put it, 'the assumption that the Open University ordinary degree is equal to the average degree of the conventional university is clearly weak' (p 266). Rumble (1976: 31) took these points on board, calculating a differential cost for non-honours and honours graduates and, in a separate calculation, allowing for the credits students transferred into the Open University.
- More recent figures on the costs per Open University graduate, including both revenue and capital costs, but excluding research costs, are given in a report prepared by the Department of Education and Science and the Open University (1991: 67), where the average cost per non-honours degree in 1989 is calculated as UK£8571, and the average cost of an honours degree as UK£11,995. Another report (Department of Education and Science, 1991) shows that the Open University's costs per part-time non-honours graduate were between 39 and 66 per cent the costs of graduates produced by three other part-time providers in the UK, while its costs per honours degree graduate were between 55 and 92 per cent of the costs of the other providers.
- Lockheed et al. (1991), in a study cited in the World Bank (1994: 34), found the Sukhothai Thammathirat Open University (STOU), Thailand, produced graduates more cheaply than traditional universities.
- Melmed et al. (1982: 238), on the basis of preliminary cost data, forecast that the cost per graduate at Israel's Everyman University (now Open University) would be US$5600 (at 1977 prices), compared with a cost of from $11,000 to $12,000 in a traditional Israeli university.
- Harwood and Kim (1985: 189) noted that the South Korean state spent the equivalent of US$10.29 millions on the Korea Air Correspondence University

in the period 1972–81, to produce 33,838 graduates at a cost of just over US$300 per graduate. In the same period the 124 traditional junior colleges graduated 28,000 students at an average cost of $675.

- Wei and Tong (1994: 97) report a 1989 study that showed that the cost per graduate at China's Radio and TV Universities was between 43 and 51 per cent of that in conventional colleges and universities, but these figures should be treated with care as they are the same as the relative cost per student cited by the same authors elsewhere in their book (p 113). Table 13.9 provides further details.

(d) Training

Distance and open learning has also proved a cost-efficient means of delivering training. Coopers and Lybrand (1990) undertook a survey of more than 50 UK companies using open learning methods for training, and prepared detailed case studies of ten of these. Although it was clear that companies' decisions to use open learning were not usually explicitly related to the relative cost of open learning, the case studies indicated that open learning was often substantially cheaper than other methods. The survey showed that open learning was in general cost efficient in relation to alternative methods. If suitable materials are *already* available, open learning can be a very cost-efficient means of training very small numbers of employees. It can also be a cost-efficient way of training very large numbers of employees, irrespective of whether this entails developing materials from scratch or buying them in. In coming to these judgements, the survey took account of the opportunity costs of studying by open learning methods: for example, Abbey National, which developed a computer-based learning course, found that the time spent on training on one course was reduced from a full day to only one to two hours, resulting in very significant savings in the costs of trainees' time. There were also savings in travel and accommodation costs. Further, at this level of activity (2700 trainees) the costs of developing the materials was cheaper than the cost of providing a lecturer. The variable cost of training was only £5.59, against £65.60 for a traditional training course. The marginal cost of training additional staff was therefore substantially less.

Muzio (1992: 78) looked at the comparative costs of providing a Certificate in Computer-based Information Services at the University of Victoria, using traditional and distance means, for different sized groups. Her study indicated the importance of off-loading the costs of e-mail use on to the students, assuming that the aim was to teach off-campus students more efficiently than on-campus ones (and thus, incidentally, supporting Nettleton's similar conclusion – see Case Study 12.1). Kemp (1995: 433) compared the costs of providing training to the Queensland Fire Service and Woodside Offshore Petroleum using traditional or flexible means. His study suggested considerable savings per 'engaged training hour' in the case of the Queensland Fire Service, but less significant savings in the case of Woodside. He concludes (p 434) with a word of caution: 'the particularized nature of industry settings, training solutions and costs emerging, reinforces Rumble's (1987) proposition that the financial outcomes of any economic study are unlikely to be of direct value to others' (ie as a guide to what outcomes might be elsewhere). Table 13.3 provides details of these studies.

13.5 The cost efficiency of mixed mode systems

Dual-mode institutions that teach both by distance and traditional means have also found distance education to be a cost-efficient option. A number of studies (see Table 13.7) throw light on this issue.

- Makau (1993: 328–31) compared the annual per student costs including capital costs of the distance-taught Bachelor of Education offered by the University of Nairobi with the residential BEd degree. He calculated that the average per capita cost with 515 enrolments was 37 per cent of the cost of a residential place. With expansion to the planned enrolment levels of 3700 in 1998, the cost per student will come down to K£856 or about 26 per cent the cost of a residential place.

- Cumming and Olaloku (1993: 369, 374) calculated the cost per student in the Correspondence and Open Studies Institute of the University of Lagos as N983, which is around two-thirds of the cost per student in the regular degree programmes in the departments of accounting and business administration, and of education. The unit cost per graduate in the distance education BSc (Education) programme is less than that of the regular programme at the same University (ibid.: 375). The unit cost per graduate of the distance education BSc (Business Administration) and BSc (Accountancy) is cheaper than the on-campus costs provided that students graduate in the minimum time, but if they take the normal maximum time to graduate (eight years) it is more expensive (p 375).

- Ansari (1992: 105) compared the per student cost of distance and on-campus studies in 15 Indian universities which have Institutes of Distance Education, showing that in 1980/81 on average the cost per distance student was just under 17 per cent of the cost of a traditional student (Rs 500 compared to RS 2962) (see Table 13.7).

- Sharma (1983) studied the relative costs of internal (conventional campus-based) and external (at a distance) study at the Royal Melbourne Institute of Technology – a dual-mode institution – in the period 1975 to 1980. He concluded that the space needs per distance-taught Equivalent Full-Time Student (EFTS) was one-third (33.6 per cent) that of a conventionally taught EFTS (p 167). Using rental as a proxy price for capital costs, this suggested that the capital cost per distance student was significantly less than for a traditionally taught student. Likewise, with a similar subject mix in both the distance and on-campus taught programmes, the direct teaching cost per distance taught EFTS was A$1115 compared with A$2202 per traditionally taught EFTS (50.6 per cent).

- Deakin University (1989) undertook a cost analysis of the average revenue cost of its on- and off-campus programmes. While there are considerable variations across courses, the study showed that on average the cost of developing and producing distance courses, and of evaluating them, together with the direct teaching costs, was not that different to the costs of on-campus courses (p 6).

Taylor and White (1991) studied the effect of using multi-media instructional materials designed for distance study to support conventional on-campus students studying at the University College of Southern Queensland (UCSQ). The original decision to use the available distance teaching materials to support *on-campus* teaching was taken in the light of the need to find alternative and effective teaching strategies to cope with expansion of student numbers and decreases in funding of higher education (p 7). They concentrated their analysis on four foundation courses. Typically, a traditional UCSQ course involved 56 hours face-to-face teaching across a 14-week semester. While one of the mixed-mode courses decided to retain the full 56 hours of contact, the other three reduced the amount of face-to-face contact significantly (to 20, 26 and 28 hours respectively) (p 13).

UCSQ's basic philosophy is to spend the same amount of money on teaching distance students as is spent on teaching on-campus students, so that if some economies of scale accrue from distance teaching, the savings are used to enhance the off-campus teaching rather than be redirected to support on-campus teaching (p 27). On the face of it, this would mean that the cost per student of the distance and on-campus modes would be about the same. The research aimed to establish if this were so. Taylor and White established the following.

- The per student costs of preparing the printed and audio materials, when spread across an average course population of 270 students (ie a class of 90 students per year over three years), was A$181, but only A$85 on courses attracting 1800 students a year over a three-year life (ie 5400 students in all). The delivery costs were estimated to be A$513 per student. The total costs of a distance-taught course were A$694 (270 students), or A$598 (5400 students) (pp 28–31).
- The per student cost of on-campus teaching (A$702) involved no materials preparation and production, but higher teaching, library, university management, capital and equipment costs.
- The mixed-mode approach involving the costs of preparation and production of materials, together with the higher university management, library, capital and equipment costs associated with students on campus was, at an average cost per student across the four courses of A$818, the most expensive option. In comparison with on-campus teaching, there were some savings on teaching costs (though not, as noted, on one of the courses).

The overall costs of the three approaches (distance, traditional on-campus face to face, and on-campus mixed mode) to teaching is given in Table 13.8.

Table 13.7 *Comparative costs of traditional and distance education methods in mixed-mode higher education level*

Institution country	Measure of cost	Number of students	Unit cost (given currency)		Efficiency ratio	Source study
			(1) Distance	(2) Conventional		
Royal Melbourne Institute of Technology, Australia	Direct teaching cost per equivalent full-time student, mean value 1975–80	n/a	A$1115	A$2202	0.51	Sharma, 1983
Deakin University, Australia	Total cost per full-time equivalent student (direct teaching cost + development, evaluation and production costs), 1988	1714 off campus; 2611 on campus	A$2882	A$2954	0.98	Deakin University, 1989
University of Nairobi External Degree Programme, Kenya	Annual per capita cost (revenue plus capital), 1988 (515 enrolments)	515	K£1235	K£3327	0.37	Makau, 1993
Correspondence and Open Studies Institute, University of Lagos, Nigeria	Average cost per student, at 2000 full-time equivalent students, 1987/88: (a) Education; (b) Accounting and Business	2000 FTE	(a) N983 (b) N983	(a) N1426 (b) N1523	(a) 0.69 (b) 0.65	Cumming and Olaloku, 1993
	Unit cost per graduate, BSc (Education)/ Education		N 3683* N 4910†	N 5035‡ N 5035‡	0.73* 0.98†	Cumming and Olaloku, 1993

Table 13.7 (continued)

Institution country	Measure of cost	Number of students	Unit cost (given currency)		Efficiency ratio	Source study
			(1) Distance	(2) Conventional		
	Unit cost per graduate, BSc (Business Administration) and BSc (Accounting)		N 4910‡	N 5525	0.89*	Cumming and Olaloku, 1993
			N 7856¥	N 5525	1.42†	
Indian universities with Institutes of Distance Education	Per student cost (1980/81)	n/a				Ansari, 1992
	(a) Allahad		Rs 520	Rs 1485	0.35	
	(b) Bombay		Rs 346	Rs 2961	0.12	
	(c) Kashmire		Rs 1085	Rs 4121	0.26	
	(d) Kerala		Rs 299	Rs 3093	0.10	
	(e) Mohan Lal Sukhadia		Rs 489	Rs 1960	0.25	
	(f) Osmania		Rs 307	Rs 3155	0.10	
	(g) Utkal		Rs 587	Rs 4627	0.13	
	(h) Andhra		Rs 238	Rs 3154	0.08	
	(i) Delhi		Rs 774	Rs 4718	0.16	
	(j) Himachal Pradesh		Rs 503	Rs 4383	0.12	
	(k) Madurai-Kamaraj		Rs 270	Rs 2778	0.10	
	(l) Mysore		Rs 927	Rs 2666	0.35	
	(m) Punjab		Rs 595	Rs 2633	0.23	
	(n) Punjabi		Rs 509	Rs 2633	0.19	
	(o) Rajasthan		Rs 446	Rs 1959	0.23	

Notes:

Correspondence and Open Studies Institute, University of Lagos: Average student costs per FTE = full-time equivalent student; unit cost per student including University overheads; Department of Education graduates: * assuming minimum time to graduate (six years); † assuming eight years to graduate; Department of Accounting and Business Administration graduates; ‡ assuming minimum time to graduate (five years); ¥ assuming eight years to graduate

Table 13.8 *Comparison of per student costs of off-campus (distance), on-campus (face-to-face) and on-campus mixed-mode (flexible) learning, University College of Southern Queensland*

	Cost per student (A$)				
	Off campus at a distance		On campus face to face	On campus flexible learning	
Activity	Average enrolment (270 students)	Large enrolment (5400 students)		Average cost across four courses	Range of costs over four courses†
Preparation (Academic input, instructional design, editing, text input, infrastructure)	137	45	no cost	137	137
Production (Audio, video, CML, print)	44	40	no cost	40*	34–130
Delivery					
(a) Teaching and examination	221	221	312	250	254–354
(b) Postage, student support, library	58	58	50	51	51
(c) University costs: management, capital and equipment	234	234	340	340	340
TOTAL	694	598	702	818	867–916†

Source: Based on Taylor and White, 1991, 33–34

Notes

* In practice recovered from the students (p 30)

† Represents the range of costs incurred across the four courses, not the sum of the figures in the column

As Taylor and White point out, 'subjective decisions have to be made in the apportionment of costs' (p 32). Thus while on the face of it the mixed mode option is the most expensive, Taylor and White totally ignored the production costs (on average A\$40) since these were recovered from the students. They also argued that the costs of preparation (A\$137) could be ignored, since these had already been incurred in developing the distance education version of the course. Finally, the costs of producing the additional copies needed to support on-campus flexible learning students might be charged at the marginal cost of running off additional copies. These adjustments would bring down the costs of the on-campus flexible learning option to below A\$650 (p 35), making it apparently very competitive with the distance and on-campus options. Moreover, there is no reason why UCSQ needed to provide the on-campus students with the amount of teaching it did. It could have provided them with exactly the same amount of contact hours as their off-campus distance colleagues, thus effecting an even greater apparent saving. This would have saved nearly A\$30 per student, arguably bringing the cost of on-campus flexible teaching down from about A\$650 to A\$620. In fact, of course, UCSQ chose to bring the cost per student back up to around A\$700 by increasing the amount of teaching.

The example shows how institutions can choose different ways of apportioning costs across joint products to gain competitive advantage (if that is the aim), or to 'justify' internal policy decisions. As Rumble (1992: 39–40) argued, the way in which costs are apportioned across joint products is not just a matter of academic interest. The ability to adopt quite legitimately different approaches to the costing of 'products' provides mixed-mode institutions with considerable flexibility, adjusting the costs to the exigencies of funding regimes, and adopting pricing strategies to gain a competitive edge in the market.

Rumble (1992: 40–41) argued that it is this very flexibility that positions dual-mode institutions so competitively. Traditional campus-based institutions have a considerable incentive to develop materials suitable for distance and open/flexible teaching, both to develop new markets among those who wish to study at a distance, and also to substitute materials for face-to-face teaching on campus, thus bringing the costs of on-campus teaching down. Given the relative ease with which materials can be developed out of lectures, it is likely that campus-based universities will have a much wider curriculum to offer at a distance: for example, the National Technological University in the US, which video-tapes traditional lecture courses at any one of its participating institutions, reckons that at any one time it can offer 200 courses drawn from a potential list of 7000 offered by its 29 participating institutions, and that it can do this economically provided that there are at least six people wishing to take the course (Fwu et al., 1992: 120, 129). Given this ability, dual-mode institutions pose a considerable competitive threat to single mode distance education institutions, since they are able to compete in their secondary business, using profits from their primary on-campus business to subsidize a competitive strategy in their secondary, off-campus, market (Rumble, 1992: 41). Single-mode institutions faced with this threat would do well either to focus on a particular market and serve it well (in which case they are likely to be smaller, specialist providers), or to themselves diversify by acquiring a campus-based operation (Rumble, 1992: 43).

What strategies should universities adopt to enter the open and distance education market? Given the potential cost saving involved, there is a prima facie case for using distance teaching methodologies to teach on-campus students as well as off-campus students. The most cost-efficient means of doing this is likely to be by video-taping the traditional lectures, and using this as the basis for an open learning version of the course. Lectures are, of course, relatively cheap to prepare. Video-taping lectures is much cheaper than developing multi-media materials from scratch. Because lectures are easy to prepare, most campus universities offer a much wider range of courses than distance teaching universities. Institutions video-taping lectures can therefore draw on the wide range of courses available to campus-based students, and so offer their off-campus students a much wider curriculum than institutions that only teach at a distance (Rumble, 1992: 36–40). While there are legitimate concerns that the quality of the materials will be less good (White, 1992: 59; Keegan, 1994: 37), would-be students are often less concerned with quality and more concerned with price and the credentialling power of the institution's name (Rumble, 1994b: 47). In any case, the argument for quality materials can be overstated: as Schramm (1977: 79) observed, 'motivated students learn from any medium if it is competently used and adapted to their needs'.

Against this argument, Keegan (1994: 37–8) and Daniel (1995: 48–9) have stressed the competitive advantage of large-scale distance teaching universities. These include:

- a significant edge in quality which smaller providers find hard to match (Keegan, 1994: 37);
- reliance on techniques of distance education based either on remote-classrooms (the China TV university system) or on the correspondence tradition (the other mega-universities) that have both yielded economies of scale (Daniel, 1995: 48);
- a clearly differentiated market based in the main on adults wishing to study from their place of work or from home (Daniel, 1995: 48);
- an ability to raise the productivity of academic staff developing the courses, using the technology of desk top publishing, and, conversely, the difficulties of diverting staff time from campus-based teaching to materials production (Keegan, 1994: 38). Against this, the availability of desk top publishing and cheap video systems has reduced scale economies in the development of materials and reduced the entry barriers for those institutions wishing to develop distance education (Daniel, 1995: 49). Indeed, Daniel (p 79) argues that the decentralization of media development, by enabling individual academics to work closer to the production system, raises the danger that large-scale distance teaching universities will lose economies of scale in the use of media;

- a proven ability to provide a wide-ranging curriculum. Keegan (1994: 38) cites the case of the Financial and Economic Institute for Distance Education in the former USSR. However, there are dangers in just counting courses. It is easy to give the appearance of a wider curriculum by categorizing very small modules as separate courses;
- the very high entry cost to distance education (in terms of establishing the infrastructure and preparing materials), which can only be justified if student numbers are high (Keegan, 1994: 38), and the difficulty of successfully implementing distance education (Daniel, 1995: 49);
- a clear cost advantage because of their size and cost structure (Daniel, 1995: 48); however, Daniel cautions that three trends may erode this cost advantage: updating courses more often, offering more courses resulting in fewer students per course and using more expensive media mixes (p 49).

In fact, the cost advantage over mixed-mode systems may not be as great as it is said to be. As other institutions adopt open learning methods, so they may challenge the cost advantage of institutions teaching only by distance means. Daniel (1995: 49) is clearly right when he says that large-scale distance teaching universities 'must pursue all cost reduction opportunities that do not sacrifice differentiation and all differentiation opportunities that are not costly'. In particular, they must pursue differentiation in areas that buyers will value, while at the same time seeking to reduce costs.

13.6 Conclusion

Distance and open education may be the only practical way of reaching some target populations. In such circumstances, whether a system is cost efficient relative to other systems will not matter. It will, of course, be important to be assured that internally it is as cost efficient as it can be. The evidence shows that distance education can be a more cost-efficient way of providing education than a traditional face-to-face institution, though much depends on the particular design, size and circumstances of the project.

When making comparisons with traditional institutions, it should be remembered that the costs of traditional institutions may vary enormously within a jurisdiction. The Universidad Estatal a Distancia had an efficiency ratio of 0.18 compared with the cost per student at the Technological Institute of Costa Rica, but an efficiency ratio of only 0.69 compared with the University of Costa Rica (Rumble, 1981).

Having said that, a word of caution is called for. The fact that in any one year a particular distance education system is less cost efficient than a comparator traditional system does not tell us a lot. It is necessary to get behind the figures and ask why this is so. For example, it may be that it is operating suboptimally. It could be that, by adding more students, the average cost could be brought down significantly, thus making it more rather than less cost efficient in comparison to the conventional system. Oliveira and Orivel (1982a: 79, 84) suggested that this was the case in respect of IRDEB. On the other hand, further economies of scale might be unachievable given the current media mix. This can be established by discovering at what point on its average cost curve the institution is operating.

One way round this problem is to calculate the average student cost taking account of the impact of expansion. Rumble (1976: 27) did this in the case of the UK Open University when he calculated the likely impact on the average student cost of an expansion in both course and student numbers from the university's 1976 base, assuming an average additional cost per course per year of £110,000 and an incremental cost per student of £248, with overheads of approximately £26.149 millions (Table 13.9).

Table 13.9 *The effects of expansion on the average cost per student at the UK Open University: 1976 forecasts*

Student numbers	Course load (planned)						
	58	62.66	73.14	77	82	84	87
51,785	505	515	537	545	554	560	567
55,000	488	499	520	528	536	542	548
60,000	468	478	498	504	512	517	523
65,000	451	461	478	485	492	497	502
70,000	437	445	462	468	474	479	484
75,000	424	432	448	453	459	464	468
80,000	413	421	435	440	446	450	455

Source: Rumble, 1976: 27

Although distance teaching institutions can bring down unit costs with expansion, there is a limit to the extent to which they can achieve economies of scale. It is clear that traditional universities are beginning to use distance teaching methods much more intensively, both to bring down the costs of their on-campus teaching and to reach new markets. Single-mode distance education systems are very vulnerable to dual-mode systems that can compete against them in breadth of curriculum and price. The extent to which they can respond to the competitive threat of dual-mode institutions will determine whether they continue to exist, or if what will emerge will be a new kind of educational institution using a mix of technologies and traditional face-to-face teaching to reach students wherever they are – at home, in the workplace, in remote classrooms or in campus classrooms. Perhaps the main lesson from experience is that the only strategy open to educational institutions in a cash-strapped mass education system is to adopt open and distance learning methods.

Chapter 14

Cost effectiveness

Effectiveness is concerned with outputs. An organization is effective to the extent that it produces outputs that are relevant to the needs and demands of its clients. This implies the existence of criteria by which the organization's success in this respect can be measured.

Organizations can be effective but not necessarily efficient. For example, Italians can be taught Russian very effectively (such that those who have done the course speak Russian like a native), but if the cost of doing this is five times the cost of any comparable programme, then it has not been very efficient. Organizations need to be both effective and efficient. An organization is *cost effective* if its outputs are relevant to the needs and demands of clients and cost less than the outputs of other institutions that meet these criteria. Organizations that pursue efficiencies to the extent that the quality of the output is jeopardized or poor may cease to be effective.

14.1 Measuring effectiveness

There are several ways in which effectiveness might be measured.

(a) Effectiveness measured against an absolute standard

Effectiveness is the ratio of the actual outcome to the possible or ideal outcome (Cowan, 1985: 236). If the effectiveness of a university's undergraduate programme is 82 per cent, then, out of every 100 possible graduates, 82 have graduated. An effectiveness of 45 per cent indicates that 55 per cent of the potential has not been realized – that is, 45 per cent of the students have passed, but 55 per cent have failed. Failure in this sense may arise from failure to pass an examination or failure as a result of drop-out prior to an examination.

Cowan measures effectiveness against an ideal situation in which every student passes, such that 'absolute' effectiveness is equivalent to 100 per cent of students passing. The pass rate at the Institut de Radio-Educative de Bahia (IRDEB) in Brazil is 37 per cent, and at the Centros APEC de Educación a Distancia in the Dominican Republic it is 58 per cent, giving effectiveness ratios of 0.37 and 0.58 respectively.

Most distance educators will make the point that in interpreting course completion and success in the examination as an indication of success, and drop-out and failure in an examination as indication of failure, an institutional, teacher-oriented, judgement is being made about what constitutes success. This may not be how the student sees it. As Holmberg (1989: 182–3) remarked:

> distance education programmes are often used by individual students who do not declare either their ultimate goals (self-actualization rather than the acquisition of competence may be their aim) or the period over which they intend to spread their study. Thus it is often impossible to say for certain, unless the students are conscious of their ultimate goals and have made their study intentions known, whether non-completion means interruption, or drop-out in the sense of failure, or if it accords with their intentions or plans.

Having said that, Bååth (1984: 32) concluded that 'it is fairly safe to say that the completion rate for this type of study [ie distance education] is often fairly low... drop-out rates round 50 per cent are not unusual'.

(b) The measurement of relative effectiveness

Another approach is to compare the *relative* effectiveness of a distance education system with traditional institutions, so that, for example, the effectiveness of IRDEB can be measured relative to traditional institutions in Brazil. In this case, the 37 per cent pass rate at the Institut de Radio-Educative de Bahia can be compared with those of institutions preparing adult students for the *madureza* by teaching them directly face to face, where the pass rate is 61 per cent, and with those who have prepared for the examination privately or with the help of a private institution, where the pass rate is 36 per cent.

There is a problem with this – in the sense that the standards achieved by traditional institutions vary one with another, so that, in principle, there are as many comparisons as there are institutions in existence. However, the situation can be exemplified by using institutions for which the data is available and comparing the standards achieved by distance education institutions with those of traditional institutions, to derive a single measure that compares the effectiveness of a distance teaching system with that of a traditional system. For example, if a traditional education system graduates 85 students out of every 100 (effectiveness ratio of 85 per cent), and a distance system graduates 40 students out of 100 (40 per cent effectiveness ratio), then a measure of the comparative effectiveness of the distance system relative to the traditional one is obtained by dividing the effectiveness ratio of the distance system by that of the traditional system (40 ÷ 85) to give a *relative effectiveness ratio* of 47 per cent. If the distance system has an effectiveness ratio of 90 per cent, then the comparative effectiveness ratio is 90 ÷ 85, giving a comparative effectiveness ratio of 1.06.

Table 14.2 provides information on the pass rates of students in the Centros APEC de Educación a Distancia in the Dominican Republic (58 per cent) compared with that in other secondary school systems in the country. In the day schools, the pass rate is 77 per cent, so the comparative effectiveness ratio of the distance system is 58/77 or 0.75. An effectiveness ratio of 1.0 indicates that the two systems are comparable in relative effectiveness. A ratio of <1.0 means that the distance system is less effective, and a ratio of >1.0 that it is more effective than the traditional system.

This approach also gives a ratio that enables direct comparison of the relative effectiveness of distance teaching institutions compared with traditional ones in Jurisdiction A, with the relative effectiveness of distance teaching institutions and traditional institutions in Jurisdiction B.

(c) Effectiveness as a measure of the quality of the student's performance

Any study of cost effectiveness must also take account of the quality of the product. The effectiveness of educational institutions can be measured by *value-added performance indicators*. The basic idea of such indicators is that institutions should be judged according to the change in their students' performance during their time at the institution. This is obtained by comparing the results of students in their final examinations with their results in an entry test taken before they started the course. Value-added performance indicators measure the difference in performance between the entry and the exit tests. Thus Cowan (1985: 237) suggests that the effectiveness of teaching can be regarded as 'the ratio of [the summation of all the learning within the class group] to [the summation of the instructional aims of that class group, in that particular period of instruction]'. However, it can be difficult to quantify a student's learning gain because of the diverse units of measurement used to measure teaching and learning effectiveness across a course. Equally, while comparisons can then be drawn across institutions, there are obviously problems where the quality of intake or output differ from one institution to another.

Given these difficulties, Cowan suggests that a way forward is to work with components of the process of education rather than with the whole entity. For example, if a lecture is devoted to the mastery of a particular concept (eg entropy), it should be easy to analyse the aspects of the concept to be mastered, to weigh them objectively and to devise a pair of matched tests that students take prior to the start of the lecture (a pre-test) and following the end of the lecture (a post-test), from which the gain ratio can be derived, such that:

$$\text{Gain ratio} = \frac{\text{Post-test score} - \text{pretest score}}{100 - \text{Pretest score}}$$

where all scores are percentages.

This gain ratio could be acceptable as a quantification of learning in that particular topic (p 238). Unfortunately, very little work has been done on the effectiveness of distance education in this sense. The rest of the chapter looks at the evidence that is available.

(d) Effectiveness measured by a weighted average across a range of variables

It is possible to calculate an *overall effectiveness ratio* across several variables. For example, Nielsen and Tatto (1993: 121) report on the effectiveness of the Universitas Terbuka's teacher training programme in Indonesia in terms of the students' scores in exit tests, compared with a comparable face-to-face programme, in four areas (subject matter knowledge, theoretical skills, practical skills and attitudes) that between them capture teacher competence and professionalism. These different scores can be weighted and a weighted average effectiveness ratio calculated, as shown in Table 14.1.

Table 14.1   *Weighted average effectiveness ratio (example)*

	Subject matter	Skills (theory)	Skills (practice)	Attitudes	Overall score
Distance					
Exit score (maths)	0.44	0.66	0.79	0.63	
Weighting	3	1	2	1	7
Total	1.32	0.66	1.58	0.63	4.19
Weighted average					4.19/7 = 0.60
Traditional					
Exit score (maths)	0.49	0.68	0.67	0.65	
Weighting	3	1	2	1	7
Total	1.47	0.68	1.34	0.65	4.14
Weighted average					4.14/7 = 0.59

14.2 Evidence of cost effectiveness in institutions teaching by distance means

Having established how effectiveness might be measured, it is time to turn to the evidence.

Table 14.2 *Student success and drop-out rates: comparative performance of distance and conventional systems*

Sector	Institution, country	Measure	Distance	Conventional	Effectiveness ratio	Notes	Source study
Schools	IRDEB, Brazil	Madurez pass rates in the town of Feira de Santanam 1976	37% 37%	61% 36%	0.61 1.03	1 2	Oliveira and Orivel, 1982a
	Centros APEC de Educación a Distancia, Dominican Republic	% of students who successfully complete the course, 1986/87	58% 58%	77% 80–85%	0.75 0.68–0.73	3 4	Muñiz Aquino, 1988
	Air Correspondence High School, Korea	Year-end test scores (% score), 1975; (a) mean, all subjects (b) Korean (c) English (d) Mathematics	(a) 56.5% (b) 51.5% (c) 36.8% (d) 44.0%	64.1% 65.8% 50.2% 75.0%	0.88 0.78 0.73 0.59		Lee et al., 1982
	Telesecundaria, Mexico	Overall pass rate	86%	(a) 79% (b) 77% (c) 73% (d) 73% (e) 74% (f) 65% (g) 64%	1.09 1.12 1.18 1.18 1.16 1.32 1.34	5	Secretaria de Educación Pública, 1981, in Arena, 1989
Teacher training	Zimbabwe Integrated Teacher Education Course Programme (ZINTEC), Zimbabwe	% of students admitted in years 1981–8 who (a) pass, (b) pass with distinction	(a) 80.0% (b) 3.2%	82.0% 4.2%	0.98 0.76		Chivore, 1993
	Basic Teacher Training, Nepal	Completion rate (% of those who entered who sat the exam), 1987–90	83.4%	n/a	n/a		Holmes et al., 1993

Table 14.2 *(continued)*

Sector	Institution, country	Measure	Distance	Conventional	Effectiveness ratio	Notes	Source study
		Pass rate, 1987–90	56.6%	94.8%	0.60		Holmes et al., 1993
	National Teachers' Institute, Nigeria	TCII national public examination pass rates, 1982–9	1982: 21.2% 1983: 72.2% 1984: 27.4% 1985: 44.0% 1986: 41.2% 1987: 38.8% 1988: 30.6% 1989: 36.1%	38.1% 65.5% 27.3% 30.2% 31.9% 29.6% 19.1% 28.6%	0.56 1.10 1.00 1.46 1.29 1.31 1.60 1.26		Bako and Rumble, 1993
Higher education	School of Correspondence and Continuing Education, University of Delhi	Academic performance of students in the School of Correspondence Courses and Continuing Education, compared with regular students of the University of Delhi: % of students gaining the degree	1984/5: 34.3% 1985/6: 37.9% 1986/7: 25.0%	63.0% 59.4% 58.8%	0.54 0.64 0.43		Ansari, 1992
		Proportion of students gaining a degree who passed in divisions 1 or 2	1984/5: 20.1% 1985/6: 16.5% 1986/7: 21.1%	32.0% 34.3% 40.2%	0.63 0.48 0.53		Ansari, 1992

Notes

(1) IRDEB, Brazil: direct teaching by qualified teachers

(2) IRDEB, Brazil: private establishments and students who have prepared for the *madureza* without having followed a formal course

(3) Centros APEC de Educación a Distancia: day school

(4) Centros APEC de Educación a Distancia: night school

(5) Telesecundaria, Mexico: Conventional systems are (a) Federal General Secondary schools, (b) State General Secondary schools, (c) private sector General Secondary schools, (d) Federal Technical Secondary schools, (e) State Technical Secondary schools, (f) private sector Technical Secondary schools, (g) Secondary Equivalency programme for Workers

(a) Schools

Some idea of the relative effectiveness of distance education systems can be obtained by looking at success and drop-out figures (see Table 14.2).

- In Brazil, IRDEB's pass rates in 1976, at 37 per cent, were much lower than the traditional adult education stream, though marginally better than private and self-prepared students (Oliveira and Orivel, 1982a: 81–2). IRDEB's relative effectiveness ratio was 0.61 compared with the pass rate of students who had been taught face to face by a qualified teacher, but at 1.03 much on a par with the pass rates of students who had not followed a formal course of study or who had received private tuition.

- In the Dominican Republic, the Centros APEC de Educación a Distancia had a relative effectiveness ratio of from 0.68 to 0.75 compared with traditional alternatives. The Centros also had a higher drop-out rate than comparable conventional systems (28 per cent against 8 to 13 per cent) (Muñiz Aquino, 1988: 39–40).

- Lee et al. (1982: 146–7) showed that the year-end test scores of students at the Air Correspondence High School (ACHS), Korea were lower than that of students at regular high schools, resulting in a relative effectiveness ratio of between 0.59 and 0.78 on three specified subjects, and a mean relative effectiveness ratio across all subjects of 0.88. They pointed out that the initial quality of the entrants to ACHS was lower, with ACHS students having a prerequisite mean score of 29.67 per cent across all subjects compared with the regular high school entrants mean score of 46.8 per cent. The poorer results of the ACHS students on exit hides the fact that their mean percentage point gain across all subjects was in fact greater than that of the regular high school students (26.83 percentage points compared to 17.3 percentage points).

- In the case of the Telesecundaria in Mexico, figures cited in Arena (1989: 51) show that the overall pass rate was better than comparable traditional systems. Table 14.2 shows the comparative data and a relative effectiveness ratio of between 1.09 and 1.34, depending on the different kinds of school with which Telesecundaria is being compared. Mayo et al. (1975b: 211) found that while ninth grade Telesecundaria students started their studies at more or less the same level as traditional students in mathematics, Spanish and chemistry, the difference between their pre- and post-test scores showed a higher gain ratio than those taught by traditional means. The Telesecundaria students were educationally disadvantaged, and general ability tests in verbal, numerical and logical skills showed them scoring below the recorded levels of secondary students in technical schools (p 213). Given this, it seems odd that the traditional students did not do better than the Telesecundaria students on subject-related achievement scores. Mayo and his colleagues concluded that the reason for this was that instructional television makes a positive difference in learning (p 215). However, they shied away from concluding that instructional television is a better instructional system while acknowledging the encouraging performance of students in the Telesecundaria (p 216).

(b) Teacher training
We now look at the evidence at the teacher training level.

- In Zimbabwe, as the Figures in Table 14.2 show, in terms of the proportion of students who pass the course, there was little difference between the examination performance of ZINTEC's distance-taught students and students who had been conventionally trained (relative effectiveness ratio of 0.98), but fewer distance students passed with distinction (Chivore, 1993: 46). The drop-out rate was 0.3 per cent against 1.3 per cent in traditional colleges, which was not statistically significant (p 53).

- In Nepal, Holmes *et al.* (1993: 161) compared the radio-based Basic Teacher Training course with the face-to-face version. The completion rate for the radio-based course was high but there were no comparable figures for the other programmes: however, direct comparison of the pass rates showed that the distance-taught programme had a markedly lower pass rate than the face-to-face course (relative effectiveness ratio of 0.6). One reason for this may be that the pass rates for the face-to-face courses were 'uniformly (and suspiciously) high' (p 161). At the same time logistical problems, competing personal demands, and towards the end of the period the political situation, disrupted the distance-taught teachers' lives. The drop-out rate was 16.6 per cent, with no comparative figures being given for traditional approaches to training.

- Bako and Rumble (1993: 218–19) compared the performance of external in-service teachers on the distance-taught TCII course offered through the National Teachers' Institute, Nigeria, and through short in-service courses, compared with internal students studying for the same examination at regular teacher training colleges. In most years the external system is more efficient than the traditional college-based system. Table 14.2 shows the comparative data and calculates a relative effectiveness ratio for each year between 1982 and 1989. There is a surprising difference in the standards applied in 1983 for which no explanation is given. NTI was more effective year-on-year, with the exception of 1984 when it was equally effective, and 1982, when it was less effective.

- Tanzania decided to adopt distance education methods in 1978 to train teachers. Quantitatively, the scheme was a success. Between 1976 and 1978 45,534 students were enrolled, of whom 37,414 sat the examination and 35,028 (93.6 per cent) passed the examination (Chale, 1993: 31).

It is fairly easy to compare the effectiveness of systems where the distance students take the same examination as the traditional students, and are thus tested against the same standards, but this is not always the case. Also, what is tested is not necessarily academic knowledge where measurement is relatively easy, but behaviours and attitudes where measurement is less easy. There is often a concern that while distance-taught students may do as well in the cognitive domain (acquisition of academic mastery in a subject), they will not perform as well in the psychomotor domain (mastery of skills) or in the affective domain (acquisition of attitudes and beliefs). This is obviously of critical importance in areas such as teacher training, and a number of studies have addressed this issue.

- Chale (1993: 31) makes the point that the quality of the teachers trained through Tanzania's teacher training at a distance programme was questioned by various observers and by the parents of the trainee teachers (p 31). He reports on two studies that looked at the actual quality of the teachers. Both studies showed that with regard to subject matter mastery, the teachers trained in residential teacher training colleges performed slightly better than the distance taught teachers in all subjects, but that the difference was only significant in science (p 32). In terms of classroom performance, one study done a year after graduation suggested that the distance-taught teachers performed better than college-trained teachers, but the other study, done three years after graduation, found no significant difference in performance, reflecting the fact that any initial difference due to differences in training will be eroded over time as experience in the classroom is gained (p 32). The performance of the students in examination did not vary significantly between distance- and college-trained teachers (though the latter were marginally more effective) (p 32). Finally, college-trained teachers were better in their mastery of educational theory (p 33).

- In the case of ZINTEC, while the assessment procedures are not identical, all the assessment procedures at teacher training colleges and at ZINTEC are moderated by the University of Zimbabwe (Chivore, 1993: 52–3). So far as effectiveness in the classroom goes, students taught by ZINTEC trained teachers did as well as those taught by teachers trained in other ways (p 55), and at least one pilot study rated the ZINTEC trained teachers as more effective than conventionally trained teachers in teaching (p 56).

- Nielsen and Tatto (1993: 111) report on the Sri Lankan distance-taught teacher education programme. Compared with in-service teachers' college programmes, the in-service distance-taught programme is more effective (in terms of adding value to its students as measured by the difference between exit and entry level scores of students) in mathematics and language subject-matter mastery, maths skills and professional attitudes, but slightly less effective in terms of language skills. Compared with pre-service college of education programmes, the distance-taught programme is more effective on this criterion in language knowledge and professional attitudes, but less effective in the other areas. The distance programme's integration of study with ongoing work as a teacher is seen as a positive strength (ibid.: 112–3). A composite index of effectiveness measured the students' gain between entry and exit levels against the total expenditure over the training cycle, and demonstrated that the cost per unit difference was lowest in the distance education programme (Table 14.3). Although the effectiveness of the distance programme was not as high as the college pre-service programme, it was significantly more effective than the campus-based in-service programme, and it also had a significant cost advantage (Nielsen and Tatto, 1991: 19; 1993: 114).

Table 14.3   *Cost effectiveness of the various teacher education programmes in Sri Lanka*

Programme	Difference in composite index, exit level – entry level	Total cost per cycle (US$)	Cost per unit difference (US$)
Colleges (pre-service)	2.36	2697	1143
Colleges (in-service)	1.08	1690	1565
Distance education	1.95	483	247

Source: Nielson, H D and Tatto, M T, 'Teacher upgrading in Sri Lanka and Indonesia', in Perraton, H (ed.) (1993) *Distance education for teacher training.* Routledge, p 114: amended by personal communication from H Dean Nielsen, 1996. Reprinted by permission.

- In Indonesia, Nielsen and Tatto (1993: 122–3) found that in respect of subject matter and theoretical and practical skills, the two-year college-taught training programme performed better than the one-year distance-taught programme in mathematics, but was on balance no more effective than the distance programme in languages. However, whereas the college-based programme had no effect on students' professional attitudes, the distance-taught programme had a negative effect on attitudes (ibid.: 123). Nielsen and Tatto (1991: 24; 1993: 123) compared the learning gain in mathematics and language of students exiting from the one-year distance-taught course and those exiting from a conventional two-year, campus-based college course, relative to the total cost of the programme (Table 14.4). Although the distance programme is much more efficient, it is not as effective, and the cost per unit difference between the entry and exit scores of students, while lower in the case of languages, is higher in the case of mathematics.

Table 14.4   *Cost effectiveness of the various teacher education programmes in Indonesia*

Programme	Difference in composite index, exit level – entry level	Total cost per cycle (US$)	Cost per unit difference (US$)
Distance education (one year)			
Mathematics	0.33	946	2867
Language	1.10	958	871
Conventional college (two years)			
Mathematics	2.21	2997	1356
Language	1.88	3314	1763

Source: Nielson, H D and Tatto, M T, 'Teacher upgrading in Sri Lanka and Indonesia', in Perraton, H (ed.) (1993) *Distance education for teacher training.* Routledge, p 123: amended by personal communication from H Dean Nielsen, 1996. Reprinted by permission.

- In Nepal, the radio-based programme was more demanding of its students (Holmes *et al.*, 1993: 163). Pre- and post-test scores indicated that the radio course improved teachers' performance from 56.5 per cent to 67.3 per cent correct answers, but there is no comparative data for the face-to-face programme (p 164). Radio-trained teachers improved in every subject, with the greatest improvement in education (53.2 per cent rising to 70.7 per cent) and the least in social studies (54.3 per cent rising to 60.8 per cent) (p 165).

(c) Higher education

Surprisingly there have been very few studies comparing drop-out and pass rates in tertiary level distance education with those found in traditional systems. That the drop-out rate is higher is usually taken as fact, but the precise extent of the difference is less well established.

- Harwood and Kim (1985: 188) indicate that of the 113,112 students enrolled between 1972 and 1981 in the Korea Air and Correspondence University's junior college, 33,848 or 29 per cent had graduated.
- Bartels (1993: 7) reports that only about 8 per cent of the students taking a degree with the Faculty of Economics at the German Fernuniversität have graduated.
- Graduation figures from the Open University (Table 14.5) require some explanation. The table shows the number of students who finally registered each year, and the proportion of these who had gained an ordinary degree within eight years, within 12 years, and by 1994. After eight years a number of students from each cohort go on graduating, but the level of additional graduations is small. Over the years, the graduation rate has been falling. One reason is that many of the students who entered in the early years of the University were teachers and lecturers (over 40 per cent in 1971), many of whom were seeking graduate teacher status. Their presence in the early years inflated the graduation rate because they were exempted from taking the full course load under the University's credit exemptions policy. Later cohorts, drawn from more educationally deprived sectors of the population, attracted less credit exemptions, with the result that the average number of years taken to graduate began to rise, and the proportion of each cohort that did graduate began to fall.
- Fleming (1982: 142–3), in his case study on the Allama Iqbal Open University, Pakistan, concluded that:

  there is no disguising the fact… that there is a serious drop-out problem because some courses are perhaps too difficult or not well prepared; because some students are perhaps ill prepared, poorly motivated, or poorly supported; or perhaps because they find it too difficult to adapt to a new system of learning that makes heavy demands on their qualities of application and self-discipline.

Table 14.5 *UK Open University: graduation rates, undergraduate students, to 1994*

	1971	1972	1973	1974	1975	1976	1977	1978	1979	1980	1981
Cohort finally registered	19,581	15,716	12,680	11,336	14,830	12,231	15,146	15,622	14,854	14,022	14,410
% graduating from cohort											
– in 8 years	54.1	48.9	49.5	48.9	44.2	45.0	43.6	39.9	42.1	40.1	40.4
– in 12 years	56.6	52.3	53.1	52.6	48.1	49.4	48.0	44.0	46.5	44.9	45.6
– by 1994	58.3	54.5	55.3	55.0	50.6	51.9	50.0	45.9	48.2	46.2	46.6

	1982	1983	1984	1985	1986	1987	1988	1989	1990	1991	1992
Cohort finally registered	18,240	18,195	15,713	13,870	14,484	16,386	18,043	16,612	17,495	18,120	20,647
% graduating from about											
– in 8 years	38.0	35.6	37.4	35.6	33.9	35.8					
– in 12 years	43.0	40.6									
– by 1994	43.6	40.6	41.8	38.8	35.7	35.8	31.9	27.3	15.1	7.1	3.5

Higher drop-out rates are a feature of distance study in dual-mode institutions as well as in those that teach only by distance means (see Table 14.2).

- A study undertaken at the Royal Melbourne Institute of Technology showed that the drop-out rate in the off-campus system was 48 per cent compared with 20 per cent in the on-campus system (Sharma, 1983).
- Ansari (1992: 107–8) looked at the academic performance of students in the School of Correspondence Courses and Continuing Education, University of Delhi, compared with regular students of the University of Delhi. He measured the proportion of students who graduated in the BA ordinary pass degree, BA (Commerce) ordinary pass degree and BA (honours degree in Commerce), the MA and the Masters of Commerce, in 1984/85, 1985/86 and 1986/87. Across these degrees, students in the correspondence school consistently performed less well. Ansari also looked at the proportions of those who passed who gained a first- or second-class degree, compared to those who gained a third-class degree. Again, the correspondence school students performed less well.

One problem in comparing the graduation rates of distance and conventional systems is that the quality of the students entering the system may be lower. Wagner (1977: 361) pointed out that 'a true measure of output should measure not just the final standard achieved but value-added, the difference between initial and final standard'. Assuming that judgements about standards are equivalent, a university that creams off the most able products of the school system may not have a higher added value (even if it achieves more first-class honours graduates) than one that takes in less qualified students and gives its students a lower overall standard of final degree.

Another problem is whether the value of a degree from one institution is the same as a degree from another. The answer to this question depends on the jurisdiction within which comparisons are made. Some jurisdictions are used to the idea that the quality of a degree varies; others resist the notion of differential quality, arguing that system-wide checks (such as an external examiner system) ensure parity of quality across the system. Most UK studies assume that the qualitative value of the degree offered by the UK Open University is the same as that of a traditional UK university. However, from time to time this view has been challenged.

- Lumsden and Ritchie (1975) pointed out that many Open University students did not take an honours degree – the normal degree of traditional UK universities (see Section 14.1). In one sense this was a quantitative difference, determined not so much by the quality of the students' work (many non-honours degree Open University students took advanced level courses and gained high marks in these), but by the fact that at that time students could graduate with a non-honours degree based on 360 credit accumulation and transfer (CATs) points, as opposed to the 480 needed to gain an honours degree. (The university has since changed its regulations, and students can graduate with honours on the basis of 360 CATs points at appropriate levels).

- Carter (1973: 69) drew attention to the fact that the educational experience of part-time Open University students who were required to study in their 'free' time was very different to the experience of full-time students in traditional universities in the UK, who were 'free from the pressures of earning a living' (a comment that would ring rather hollow with today's students in the UK, who often work long hours at poor wages to meet their fees and expenses). Such a comment is in itself a product of the society within which it is made. In conventional Latin American universities, for example, it is quite normal for students to attend part time, so that the time taken by a student to complete a degree is invariably longer than the time scheduled for completion if students studied full time (Hennessy, 1979: 152).
- Carnoy and Levin (1975: 396) went further, suggesting that the cost savings of the Open University system might be 'obliterated by a smaller educational product'. They argued that the average university student 'receives not only instruction and instructional materials, but he receives substantially more tutorial services, contact with fellow students, access to libraries, computers and campus lectures than does his Open University counterpart'.
- Escotet (1980: 11–12, 15–17), drawing on his experience of the Universidad Nacional Abierta in Venezuela, found distance teaching universities deficient in the provision of cultural and social learning. He does not deny that what he calls distance *instruction* systems 'can fulfil the information role that the university actually has, with better quality, less cost, and a greater number of users', but, he argues, that is not *education* (pp 15–16).

Lumsden and Scott (1982) sought to answer some of these issues by looking at the level of comprehension demonstrated by Open University students taking two second-level economics courses (D222 in microeconomics and D282 in macroeconomics), compared with the level demonstrated by students completing economics courses in a conventional university. Multiple choice questions used to test students' comprehension of economics in traditional universities were administered to Open University students on D222 and D282. Subsequently, the conventional students were set two of the final examination essay questions drawn from the Open University's examinations.

- The results for the first test, involving OU students' responses to the multiple choice questions, showed that overall the Open University's second-level economics students had significantly higher levels of comprehension than first-year conventional university students, and were on a par with second- and third-year conventional students (p 575). There was a difference in the subjects: in microeconomics OU students scored the same as first-year conventional students, and significantly less than second- and third-year students; in macroeconomics they scored significantly more than third-year conventional university students.
- Both essay questions dealt with aspects of macroeconomics. The results showed that there was no significant difference between OU and conventional students on one of these questions, but the performance of OU students was significantly better on the other question (pp 576–7).

- Further research showed that the OU students had better pre-test scores than the conventional students. Given that a smaller percentage of them had an Advanced level school leaving certificate in economics (27 per cent against 34 per cent of the conventional university sample), this suggested that both their life experience and their exposure to some economics in the prerequisite social science foundation course had helped them (pp 579–80).

Overall there was no evidence to suggest that OU economics students were 'superior' to the conventional university ones, but equally it was impossible to say that OU teaching methods contributed to their better performance.

Studies such as Lumsden and Scott's do not specifically relate the learning scores and learning gains to costs. Wagner (1982: 43–4) provides the basis for an example that explains the difficulties involved, and the way in which the results can be interpreted in different ways. Suppose that University X spends £5000 on teaching 25 students economics, and that the learning gain shows an increase of 25 per cent based on the difference between an average entry test score of 30 per cent and an average exit score of 55 per cent. And suppose that University Z spends £10,000 teaching 60 students economics and that the same tests show a learning gain of 15 percentage points between an average entry test score of 45 per cent and an average exit test score of 60 per cent (see Table 14.6). In cost terms, Z is the cheaper (more efficient) university because although its total cost is twice that of University X, it teaches more than twice the number of students. This relative cost efficiency is reflected in the average cost per student, which is £167 for University Z compared with £200 for University X. Further, University Z graduates students with a better final score than University X (60 per cent as opposed to 55 per cent). Using normally accepted measures, Z is the more efficient and effective university because it has a lower average cost per student and a higher final examination score.

However, looking at the learning gain, University X is the more cost-effective university, with an average learning gain of 25 percentage points against University Z's learning gain of 15 per cent. Further, dividing the average cost per student by the average percentage point learning gain in each university, shows that University X spends £8.00 per learning point gain against £11.13 in University Z. On this criterion, University Z is the less cost-effective university.

14.3 The relative effectiveness of technologies

The studies cited above look at the overall cost effectiveness of different systems using particular configurations of technology. It can be very difficult to separate out the impact different media have on overall results. Much of the basic research in this area was done in the 1960s and 1970s and has been generally confirmed in the distance education literature since then (cf Clark, 1983, 1994). The contention that the research suggests that media choice has little impact on student's cognitive learning is supported by:

Table 14.6 *Efficiency and effectiveness – an example*

University	Total cost	Number of students	Average cost per student	Entry test average score	Exit test average score	Learning gain (% points)	Average cost per learning point gain
X	5000	25	200	30	55	25	8.00
Z	10000	60	167	45	60	15	11.13

- Schramm's (1977: 79) observation that 'motivated students learn from any medium if it is competently used and adapted to their needs' that has already been cited;
- Wells (1976: 270), who held that 'there are no significant differences (on cognitive measures of student learning) among a variety of technologies and instructional methods';
- Jamison et al.'s conclusion (1974: 56), reporting on the research literature on instructional technologies, that 'instructional radio, supplemented with appropriate printed material, is about as effective as traditional instruction', while 'there is strong evidence that instructional television, used in a way that closely simulates traditional instruction, is as effective, on average, as traditional instruction for all grade levels and subject matters'.

If so, there would seem to be a case for always adopting the cheapest technology available provided that (a) students can access the technology, and (b) the medium used allows the pedagogic objectives to be realized. In any case, within any one medium there is a strong argument for simplicity of presentation. In respect of educational broadcasting, for example, Schramm (1977) challenged the need for professional production techniques:

> The general conclusion that emerges from the studies of simple vs complex treatments of material in the audio-visual media is one that should gladden the heart of a budget officer or an executive producer. More often than not, there is no learning advantage to be gained by a fancier, more complex treatment (p 55).

> Visual embellishments do not usually help learning unless (like directional arrows) they help organize content that is not inherently well organized or (like animation) help a viewer to understand a process or concept that is very hard to understand without such simplification. In other words, visual embellishments *per se* are not especially useful in instructional materials (p 65).

> No learning advantage has been demonstrated for 'professional' or 'artistic' production techniques such as dollying rather than cutting, key rather than flat lighting, dissolves, wipes, fades etc (p 65).

Schramm (1977: 66) did however find that active participation by the student, 'either overt or covert, spoken or written or done through practice with a model or a device; button pushing or asking or answering questions, or finishing what the instructor has begun to say' is important and 'is more effective if the students are given immediate knowledge of results – that is, told whether their responses are correct'.

While a recent literature review by Carter (1996) suggests that distance educators have on the whole accepted the proposition that motivated students learn from any medium that is competently used, Carter points to other evidence suggesting that neurological responses to different media vary (p 35) and presses for research into the influence of different media on learning (p 38).

There are a number of possible criteria governing media choice, including access and participation rates, student success and cost. How would one choose between a technology based system which had, for example, a participation rate of 75 per cent and a success rate of 30 per cent, and cost twice as much as another which had a participation rate of 35 per cent and a success rate of 45 per cent? One way is to weight the various criteria in some way – a procedure proposed by Klees and Wells (1977). However, such approaches have been criticized on the grounds that they are extremely sensitive to the weights applied (Wagner, 1982: 58), and that they tend to focus on what is easily measurable – for example, participation rates, exit test scores, earnings and costs – and not to take account of less measurable outcomes such as the development of attitudes, socialization, and general satisfaction with the experience undergone (Carnoy and Levin, 1975).

Even putting these issues to one side, there are very considerable difficulties in unpacking the likely effects of technological interventions on students' performance, and relating this to the costs involved. A study by Levin *et al.* (1984) sought to compare the cost effectiveness of four interventions in education (computer assisted instruction (CAI), cross-age tutoring, reduced class size and a longer school day). In each case the intervention represented an addition to rather than a replacement for the basic instructional services provided. A control group continued to receive the basic package. To measure the effect of the interventions, the study compared the difference of the mean of the experimental group minus the mean of the control group, divided by the standard deviation of the control group. This measure, called an 'effect size', sought to measure the 'gain' in months of additional achievement in the progress of students, such that an effect size of 1.0 represented a gain of a whole academic year (of ten months), while an effect size of 0.1 represented a gain of one month in academic achievement (Table 14.7). However, there are insufficient studies for any firm conclusions to be drawn.

The evidence available suggests that open and distance learning can be as effective as traditional methods but, as Laurillard (1993: 223) comments, 'our use of IT-based media over the last 20 years has been prodigious but is not matched by our understanding of it, because the emphasis has been on development and use rather than on research and evaluation'. Further:

> because new technology materials are developed in isolation from a particular course, and necessarily so, they tend to be modular in nature, and require some particular prior preparation and follow-up by the teacher. In addition, materials are usually developed for one medium, rather than a combination. Both these features have the consequence that the materials so developed cannot usually address all essential aspects of the learning process... In order for students to learn from these materials, they have to contribute these other aspects for themselves. Many of them will be capable of doing this... However, many students do not find this easy; they are even more unlikely to do so when they are finding the subject matter difficult... (p 226).

The effective use of educational technologies, and hence of open and distance learning methodologies, requires teachers to be alive to ways of effectively defining

Table 14.7 Comparison of effectiveness of four educational interventions

	Estimated effectiveness in months of additional achievement gain		Annual additional cost per student of intervention ($)	Estimated effectiveness in months of additional achievement gain per each additional $100 per student	
	Mathematics	Reading		Mathematics	Reading
CAI*	1.2	2.3	119	1.0	1.9
Cross-age tutoring:					
– peer component	9.7	4.8	212	4.6	2.2
– adult component	6.7	3.8	827	0.8	0.5
Increasing instructional time	0.3	0.7	61	0.5	1.2
Reducing class size from:					
35 to 30	0.6	0.3	45	1.4	0.7
30 to 25	0.7	0.4	63	1.2	0.6
25 to 20	0.9	0.5	94	1.0	0.5
35 to 20	2.2	1.1	201	1.1	0.6

* Students worked with drill and practice exercises on an average of ten minutes a day

learning materials, starting with the definition of objectives and the analysis of student learning needs, and moving on from this to the design of learning activities that will result in students' attaining the desired outcomes (Laurillard, 1993: 181–202). Laurillard contends that the best approach is likely to be the use of several media together, in an integrated way (p 208), while paying attention to the context within which the technologies will be used (pp 221–2). Unfortunately, while the use of educational technologies within distance and open learning contexts can be cost effective, as the research demonstrates, this does not necessarily explain why they are effective. Equally, the fact that they are ineffective in particular circumstances, in the sense that few students succeed and learn effectively, does not mean that they are inherently ineffective. It may only mean that they have been used poorly and inappropriately by those who have designed and implemented the system. Economists can show that educational technology can be cost effective. How the organizational infrastructure is designed and how appropriate teaching strategies are developed to guarantee that this is so without excessive cost is beyond the scope of this book.

14.4 Conclusion

Distance and open learning can be effective, but in general far less is known about its effectiveness than about its efficiency. Recent studies have begun to address this issue rather more (for example, some of the studies in Perraton, 1993). However, cause and effect are difficult to disentangle and there is little clear research available to guide educational planners and course developers in the choice of the most cost-effective media.

Chapter 15

Cost benefit

Cost benefit seeks to measure in economic terms the benefits of education to the individual and to society. Two benefits of education are identified in the literature.

1. The private rate of return to the individual. The basic idea is that education provides individuals with utility (that is, pleasure and satisfaction from consuming goods and services), like any other goods or services. This may be reflected in the higher levels of income that those who are more highly educated can obtain over their lifetime; in non-monetary consumptive benefits associated with education such as participation in cultural events and the enjoyment of leisure reading; and in some of the benefits that educated people pass on to their children. The decision to spend private resources on education is an investment decision. Individuals choose from alternative investments, selecting education when the expected yield from lifetime earnings exceeds the costs by a margin sufficient to give a rate of return greater than anticipated returns from alternatives.

2. The social rate of return, reflected in the extent to, which society as a whole benefits from its investment in education. The economic study of education gained importance within the context of human capital theory. This concept arose out of the inability of conventional economic analysis to account for the differences in national income growth between rich and poor countries.

The study of the cost benefits of education raises the issue that Wagner (1982: 3) called 'the general problem of attributing causation': what certainty is there that the benefits people and society enjoy stem from their investment in education, as opposed to some other factor?

15.1 Private rates of return: The theoretical background

The private rate of return on education is the annual value of the (discounted lifetime) gains due to an individual's education expressed as a percentage of the (discounted) cost *to the individual* of acquiring that education (Johnes, 1993: 28). The cost of education typically consists of foregone earnings (though this is less true of part-time education and hence of much open and distance learning) and other costs incurred by the student. There are basically three ways of measuring the monetary yield of an education to the individual (Leslie and Brinkman, 1988: 41–8):

1. Earnings differentials. This approach measures the difference in earnings between individuals who have had different levels of education. Put simply, how much on average does a university graduate earn in comparison with a non-graduate? How much does someone with a higher secondary school qualification earn in comparison to someone without one? The assumption is that the earnings differentials between educated and under-educated individuals are entirely due to education and not to other factors. This is, of course, not always the case. Nevertheless, the earnings differential approach has the virtue of simplicity. The main problem is that it takes no account of the costs of education, and hence is of little value in calculating the expected yield on investment in education.
2. Net present value (NPV) calculations. Present value is the discounted value of a financial sum arising at some future period. Thus if the discount rate is 10 per cent, the present value this year of £110 earned next year is £100 since £100 invested now will yield £110 in a year's time. The approach seeks to establish the NPV of an education after costs are subtracted and corrections made to adjust for the effects of changes in the value of money. The assumption underlying NPV is that £1 spent today on education is worth more, considering foregone interest, than £1 earned at some later date. The main problem with this approach is that of selecting an appropriate interest rate for calculating NPVs.
3. Internal rates of return (IRR). Conceptually, the IRR is the NPV in reverse. It is calculated by estimating from workers' earnings the expected lifetime earnings for graduates and non-graduates, year on year, and from institutional cost data, the cost of an education. After correcting costs to current pounds through compounding, the interest or discount rate that would set the earnings value equal to the cost value is calculated. This rate is the IRR. The IRR can be compared to potential yields. The assumption is that investment in education should take place so long as the IRR exceeds the market interest rate. Interest rates naturally vary but most IRR literature compares IRR estimates with a 10 per cent rate of return on investments (Leslie and Brinkman, 1988: 45–6).

The weakness of IRR studies lies in their sensitivity to the costs of education. This is because variations in cost of only a few hundred pounds or dollars a year may represent a large proportion of total college costs, but are likely to represent a small proportion of post-college earnings; and because costs are compounded forward and earnings are discounted backwards, the same few hundred dollars or pounds spent in an individual's late teens or early twenties represents a much higher amount later, while the same amount earned in the future will decrease greatly when reduced to present value (ibid: 57). Leslie and Brinkman (1988: 57) comment, 'to our knowledge, no one has ever emphasized that the explanation is cost difference, not benefit difference'. This leads them to conclude that 'private IRRs are an inappropriate base for determining public support levels for higher education, not only because these rates pertain to private circumstances, but because what they reflect is primarily how generous society has been, not how valuable the higher education enterprise may be' (p 58).

15.2 Social rates of return: The theoretical background

The social rate of return on education measures the extent to which society receives a positive payoff on its investment in education. It differs from the private rate of return in that it takes account of the costs of providing education borne by the rest of society (usually through taxes), *as well as* those private costs borne by the individual (such as foregone earnings and the direct costs paid by the individual). On the other hand, the benefits are private benefits only (before taxes).

Since education is usually heavily subsidized by government, in many cases the social rate of return is likely to be much lower than the private rate of return. However, the assumption that all the social benefits are captured by the graduate, and that there are no societal benefits beyond the untaxed income of the individual, is clearly wrong, reflecting the narrow definition accorded it in the education rate-of-return literature. Equally, the inclusion of private costs in the social cost seems illogical.

From a policy point of view, the social rate of return is a better basis for public policy decisions on the level of investment in education. As Schultz (1971: 171) observed, 'the price that the student pays for educational services is only remotely connected to the real cost of producing them, and therefore private choices by students, however efficient they are privately, are not necessarily efficient socially'. However, the methodological limitations mentioned above limit the utility of the social rate of return as an instrument for policy analysis. For example, ignoring the societal benefits other than tax raised on the (higher) income of more educated individuals and including private costs in the cost side, tends to widen the gap between private and social rates of return and gives credence to the argument that individuals should be prepared to pay a greater share of the costs of higher levels of education.

Further, since social rates of return build on the same figures as private rates of return, any unreliability in the figures will affect both. However, on the benefits side the omissions are more serious. Monetary benefits to others are excluded, as are all the non-monetary benefits such as the fact that higher levels of education are associated with lower crime rates, lower fertility rates, lower levels of health problems, lower infant and child mortality etc.

There are a number of possible ways of compensating for the omission of social benefits. These include calculating:

- the percentage of national income growth deriving from education and higher education. Growth is traditionally dependent on land, labour and capital. A proportion of labour's contribution to growth must result from education. In the United States, Leslie and Brinkman (1988: 71) suggested that this was in the range of 15–20 per cent for education as a whole, and 4–5 per cent for higher education. Those interested in the methodology giving rise to these estimates and in the criticisms levelled against the approach are referred to Leslie and Brinkman (1988: 82–6);
- the economic impact of colleges upon their communities, which Leslie and Brinkman (1988: 71) suggested was worth $1.50 to $1.60 for every dollar spent on college operating expenses, and 59 jobs created per each $1 million of college budget;
- the reduction in training and the reduction in lost productivity arising from staff being diverted from productive work to training if, as Thurow (1975) suggests, employers tend to fill jobs with those on whom they will have to spend the least money in further training. There is, of course, a need to ensure that workers retain their skills once hired. Training will enhance or maintain a worker's productivity in the face of change. There is a cost to training which includes not just the cost of providing training, but also the cost of lost productivity while the worker is taken off the job. Any system of training that can pass on part of the cost of training time to the employee, by cutting into the employee's leisure time as opposed to working time, has benefits to the employer. Open, flexible and distance training is of benefit to employers for precisely this reason.

15.3 Private and social rates of return in practice

Psacharopoulos (1985) provides estimates for the private and social rates of return to primary, secondary and tertiary education for a selection of countries.

- Not surprisingly, private rates of return almost always exceed the social rate of return, given the extent to which the education of private individuals is subsidized by the state.
- in general, the rates of return on education are higher in less developed countries than in intermediate and advanced economies, reflecting the relative lack of access to education in less developed countries.

- in most of the countries studied by Psacharopoulos, the private and social rates of return of primary education are greater than that of secondary education.
- in less developed countries, the rates of return of primary schooling exceed those of higher education, giving rise to a belief on the part of some that resources should be reallocated away from tertiary to primary education.
- in advanced countries where basic literacy is an absolute necessity, the private and social rates of return of primary education rise to infinity since the acquisition of basic skills is a prerequisite for productive employment.
- so far as higher education goes, the private rate of return exceeds that of secondary education in many countries, but this is the result of heavy subsidy by the state.
- in advanced countries the social rate of return to higher education is also frequently greater than the social rate of return of secondary schooling, reflecting the fact that higher education is often rationed.

Because college education is so much more expensive than primary and secondary level education, and because college-based students are charged for income foregone whereas primary and to an extent secondary school children are not (given the existence of laws forbidding child labour), the private rates of return of higher level education tend to be lower (though there are considerable differences from country to country. However, the salary benefits of a college-based education remain considerable: in 1983, male median money income in the United States was $10,308 for those with an eighth-grade education, $17,568 for those with four years of high school, and $26,152 for those with four years of college. On this basis, the benefit that each additional year of education provides can be calculated (see Table 15.1).

Where education is heavily subsidized by the state, the private rates of return on which individuals base their demand will differ markedly from the social rate of return. Further, those in receipt of subsidies will have a higher rate of return than those who are not subsidized, thus Wachtel (1975: 158–62) showed that those who benefited from the GI Bill after the Second World War, and received grants to help them through college, had a rate of return that was almost twice that of non-recipients.

There is some evidence that individuals' choice of courses is partly determined by whether their chosen field of study will assure them of a job – and preferably a highly paid job – on graduation. Freeman (1976b) propounded a model that suggested that a shortage of graduates in a particular field may lead to an increase in wages as firms compete for the products of a finite pool of qualified labour, leading to a consequential rise in student demand for these fields of study. Unfortunately, of course, the decision to enter a particular field is taken several years before graduation and, by the time they graduate, the labour market in the chosen field may have changed, with an over-supply of graduates leading to a fall in wages. Low wages will depress demand just as high wages will encourage demand to study a particular subject area, leading to an oscillation in the demand figures. There is evidence in support of Freeman's model, more especially in the

Table 15.1 *Male mean money income derived from each additional year of education in the United States, 1983*

Level of education achieved	Median male money income for persons with this level, 1983	Money income attributable to lower levels	Net increase in money income	Number of years invested in education at this level	Income per year invested at this level
8th grade primary	10,308	–	–	8	1289
4th grade high school	17,568	10,308	7260	4	1815
4th year college	26,152	17,568	8584	4	2146

Source: Based on Leslie and Brinkman, 1988: 57–8

fields of science and engineering, but, for substantial numbers of students, the level of financial return is not the prime consideration governing their choice of course (Bosworth and Ford, 1985). Indeed, if, as Thurow (1975) suggests, employers tend to fill jobs with those on whom they will have to spend the least money in further training, the decision to go on to higher education turns not so much on the higher wages likely to be paid to those with more education, but on the fact that the absence of education reduces one's chances of being selected for a job (Tsang and Levin, 1985).

Overall, the private rate of return from higher education can be expected to fluctuate. Evidence from UK experience indicates that the rates of return of higher education fell during the 1980s and 1990s, initially because the recession of the early 1980s led new graduates to accept lower paid jobs, and then as a result of the marked increase in the supply of graduates as, using Trow's (1973) classification, the UK's higher education system moved from an elite to a mass system. This general conclusion seems to be supported by Freeman's (1976a) findings that in the United States in the mid-1970s the rate of return to higher education fell. Freeman saw this as a problem of over-education. As the market for graduate labour became depressed, so the number of secondary school graduates enrolling in colleges fell. Overall, however, in the United States the decline in the profitability of the college degree in the 1970s was temporary (Liberman, 1979; Mattila, 1982) so that by the latter half of the 1980s Leslie and Brinkman (1988: 56) were able to conclude that the first degree remains a good investment, while Psacharopoulos's findings suggest that primary and, increasingly, secondary education is an absolute necessity for obtaining gainful employment (Psacharopoulos, 1985).

15.4 Private rates of return from distance and open learning

Lee et al. (1982: 158–62) sought to establish the relative cost benefits of the Air Correspondence High School compared with regular high schools in Korea. To do this they modelled the costs of a regular high school starting at the same time and on the same scale as the ACHS. They took account of the capital costs of the projects, their recurrent operating costs, the foregone earnings of students (an important consideration given that 70 per cent of ACHS's students were earning) and the assumed benefits accruing to students of the two systems over their working lives. They concluded that the private rate of return on the regular high school would be about 10 per cent, but that on the ACHS would be about 27 per cent, nearly three times as high. Moreover, as Lee and his colleagues commented, 'since the major beneficiaries of the project are the poorer in the national income scale, the social rate of return – with appropriate social weights attached to the benefits of the target groups – would be much higher' (p 161). They therefore concluded tentatively that 'despite the low internal efficiency, ACHS is a socially viable and economically profitable project' (p. 161).

The benefits of education are reflected in the individual's earnings over a lifetime of employment. The number of years of employment is therefore crucial to the calculation of benefits, as is the extent to which earnings are foregone during the period of education. Mace (1978: 299) questioned whether UK Open University graduates will enjoy the same increased earnings as do the graduates of traditional universities. Since the average age of Open University graduates was 37 in 1975, and that of traditional university graduates 22, the period during which Open University graduates might enjoy increased earnings is severely reduced – being one-third shorter assuming a retirement age of 65. Further, by the age of 37 'most people are established in their jobs, and in addition there are powerful institutional forces, such as internal labour markets, that will inhibit mobility'. So the economic value of an Open University degree will be less than that of a traditional university degree (p 300). Ansari (1992: 109) also points to the fact that students in the University of Delhi's School of Correspondence Courses and Continuing Education are older (generally over 30 years) than students in the regular schools (mostly aged 18–23 years).

Mace (1978: 298–9) also points to the very different learning experience of Open University and traditional university students, and queries whether Open University graduates will be as successful in the labour market as conventional university graduates. Carnoy and Levin, in their critique of the value of a degree gained by distance study relative to one gained through traditional means, pointed to the credentialling effects of higher education and argued that 'to assume that the value of an Open University degree will be similar to one from Oxbridge [ie Oxford or Cambridge] or the "Red Bricks" [the nineteenth- and early twentieth-century city universities in the UK, such as Birmingham, Manchester, and Leeds] … simply ignores the credentialling effect of higher education institutions' (Carnoy and Levin, 1975: 390). They suggested that 'the Open University seems to be a solution to pressures for university training for working-class youths, but only for a university training which increases some competencies without necessarily providing credentials for higher paying jobs which are reserved for graduates from the "real" universities' (p 402). They concluded that:

> a more realistic premise is that the limited nature of the Open University education as well as the credential effect of particular institutions on earnings and occupational attainments would suggest that the Open University graduate is not likely to receive either consumption or income benefits from his education that are as high as those of the person from the more conventional university setting (p 396).

A survey of employers' attitudes towards the qualifications gained by Open University students asked employers to rank Open University qualifications against those of other UK universities on a five point scale ranging from +5 (much better) to +1 (a lot worse), with the mean score of 3.0 indicating that the institutions were thought to be the same. Employers scored the Open University's qualifications as a little worse than Oxbridge qualifications (mean score 2.5), marginally worse than 'redbrick' universities (2.8) and 'new' universities (those set up in the 1960s) (2.9), and marginally better than the old polytechnic sector (3.1). When asked to say how an Open University degree compared with that from other universities, two out of three employers (69 per cent) felt that the Open University degree was about the same as other degrees; 4 per cent thought it was better; 19 per cent thought it was inferior; and 7 per cent spontaneously said it was better than some degrees but not as good as others (MAI Research for Marketing, 1992: 33). When recruiting, 80 per cent viewed candidates with an Open University degree as the same as graduates with a degree from another university; 8 per cent rated Open University graduates more highly; and 12 per cent rated them less highly (ibid: 34).

Many distance teaching institutions are specifically aimed at the needs of adults and hence the benefits accruing to their graduates will be different to those accruing to younger students. For example, a survey of Open University graduates who had obtained their Bachelor's degree between 1985 and 1989 indicated that 74 per cent of them were in full-time employment when they commenced their studies, and 8 per cent in part-time employment (Woodley, 1995: 38). Individuals may move in and out of work during their studies, and the survey showed that 34 per cent had in fact moved from one occupational category to another. Those who had moved within an occupational category were not identified. Occupational mobility in this sense varied with only 8 per cent of the health professionals and 9 per cent of teachers in schools indicating a change of occupation, against 62 per cent of graduates who had started their studies in a clerical job, 63 per cent who had started in a secretarial job, and 68 per cent who had started in a personal services occupation. Column 2 of Table 15.2 provides more details. The table also shows in column 3 the destination occupation of those who had moved, thus of all those who had moved, 28 per cent had moved into management and 10 per cent into teaching in schools. Table 15.2 provides more details. Overall more than four in ten of the Open University graduates reported some kind of occupational benefit (see Table 15.3). However, the survey does not indicate the level of financial benefit enjoyed by graduates, nor their age at the time that they began to enjoy this benefit. It is also the case that the benefit might have occurred without studying with the Open University.

Apart from these occupational benefits, students reported a range of personal benefits (eg increased self-confidence, self-awareness and maturity, expanded horizons and new interests) and some beneficial impacts on others (eg encouragement to children to study hard, and greater involvement by themselves in political, cultural, community and voluntary activities). Negative effects reported by some were a strain on their relationship with their partner.

15.5 Benefits to the employer from open and distance learning

A number of studies have shown that use of distance teaching methods can help reduce employers' costs by avoiding some of the costs of face-to-face

Table 15.2   *Occupational change following study at the UK Open University*

Occupational category	% of all students surveyed who changed occupation	% of those who changed occupation moving into this occupation
Corporate managers/administrators and managers/proprietors in agriculture and services	23	28
Science and engineering professionals	24	10
Science and engineering associate professionals	55	8
Health professionals	8	1
Health associate professionals	29	2
Teaching professionals in schools	9	10
Teaching professionals in further and higher education	12	11
Other teaching professionals	34	3
Other professionals	29	7
Other associate professionals	37	8
Clerical occupations	62	5
Secretarial occupations	63	2
Skilled manual trades	55	1
Protective services occupations	55	0
Personal services occupations	69	2
Buyers, brokers and other sales occupations	68	2
Industrial plant and machine operators, assemblers, drivers and mobile machine operatives, and other occupations in agriculture, forestry and fishing	61	1
ALL	34	100

Source: Woodley, A (1995) 'The experience of older graduates from the British Open University'. *International Journal of University Adult Education*, p 45. Reprinted with permission.

teaching. Moore and Thompson and their colleagues (1990: 29–30) report on several American studies (Table 15.4) that bear out the experience of many of the UK firms surveyed by Coopers and Lybrand (1990) that open learning methods can be more cost efficient than traditional training methods (see Table 13.3).

A survey (MAI Research for Marketing, 1992: 33–4) in the UK of 426 employers showed that all but two companies used at least one of the following forms of training: in-house, residential courses, day release, open learning, distance learning or another kind of training. However, while virtually all the companies (96 per cent) used in-house training and most used day release (86 per cent) and residential courses (83 per cent), open and distance learning was used by a smaller proportion of companies (57 per cent in both cases). The study asked employers

Table 15.3 *Occupation-related benefits of Open University study*

Better pay/extra increment	24%
Promotion to a higher grade	16%
New occupation	17%
More specialist job in same occupation	12%
Switch of specialization within same occupation	8%
Re-entered paid employment	6%
Became self-employed	1%
Achieved management status	9%
Moved to a new firm/organization	11%
Any of the above	43%

Source: Woodley (1995) ibid. p 44. Reprinted with permission.

to identify which kind of employee the various approaches were most appropriate for. While in-house training was seen as appropriate for everyone, open and distance learning was seen to be particularly suitable for middle and senior management (88 and 83 per cent respectively). The research, which was carried out for the UK Open University, confirmed that the main advantage perceived by employers for open and distance learning was that the learning could be done in the individual's own time and at their own pace (27 per cent), thus enabling individuals to work and study at the same time (20 per cent).

15.6 Conclusion

This chapter has hinted at some of the issues that need to be addressed in any study of the cost benefits of distance education. At the time of writing this is an area where much more research is needed. As open and distance learning methods come to be used more widely, so it becomes increasingly important that economists should begin to address the issues raised here.

Table 15.4 *Benefits to employers: cost avoidance*

System	Instructional method	System description	Costs avoided	Cost avoidance ($)	Source study
US Air Force Institute of Technology	Teleteaching remote site students compared with residential instruction	2982 students over two years, 1247 at remote sites. System costs US$497,139 over two years	Transportation costs to on-site training	Cost avoidance estimated at US$1,490,980	Christopher, 1982
Continuing professional education	Audio-teleconferencing	5377 contact hours. Cost of teleconferencing US$69,635	Cost of travel of consultants to deliver training	Cost savings of US$86,636	Showalter, 1983
AT&T	Teletraining	3176 students. System cost US$234,900	Travels, meals and lodging costs for Cincinnati-based training. Avoidance of non-productive time (six hours/student)	Cost saving: US$1,588,000. Cost saving: US$457,300	Chute *et al.*, 1987

Chapter 16

Costs, prices, demand and funding

Section 1.1 noted the high level of concern about the cost of education. Who funds what is a major political issue. While public institutions will no doubt continue to educate the majority of the world's students, governments are seeking, particularly at the higher education level, to mobilize a greater proportion of total funding from private sources, by increasing the proportion of educational costs that are borne by the students, or by encouraging increased private sponsorship of education. Private institutions are also an important element in the total provision of education, both at secondary and at higher education levels (UNESCO, 1995: Table 10; World Bank, 1994: 34–6). At the same time, there is a strong tradition of private provision of distance education, arising from the nineteenth-century development of commercial correspondence colleges.

Radical new proposals for the funding of education have been proposed. These include:

- auctions, under which educational institutions bid for student places funded by government; other things being equal, the places go to the institution offering places at the lowest cost per student;
- voucher schemes, where each consumer is given a voucher by the government to be used at their own choice of institution;
- approaches which provide for a mix of any one, two or three of the following: grants, loans and graduate taxes.

It is not the purpose of this book to look at the various solutions to the funding of education in detail, but instead to look at some of the issues that need to be raised when governments and institutions consider the funding of distance education.

16.1 Prices, demand and what the student can afford

To an extent, institutions under financial pressure can respond by reducing costs or increasing fees. However, studies of non-registration and drop-out in the UK Open University identified lack of money and inability to pay fees as one of the factors leading to either a failure to enter the programme or to a decision to drop-out from the programme once the student has embarked on it.

- 24.6 per cent of a survey of people who did not apply to study with the British Open University cited as a reason that, for them, the financial commitment was too great (Woodley and McIntosh, 1977: 21).
- 28 per cent of a survey of people who declined to accept the offer of a place on the Open University's undergraduate programme in 1983 gave as one of the reasons the fact that they could not afford to accept the offer (Woodley, 1983: 2).
- 36 per cent of new students entering the Open University in 1986, and 32 per cent of continuing students, experienced severe hardship or found it 'quite difficult' to pay their tuition fees. Women were more likely than men to experience difficulty in finding the money to pay their fees, and those on low incomes were, not surprisingly, likely to have more difficulty than those on high incomes (Kirkwood, 1988: 11–15).
- Woodley (1990) found that of the students who had entered the Open University between 1981 and 1987, had taken a course in 1987, had successfully completed at least one course, but who had not studied in 1988 or 1989, 17 per cent were not doing so because they could not meet the costs of Open University study. Six per cent of this same group said they would resume study when they could afford it. He also found that 13 per cent of students who had entered the Open University between 1981 and 1987, had taken a course in 1987, had not passed any courses and had not studied in 1988 or 1989, were not doing so because they could not meet the costs of Open University study. Ten per cent of this group said they would resume study when they could afford it. Of those with some credit, 46 per cent reported that it had been 'quite difficult' or a 'severe hardship' to finance their studies, while 58 per cent of those without any academic credit reported the same.

If cost is the reason and not the excuse for not studying, this is particularly challenging to an institution established to open up educational opportunities to the disadvantaged.

A number of stake-holders are engaged in the demand for and supply of distance and open education, including:

- the students demanding open, flexible and distance education;
- the institutions providing open, flexible and distance education;
- companies, which may be on the demand or the supply side;
- government, which provides incentives and structures within which the other three stakeholders operate.

Most studies on the relative cost efficiency of distance education are undertaken from the point of view of government, or companies as consumers of open, flexible and distance training, or the providers. There have been no significant studies on whether students as consumers see distance education as a route to a lower cost education for themselves. Traditional and distance systems of education have different characteristics that may individually or collectively appeal to or put off potential learners: indeed, distance educators naturally stress those characteristics (flexibility, high quality learning materials etc) that they think will appeal to potential students, while critics have queried the off-putting aspects, such as the credentialling power of institutions teaching by distance means (see Section 15.4). But while it is recognized that students can distinguish between the two forms of education, and hence regard them as different 'products', it is not known how these perceptions affect willingness to pay, nor how different price structures may affect student choice. In India, Shanmugasundaram (1995), in a study of the costs of BEd students studying by distance and by conventional means, found that, whereas the tuition costs of the distance BEd students was 4.44 times that of conventional learners, conventional learners incurred greater non-tuition fees (2.63 times their distance-taught colleagues); and Panda *et al.*, (1996: 138–9) found that the net private cost of education to traditional students was 1.38 times that to distance learners. However, it is not known in these cases whether the different cost of entry to the programmes affected the students' choice of product.

Bolwig (1993: 2) looked at the case of the Nandelshøjskole Syd in Southern Jutland where the introduction of a part-time distance-taught course in advanced business English and German led to a marked fall in enrolments for the traditional course – to the extent that the latter had to be dropped because of lack of demand. One reason was clearly that students had to travel to attend the traditional course: the average distance between the school and the student's home was 105 kilometres, with only 20 students living less than 60 kilometres from the school. Bolwig argues that students, as individuals, will wish to maximize their utility, welfare or satisfaction. The decision to purchase a distance course will depend on:

- the individual's real income;
- the price of the distance education course relative to other prices in the economy (eg the price of traditional forms of education, the wage rate etc);
- the individual's preferences.

However, it is not known to what extent the difference in the cost of distance education as against traditional education will affect individual's perceptions of the benefits or their willingness to pay for different options. As Bolwig (1993: 9) remarks, 'the reason why we always hear a lot about costs of distance learning and virtually nothing about the benefits accruing to individuals and society is of course that it is very difficult to measure benefits and quite easy to measure costs'. One reason is that the benefits to the student may not all be monetary ones reflected in the price of the course and the associated costs of studying it (such as the cost of travel). Other factors, such as use of time, may come into the equation as well. The value of the time one gives up on one activity in order to undertake another represents the opportunity cost of time. The usual proxy value for an individual's time is the value of what they might have earned if they had chosen to work instead. But, of course, this proxy value may be entirely bogus from the student's point of view. (Such opportunity costs are of course very important when one comes to consider the savings on staff time firms can achieve by transferring the cost of training from the firm's time to the student's personal time.) That there is a demand curve (the graphical representation of a schedule listing the quantities of a commodity a consumer would be willing to buy at various prices) for open and distance education, and that this will probably differ from that for traditional forms of education, is self-evident – but what this might be in specific cases and whether it is possible to generalize any findings is unknown.

There is a tendency for institutions to equate student costs with the fees charged to the student, but in fact students may have to incur all sorts of other costs in order to study. The cost of tuition fees and other fees and charges are, of course, a starting point, but practice varies enormously, with some institutions charging for the materials used by students separately from the costs of tuition, and others charging a single fee that covers the costs of materials and tuition. Yet others may charge a range of fees for special services. The cost of fees to the student can usually be computed fairly readily. However, other costs that students may incur include supplies and consumables associated with their course (stationery, books, paper); communication costs (postage, telephone); travel to and from local study centres and for other reasons associated with their studies; and, perhaps above all, the costs of buying and using the various technologies used by the institution. The latter can be significant. Chapter 12 (Case Study 12.2) reported on the costs of the Open University's introduction of computer-mediated communications to a course, and indicated (Table 12.2) the kinds of costs borne by students. Notwithstanding the fact that the computer, once acquired, could be used on subsequent courses, the cost of buying a machine (£630 at the time of the study) represented a significant cash outlay for each student on top of the normal course fees and other costs, including those associated with the computing element (Rumble, 1989b: 155).

The question of what a student is prepared to pay, in the widest sense, obviously has a direct relationship to their income, other demands on their income and preferences. Equally it has important implications for access. Many open, flexible and distance education systems include among their objectives reaching disadvantaged sectors of the population. If fees and costs are set at levels too high for the target population to afford, the achievement of social justice objectives is put at risk. Some institutions (the UK Open University is one) may set aside money to help some impoverished students pay their fees. But the issue of ability to pay is clearly crucial when considering the viability of projects operating in countries where the average level of income is low, as in the case of the Bangladesh Open University, which faces the additional challenge that it is expected in the long term to meet a substantial amount of its costs from fees (Shamsher Ali, *et al.*, 1997).

Although it is known that price will affect demand, from evidence from surveys looking at why people do not enrol and why they drop-out, and because there is no reason to believe that education is any different to any other product for which people have to pay, there is no information on the extent to which increases in student costs deter students from completing their study, or whether students value distance education because it is often the cheaper option for them, or for other reasons. This is, therefore, an area where research might be focused.

16.2 The state as a source of finance

Governments have seen open, flexible and distance education as a cheaper way of financing educational expansion and educational provision. In this sense, distance education is seen as potentially a more efficient way of providing education (see Chapter 13). At the same time, a growing number of governments have been seeking to encourage greater private funding of education and particularly higher education by getting students themselves or their parents to pay a greater share of the costs of education (World Bank, 1994: 41). The previous section noted some of the problems arising when students are expected to undertake a greater share of the cost of distance education.

But even where governments hope that a greater proportion of the overall costs of distance education will be carried by the students, start-up money is needed in advance of any enrolments to pay for the development of the infrastructure and the course materials. While some institutions have required little capital investment to start, the scale of the initial operations has been small and their development relatively slow. Thus Hermods correspondence school – now one of the biggest in Europe – started when its founder, H S Hermods, began helping an individual student who was moving away from Malmo to continue his course by post. In contrast, the cost of setting up a large-scale operation can be significant: for example, in 1992 the Asian Development Bank loaned the Government of Bangladesh US $33.93 millions to set up the Bangladesh Open University – while recognizing that even during the development period there would need to be some additional funding from the Government of Bangladesh and from student fee income. Given the lead-in times required to develop the infrastructure and courses, it usually takes at least two to three years before any income from student fees begins to flow into a project, and several more before the proportion of government funding begins to fall. In India, the government had initially to meet the full cost of developing the Indira Gandhi National Open University (IGNOU) when it was set up in September 1985. In 1987/88, with enrolments started, the government was meeting 93 per cent of IGNOU's costs, with 6.9 per cent of its funding coming from student fees (UNESCO/ICDE, nd: 29). By 1991/92 the government's contribution had fallen to 68 per cent as enrolments expanded.

The amount required to set up a project can easily be underestimated: when the UK Government was thinking about setting up the Open University, it asked Lord Goodman, a distinguished lawyer, to undertake a realistic assessment of the costs of launching the University. He estimated the initial costs (in 1966 prices) at £3.5 million annually, with an initial capital expenditure of just over £1 million. In 1974, speaking in the House of Lords, he acknowledged that he had seriously underestimated the costs of the project, but had he not, the University might never have been established at all (Perry, 1976: 20, 227). Such high initial costs make it difficult for private investors to enter the field, except at a modest level.

Governments also find it difficult to understand the cost structure and funding needs of large-scale projects. Snowden and Daniel (1980: 76), reflecting their experience at Athabasca University in Alberta, Canada, wrote of: 'the considerable difficulty we have in describing the institution's operations and its economics to officials in government and funding agencies, to members of other (conventional) institutions and, to some extent, to our own counterparts in other SDEs [small distance education systems]'.

Swinerton and Hogan (1981: 1) pointed out that non-traditional programmes cannot be driven by 'the same financial flywheels as the more customary academic programs'. Generally 'the budget for a non-traditional degree program is a nightmare for everyone involved'. In those cases where it is funded 'by the same mechanisms as traditional programs... there is an inevitable pressure to mould the program itself to fit traditional funding formula'.

In Britain, the government found it difficult to understand the funding of the Open University and pressed the University to develop a funding methodology that would be acceptable to both parties, and that would define the resource needs of the institution relative to its plans. As Perry (1976: 228) points out, it was clear that there were no norms to guide anyone on the funding of the Open University. This led to the decision, in its early years, to fund the institution directly from the Department of Education and Science, and not through the normal mechanisms for university funding in Britain. Initially, in the absence of any funding norms, the University negotiated each development with officials at the Department of Education and Science (Perry, 1976: 230), but during 1974–5 the University began to envisage a point at which the development of its undergraduate programme might for the foreseeable future reach a steady state, at least in relation to the size of its curriculum. The time was therefore ripe to develop a funding formula that reflected the main cost drivers of the University: the number of courses, the number of students and the size of its institutional overheads. The University analysed its 1975 costs into student-related, course-related and overhead costs, using this data to inform the development of a funding formula reflecting its current expenditure (Equation 16.1).

$$E = 192S + 80000C + 5260000 \qquad \text{[Eq. 16.1]}$$

where:

E = the total expenditure in the Open University in a plateau situation (at June 1975 prices)
S = the number of finally registered students in each academic year
C = the number of standard length courses presented in each year

and where:

- the direct (marginal) cost per student was £192;
- the average annual cost per course presented was £80,000;
- the overheads were £5.26 millions.

This formula was endorsed by an independently chaired committee (Open University, 1975). The University then agreed a curriculum plan that would enable it to present a 'steady state' curriculum of 87 Open University 'full credit' courses (courses involving on average 12 hours study over about 34 weeks), with an annual remake load based on the total remaking of each course every eight years, and a general course maintenance load of about 10 per cent of the effort required to launch the courses in the first place, and sought government approval of this plan. The other main driver of costs was controlled by the government, which set the level of new students taken into the programme each year, and hence in effect the total number of students. Finally, the institutional overhead was agreed. This formula was used for several years to determine the funding of the University, but broke down in the 1980s as the University diversified into other areas and the Thatcher government sought to reduce the costs of higher education.

Currently, the Open University is funded on a student number basis that does not adequately reflect the cost structure of the University, and in particular the extent to which costs are driven by factors other than student numbers. The way in which student numbers are used to determine funding may also be misguided. It is quite common (see, for example, the case cited in Section 8.2) for different funding weights to be given to students studying part time as opposed to full time, or by different modes, so that, for example, a full-time student will generally be weighted 1.0, a part-time student might be weighted, say, 0.5 of a full time student, and a distance learning student might have another weight. In such circumstances, if a full-time student attracted government funding of, say, £1400, a part-time student weighted as 0.5 full-time equivalent might on a strictly pro rata basis attract £700 funding. Where costs are closely attached to the time spent by students in class, as is the case with part-time students who are taught in class, the use of full-time equivalent weights is reasonable. But in the case of distance learning students who spend little time in class, it is not. The average cost (AC) of a distance learning student is based on the variable cost per student (V) (ie direct cost of materials, assessment, tuition, postage etc) plus the fixed costs (FC) divided by the number of students enrolled (N):

$$AC = V + (FC/N) \qquad \text{[see Eq. 5.3]}$$

Clearly, if there are large numbers of students (N) enrolled relative to the fixed costs, the average cost per student will be low; if numbers are low, the average cost will be high. The relationship of the average cost per distance student to the average cost of a traditional student will vary depending among other things on the number of students enrolled, as is clear from an examination of the efficiency ratios given in Table 13.3. To define a funding weight per student that does not take account of the very different cost structure of teaching by distance and open means will constrain the range of courses offered to distance students, and disadvantage the development of distance teaching. Yet, at the time of writing, this was precisely what was being suggested in the UK, where the Higher Education Funding Council had issued a consultative paper on funding methods under which:

> the price fixed (ie the government funds given to an institution) will be the standard price for a full-time equivalent (FTE) student... Weights will be attached to a number of student-related factors... part-time students will attract a small additional weight, to recognize the additional costs of providing for them. On the other hand, distance learners will be differentiated from other part-time students and given a lower weight to reflect their lower costs (Higher Education Funding Council for England, 1996: 5).

Nothing could illustrate better the fundamental misunderstanding of the cost structures of distance and open education held by funding agencies that deal primarily with the funding of classroom-based teaching.

Recent papers provide information on the level of government subsidy of higher distance education in some countries. Governments would seem to be seeking to reduce their funding of all kinds of education. In practice there is wide variation in the proportion of the costs of distance education systems carried by government, though Daniel (1995: 47) argues that governments are now minority providers of funds for most large-scale distance teaching universities.

- Distance teaching universities reliant to a considerable degree on fee income include the Universidad Nacional de Educación a Distancia in Spain (60 per cent), the Centre National d'Enseignement à Distance in France (60 per cent), the Universitas Terbuka in Indonesia (66 per cent) and Anadolu University, Turkey (76 per cent) (Daniel, 1995: 16).
- In 1993, the Government of Thailand contributed about 30.1 per cent of the total budget of the Sukhothai Thammathirat Open University, with 70 per cent coming from fees (Teswanitch and Thanavibulchai, 1993: 21). However, only 3.9 per cent of the total costs of the Sukhothai Thammathirat Open University postgraduate studies programme comes from government, with 64.3 per cent coming from tuition fees and 31.8 per cent from other sources, whereas in the other universities 80 per cent of the costs of postgraduate studies are born by government, and 20 per cent by students (Silphiphat and Tamey, 1993: 16).
- Wei and Tong (1994: 97–8) point out that 59 per cent of the costs of the Chinese Radio and Television Universities (RTVU) comes from central and

local government sources, 4 per cent from student fees and the rest from industries, companies and public services running RTVU classes.

- Jung (1993: 62) indicated that student fees met 62 per cent of the Korea Air and Correspondence University budget in 1993.
- In India, 68 per cent of the income of the Indira Gandhi National Open University's 1991–2 budget came from government sources and 32 per cent from fees. The level of government subsidy to IGNOU is within the range (60–95 per cent) found in conventional universities in India, and considerably higher than the subsidy provided the Dr B R Ambedkar Open University in Andhra Pradesh (27 per cent), the Kota Open University (48 per cent), and a selected group of distance education institutes (8 per cent) (Ansari, 1993: 114).
- Over the years, the proportion of the UK Open University's costs met by government has fallen, while that met through fees has risen: in 1971, when the University launched its undergraduate programme, government grant met 88.5 per cent of the University's expenditure while fees met 11.5 per cent (Perry, 1976: 235); by 1981 grant provided for 84.3 per cent of undergraduate programme costs, with fees meeting 15.7 per cent of costs (Department of Education and Science and The Open University, 1991: 69); by 1989 this had become 77.5 and 22.5 per cent respectively (ibid: 69); and by 1995 government grant accounted for 60 per cent of the University's income, fees constituted 31 per cent, and 9 per cent came from other sources (Daniel, 1995: 16).

Ansari (1992: 77) points out that government subsidy of distance education programmes located within mixed-mode Indian universities is lower than the subsidy given to on-campus education. In 1980/81 the government met on average 18 per cent of the costs of distance education provided through the correspondence directorates, with 73 per cent of costs being met by fees and 9 per cent from other sources. In contrast, 72 per cent of the costs of the conventional system was funded by government, with 13 per cent coming from fees and 14 per cent from other sources (see Table 16.1).

Table 16.1 *Source of income of distance and on-campus systems in mixed-mode Indian universities*

| Year | Sample size | Mode | % of total income from: | | |
			Fees	Government	Other
1980/81	All-India	Correspondence	72.6	18.3	9.1
		Traditional	13.5	72.4	14.1
1986/87	Sample of six	Correspondence	74.1	25.9	

Source: Based on Ansari, 1992: 77, 80

It would be dangerous to generalize from the figures given in this section. The degree of state subsidy of distance education may depend on a number of factors: the stage of development of the institution – in the early years of development the proportion of subsidy is likely to be high, the extent to which the institution's target population is acknowledged to need state subsidy towards fee levels, and the philosophy adopted by the state towards educational subsidies. However, it may be that not only does distance education enable governments to reduce their per capita funding of education, but also, because of the very different student experience, to reduce the overall proportion of institutional costs that they meet.

16.3 Conclusion

It is not necessarily the case that distance and open learning are cheaper than traditional approaches to teaching. Approaches to funding need to recognize this, and also the fact that the costs of distance and open learning are driven by a range of factors, not simply by a formula that links total costs to teaching loads.

Governments may be seeking to reduce the amount of money they put into education by driving down the unit price they are prepared to pay to institutions for educating students; and institutions are increasingly looking for sources of funding other than those derived from government. The major alternative is student fees, whether these are met from available resources or from loans. In either case, there is a danger that the fees, coupled with the other costs of study that students have to bear, will rise to levels that increasing numbers of students will not pay. Inevitably, it will be poorer and more disadvantaged students who are affected first. This will challenge those distance and open learning systems that were set up to meet the needs of disadvantaged sectors of society, and that are often driven by a keen sense of their social mission. Increased efficiencies may for a while bridge the gap between funding and expenditure, but at some point real damage will be done to the 'fabric' of the institution, leading to a choice between niche marketing for the well-off, and the worst kind of provision for the poor. The latter could well be reminiscent of the worst of nineteenth-century correspondence education – poor quality materials, little or no student support, payment of fees up-front, and high drop-out rates.

Such a scenario is not in the interests of distance and open educators, who have struggled hard to establish reputations for quality; nor is it in the interests of the students; nor, ultimately, is it in the interests of those governments that are seeking cost-effective methods of providing education and training. It is therefore very important that policies impacting on funding, fees and the other costs borne by students are carefully thought out.

Chapter 17

Conclusions

There are wide variations in distance education systems, both in their size and in the range of technologies they use. In sharp contrast to Daniel's (1995) focus on the mega-universities, Hallak (1990: 187) points out that although the large-scale distance education systems enjoy a great deal of visibility, only one in three (35 per cent) of institutions teaching only at a distance and listed in the International Centre for Distance Learning's database in 1989 had more than 10,000 students, while one in four of these (25 per cent) had less than 1000 students; of the dual-mode systems, only 1 per cent had over 10,000 students, and 60 per cent had under 1000 students. Structurally, the majority of institutions teaching by distance means are mixed mode, using distance education as one delivery system among a range of possible options, including traditional classroom-based teaching. In such institutions, the distinction between class-based and resource-based, and on-campus and at-a-distance education, is being eroded as institutions seek the most appropriate way to achieve further efficiencies (Section 13.4). This merely continues a process of searching for efficiencies in education that began a long time ago (Section 1.1).

Within distance and open learning, there are wide differences in the choice and mix of media and technologies, in working practices, in the terms and conditions of employment of staff, in production standards, in the range of student support services offered and in the range and sophistication of the institutional 'overheads' that support the prime function of teaching open and distance learning students (Chapters 10–12). This makes it difficult to reach any hard and fast conclusions – beyond the level of generalities – about the costs of different approaches (Sections 11.5 and 12.3).

It is not technically difficult to cost distance and open learning systems (Chapters 2–8), though there are particular difficulties about the analysis of overhead costs (Chapter 7), and technical choices over the treatment of capital costs, notably annualization (Section 6. 3), and the attribution of costs to joint products (Chapter

8). There may be a number of practical difficulties in costing and particularly in comparing the costs of one system with another (Section 13.2). What is important is the need to be absolutely clear about the purpose of the analysis, and to be methodical in carrying it out (Chapter 9).

There is plenty of evidence that open and distance education can be more cost efficient than traditional forms of education (Chapter 13), but this is not necessarily the case. Much depends on the number of students being served by the system, but this is not the only factor. The cost-efficiency ratios in Tables 13.3 and 13.4 hide all kinds of factors including media mix (each medium and each technology has its own cost structure), working practices, differential standards and the breadth of investment in the curriculum. It is important not to draw facile conclusions or make extravagant claims. Perhaps the most that can be said is that 'there are circumstances in which distance teaching looks attractive from an economic point of view' (Perraton, 1982: 61).

There is evidence too that students learn effectively using open and distance methods, but again, this is not always the case (Chapter 14).

Although there is almost no research on differentials between the private and social rates of return of open and distance education compared to traditional methods, it is clear that students do benefit from their studies (Chapter 15). It is also clear that open and distance methods of training are not only potentially more cost efficient from the firm's point of view (Table 13.3), but also have the benefit that the cost of time used for training is transferred from the employer to the employee (Section 15.5).

Distance education is a way of reducing the costs of education to the state, to the providing institution, and to the employer. There is a danger that costs will be transferred to the users, and Chapter 16 discusses the issues around the questions of demand, price, the funding of distance education and the implication of this for access. Funding agencies need to bear in mind that the cost structures of open and distance education systems are very different to traditional approaches based on the classroom. Funding mechanisms must recognize this if distance and open learning is to be given the chance to flourish and achieve the efficiencies that the policy-makers want. The use of traditional funding mechanisms to determine the funds available for distance and open learning can jeopardize investment in the development of new course materials, and hence ultimately threaten academic quality.

Perhaps the main message from this book is that, behind the wealth of figures and the vast number of studies that have been undertaken concerning costs, there is little that can be concluded with certainty. Policy-makers and institutional leaders should beware of lifting solutions off the shelf, hoping that the economic benefits that may be said to apply in one socio-economic environment will transfer, along with the media and the technologies, to another. There is no substitute for management; for active involvement in planning and costing a project. Experience shows that although it may not be easy it is possible to design systems that will reap efficiencies and be cost effective.

References

Ansari, M M (1992) *Economics of Distance Higher Education*, Concept Publishing Company, New Delhi.

Ansari, M M (1993) 'Economics of distance education in India', in Asian Association of Open Universities *Economics of Distance Education: AAOU VIIth Annual Conference*, Open Learning Institute of Hong Kong, Hong Kong.

Arena, E (1989) 'Actualización del cálculo del costo de la Telesecundaria Mexicana', in J B Oliveira and G Rumble (eds) (1992) *Educación a Distancia en América Latina: Análisis de costo-efectividad*, World Bank, Washington, DC.

Bååth, J (1984) 'Research on completion and discontinuation in distance education', *Epistolodidaktika* 1–2, 31–43.

Bako, C I and Rumble, G (1993) 'The National Teachers' Institute, Nigeria', in H Perraton (ed) *Distance Education for Teacher Training*, Routledge, London.

Bartels, J (1993) *Absolventen des Fachbereichs Wirtschaftswissenschaft: Ergebnisse einer Repräsentativbefragung*, Zentrum für Fernstudienentwicklung Berichte und Materialien, Fernuniversität.

Bates, A W (1995) *Technology, Open Learning and Distance Education*, Routledge, London.

Birch, D W and Cuthbert, R E (1981) *Costing Open Learning in Further Education*, Council for Educational Technology, London.

Birch, D W and Cuthbert, R E (1982) 'Academic staff costs in open and distance learning', in Scottish Education Department, *Distance No Object: Examples of Open Learning in Scotland*, HMSO, Edinburgh.

Bolwig, N G (1993) 'The economics of distance teaching: short and long run analysis', in H Siggard Jensen and S Siggard Jensen (eds) *Organization, Technology and Economics of Education: Proceedings of the COSTEL Workshop, Copenhagen, 11–12 January*, Copenhagen.

Bosworth, D and Ford, J (1985) 'Perceptions of higher education by university entrants: An exploratory study', *Studies in Higher Education* 10 (3), 257–67.

Bynner, J (1985) 'Collaborative schemes and the ethos of distance education: A study of Australian and New Zealand universities', *Higher Education* 14 (5), 513–33.

Carnoy, M and Levin, H M (1975) 'Evaluation of educational media: Some issues', *Instructional Science* 4 (2), 385–406.

Carter, C F (1973) 'The economics of the Open University: A comment', *Higher Education* 2 (1), 69–70.

Carter, V (1996) 'Do media influence learning? Revisiting the debate in the context of distance education', *Open Learning* 11 (1), 31–40.

Cavanagh, A K and J Tucker (1993) 'Costing of off-campus library services', in C J Jacob (ed) *The Sixth Off-Campus Library Services Conference*, Kansas City, Missouri, 6–8 October, Central Michigan University, Mount Pleasant, Michigan.

Chale, E M (1993) 'Tanzania's distance-teaching programme', in H Perraton (ed) *Distance Education for Teacher Training*, Routledge, London.

Chambers, E (1993) 'The economics of collaborative publishing in distance education', in Asian Association of Open Universities, *Economics of Distance Education: AAOU VIIth Annual Conference*, Open Learning Institute of Hong Kong, Hong Kong.

Charbonneau, J and Cunningham, C (1993) 'Videoconferencing in distance education: economic and pedagogical considerations', in Asian Association of Open Universities, *Economics of Distance Education: AAOU VIIth Annual Conference*, Open Learning Institute of Hong Kong, Hong Kong.

Checkland, P (1981) *Systems Thinking, Systems Practice*, John Wiley & Sons, Chichester.

Chivore, B R S (1993) 'The Zimbabwe Integrated Teacher Education Course', in H Perraton (ed) *Distance Education for Teacher Training*, Routledge, London.

Christopher, G R (1982) 'The Air Force Institute of Technology: The Air Force reaches out through media: An update', in L Parker and C Olgren (eds) *Teleconferencing and Electronic Communications*, Center for Interactive Programs, University of Wisconsin-Extension, Madison, Wisconsin.

Chute, A G, Hulik, M and Palmer, C (1987) *Teletraining Productivity at AT&T: Paper presented at the International Teleconferencing Association Annual Convention*, Washington DC, 5 May, AT&T Communications, Cincinnati, Ohio.

Clark, R (1983) 'Reconsidering research on learning from media', *Review of Educational Research* 53 (4), 445–59.

Clark, R (1994) 'Media will never influence learning', *Educational Technology* 31 (2), 34–8.

Committee on the Establishment of an Open University (1982) *Towards an Open Learning System*, Osmania University Department of Publications and Press, Hyderabad, Andhra Pradesh.

Coopers and Lybrand in association with the Open University (1990) *A Report into the Relative Costs of Open Learning*, The Open University, Milton Keynes.

Cowan, J (1985) 'Effectiveness and efficiency in higher education', *Higher Education* 14, 235–9.

Crabb, G (ed) (1990) *Costing Open and Flexible Learning: A Practical Guide*, National Council for Educational Technology, London.

Crosson, P (1983) *Public Service in Higher Education: Practices and Priorities*, Association for the Study of Higher Education, Washington.

Cumming, C and Olaloku, F A (1993) 'The Correspondence and Open Studies Institute, University of Lagos', in H Perraton (ed) *Distance Education for Teacher Training*, Routledge, London.

Curran, C (1993) 'Scale, cost and quality in small distance teaching universities', in H Siggard Jensen and S Siggard Jensen (eds) *Organization, Technology and Economics of Education: Proceedings of the COSTEL Workshop, Copenhagen, 11–12 January*, Copenhagen.

Daniel, J S (1995) *The Mega-universities and the Knowledge Media: Implications of New Technologies for Large Distance Teaching Universities. Thesis in partial fulfilment of the requirements for the Degree of Master of Arts (Educational Technology)*, Concordia University, Montreal.

Deakin University (1988) *Application for a Designation as a Distance Education Centre*, Deakin University, Geelong.

Deakin University (1989) *Further Investigations into Activity Costing in a Mixed-mode Institution*, Department of Employment, Education and Training, Commonwealth of Australia.

Delors, J, al Mufti, I, Amagi, I *et al.* (1996) *L'Éducation: Un Trésor est Caché Dedans*, Éditions UNESCO and Éditions Odile Jacob, Paris.

Department of Education and Science (1991) *Open University Review: Study of the Costs of Part-time Higher Provision in Three Comparator Institutions. Final Report.* April.

Department of Education and Science and the Open University (1991) *Review of the Open University*, Open University, Milton Keynes.

Ding Xingfu (1993) 'Economic analysis of Radio and TV universities education in China', in Asian Association of Open Universities, *Economics of Distance Education: AAOU VIIth Annual Conference*, Open Learning Institute of Hong Kong, Hong Kong.

Dudézert, J-P (1993) '"Formations ouvertes": Le rapport coût-efficacité', *LEADER* (Lettre de l'Education a Distance en Reseaux), March–April, 16–22.

Eicher, J-C (1978) 'Quelques réflexions sur l'analyse économique des moyens modernes d'enseignement', Paper presented to the International Conference on Economic Analysis for Education Technology Decisions, University of Dijon, Institut de Recherches sur l'Economie de l'Education, 19–23 June.

Eicher, J-C (1980) 'Some thoughts on the economic analysis of new educational media', in UNESCO *The economics of New Educational Media, Vol. 2: Cost and Effectiveness*, UNESCO Press, Paris.

Eicher, J-C, Hawkridge, D, McAnany, E *et al.* (1982) *The Economics of New Educational Media. Volume 3: Cost and Effectiveness Overview and Synthesis*, UNESCO Press, Paris.

Ekins, J (1993) 'The economics of different models for the use of distance learning courses from other institutions in terms of human resources', in Asian Association of Open Universities, *Economics of Distance Education. AAOU VIIth Annual Conference*, Open Learning Institute of Hong Kong, Hong Kong.

Escotet, M A (1980) *Tendencias de la educación superior a distancia*, Editorial Universidad Estatal a Distancia, San José, Costa Rica.

Fleming, A (1982) 'The Allama Iqbal Open University, Pakistan', in G Rumble and K Harry (eds) *The Distance Teaching Universities*, Croom Helm, London.

Freeman, R B (1976a) *The Over-educated American*, New York, Academic Press.

Freeman, R B (1976b) 'A cobweb model of the supply and starting salary of new engineers', *Industrial and Labor Relations Review* 29, 236–48.

Fwu, B-j, Jamison, D, Livingston, R *et al.* (1992) 'The National Technological University', in G Rumble and J Oliveira (eds) *Vocational Education at a Distance: International Perspectives*, Kogan Page in association with the International Labour Office, London.

Hall, N (1994) 'Academy in the ether', *The Times Higher Education Supplement, Multimedia Features*, 16 September, xii.

Hallak, J (1990) *Investing in the Future: Setting Educational Priorities in the Developing World*, UNESCO: International Institute for Educational Planning and Pergamon Press, Paris.

Harwood, R F and Kim, S H (1985) 'Seoul's Super School', in Institute of Lifelong Learning, Korea Air and Correspondence University (nd, c 1987) *Articles on Korea Air and Correspondence University and Related Issues*, np, Institute of Lifelong Learning, Korea Air and Correspondence University. (This article was first published in the International Council for Distance Education's *ICDE Bulletin* Vol 8 (May 1985).)

Hawkridge, D, P Kinyanjui, J Nkinyangi and F Orivel (1982) 'In-service teacher education in Kenya', in H Perraton, *Alternative Routes to Formal Education: Distance Teaching for School Equivalency*, John S Hopkins University Press, Baltimore.

Hennessy, A (1979) 'Students in the Latin American university', in J Maier and R W Weatherhead, *The Latin American University*, University of New Mexico Press, Albuquerque.

Higher Education Funding Council for England (1994) *Average Units of Council Funding for Academic Year 1993-94*. Report 1/94, August.

Higher Education Funding Council for England (1996) *Funding Method for Teaching*, HEFCE Consultation Paper 1/96.

Holmberg, B (1989) *Theory and Practice of Distance Education*, Routledge, London.

Holmes, D R, Karmacharya, D M and Mayo, J K (1993) 'Radio education in Nepal', in H Perraton (ed) *Distance Education for Teacher Training*, Routledge, London.

Jamison, D T (1977) *Cost Factors in Planning Educational Technology Systems*, UNESCO, International Institute for Educational Planning, Paris.

Jamison, D T, Klees, S J and Wells, S J (1975) *Cost Analysis for Educational Planning and Evaluation: Methodology and Application to Instructional Technology*, Princeton, Economics and Educational Planning Group, Educational Testing Service; reproduced in UNESCO (1977) *The Economics of New Educational Media: Present Status of Research and Trends*, UNESCO, Paris.

Jamison, D T, Klees, S J and Wells, S J (1978) *The Costs of Educational Media. Guidelines for Planning and Evaluation*, Sage Publications, Beverly Hills.

Jamison, D T and E G McAnany (1978) *Radio for Education and Development*, Sage Publications, Beverly Hills.

Jamison, D T and F Orivel (1978) 'The cost effectiveness of distance teaching projects', *Educational Broadcasting International*, December, 169–75.

Jamison, D T, Suppes, P and Wells, S (1974) 'The effectiveness of alternative media: A survey', *Review of Educational Research* 44 (1), 1–67.

Jennings, P L and Ottewill, R (1996) 'Integrating open learning with face-to-face tuition: A strategy for competitive advantage', *Open Learning* 11 (2), 13–19.

Johnes, G (1993) *The Economics of Education*, The Macmillan Press, London.

Johnson, H T and Kaplan, R S (1987) *Relevance Lost: The Rise and Fall of Management Accounting*, Harvard Business School Press, Boston.

Jung, I (1993) 'Improving the economics of budget allocation in distance education: A case study of Korea Air and Correspondence University', in Asian Association of Open Universities, *Economics of Distance Education: AAOU VIIth Annual Conference*, Open Learning Institute of Hong Kong, Hong Kong.

Keegan, D (1994) 'The competitive advantages of distance teaching universities', *Open Learning* 9 (2), 36–9.

Kemp, J E (1995) 'Costing training delivery distance education and face to face options: a methodology and case studies', in Sewart, D (ed) *One World, Many Voices: Quality in Open and Distance Learning. Papers of the 17th World Conference for Distance Education, Birmingham, 26–30 June*, International Council for Distance Education and Open University, Milton Keynes.

Kirkwood, A (1988) *Students' Costs and Hardship in 1986: Findings from the Costs/Access Survey 1986*, Open University, Institute of Educational Technology, Student Research Centre, Milton Keynes.

Klees, S J and Wells, S J (1977) *Cost effectiveness and Cost-benefit Analysis for Educational Planning and Evaluation: Methodology and Application to Instructional Technology*, Agency for International Development, Washington DC, US.

Laidlaw, B and Layard, R (1974) 'Traditional versus Open University teaching methods: A cost comparison', *Higher Education* 3 (4), 439–68.

Laurillard, D (1993) *Rethinking University Teaching: A Framework for the Effective Use of Educational Technology*, Routledge, London.

Layard, P R G and Verry, D (1973) *Cost Functions for Teaching and Research in UK Universities*, mimeo, London School of Economics, Higher Education Research Unit, London.

Lee, K-W, Futagami, S and Braithwaite, B (1982) 'The Korean Air-Correspondence High School', in H Perraton, *Alternative Routes to Formal Education: Distance Teaching for School Equivalency*, Johns Hopkins University Press, Baltimore.

Leslie, L L and Brinkman, P T (1988) *The Economic Value of Higher Education*, American Council on Education and Macmillan, New York.

Levin, H M (1983) *Cost effectiveness: A Primer*, Sage Publications, Beverly Hills.

Levin, H M, Glass, G V and Meister, G (1984) *Cost-effectiveness of Four Educational Interventions. Project Report 84–A11.* School of Education, Stanford University, Stanford CERAS.

Lewis, R (1990) 'Open learning and the misuse of language: A response to Greville Rumble', *Open Learning* 5 (1), 3–18.

Liberman, J (1979) The rates of return to schooling: 1958–76, Faculty Working Paper, University of Illinois, Department of Finance, cited in L L Leslie and P T Brinkman (1988) *The Economic Value of Higher Education*, American Council on Education and Macmillan, New York.

Lockheed, M, Middleton, E J and Nettleton, G (eds) (1991) *Educational Technology: Sustainability and Effective Use*, World Bank, Population and Human Resources Department, Education and Employment Division, Background paper Series PHREE/91/32, Washington DC.

Lockwood, G (1993) 'Cost-effective methods of materials production', in Asian Association of Open Universities, *Economics of Distance Education: AAOU VIIth Annual Conference*, Open Learning Institute of Hong Kong, Hong Kong.

Lumsden, K G and Ritchie, C (1975) 'The Open University: A survey and economic analysis', *Instructional Science* 4 (2), 237–91.

Lumsden, K G and Scott, A (1982) 'An output comparison of Open University and conventional university students', *Higher Education* 11 (5), 573–91.

Macdonald-Ross, M and Waller, R (1969), 'The transformer', in *Penrose Graphic Arts International Annual*, Northwood Publications, London.

Mace, J (1978) 'Mythology in the making: Is the Open University really cost effective?', *Higher Education* 7 (3), 295–309.

MAI Research for Marketing (1992) *OU Employers' Study 1992. The report*, MAI Research for Marketing, London.

Makau, B (1993) 'The external degree programme at the University of Nairobi', in H Perraton (ed) *Distance Education for Teacher Training*, Routledge, London.

Mason, R (1994) *Using Communications Media in Open and Flexible Learning*, Kogan Page, London.

Mattila, J P (1982) 'Determinants of male school enrolments: A time series analysis', *Review of Economics and Statistics* 64, 242–51.

Mayo, J, McAnany, E and Klees, S (1975a) 'Estimación de costos unitarios del sistema nacional de telesecundaria', in A Montayo and M A Rebeil (eds) (1981) *Televisión y enseñanza media en México: el caso de la Telesecundaria*, Mexico, CNTE-GEFE, 2 volumes. Cited in E Arena (1989) 'Actualización del cálculo del costo de la Telesecundaria Mexicana', in J B Oliveira and G Rumble (eds) (1992) *Educación a Distancia en América Latina: Análisis de costo-efectividad*, World Bank, Washington DC.

Mayo, J, E McAnany and Klees, S (1975b) 'The Mexican Telescundaria: A cost-effectiveness analysis', *Instructional Science* 4, 193–236.

Melmed, A S, Ellenbogen, B, Jamison, D T and Turniansky, U (1982) Everyman University in Israel: The first two years', in H Perraton, *Alternative Routes to Formal Education: Distance Teaching for School Equivalency*, Johns Hopkins University Press, Baltimore.

Miller, E J and Rice, A K (1967) *Systems of Organisation: The Control of Task and Sentient Boundaries*, Tavistock Publications, London.

Molina, R (1981) 'Estimación de costos unitarios del Sistema Nacional de Telesecundaria', in A Montayo and M A Rebeil (eds) *Televisión y enseñanza en México: el caso de la Telesecundaria,* Mexico, CNTE-GEFE. 2 volumes. Cited in E Arena (1989) 'Actualización del cálculo del costo de la Telesecundaria Mexicana', in J B Oliveira and G Rumble (eds) (1992) *Educación a Distancia en América Latina: Análisis de costo-efectividad*, World Bank, Washington DC.

Moore, M G and Thompson, M M with Quigly, B A, Clark, G C and Goff, G G (1990) *The Effects of Distance Learning: A Summary of the Literature*, University Park, Pennsylvania State University, American Center for the Study of Distance Education.

Muñiz Aquino, G (1988) 'Análisis de la eficacia en función del costo de un proyecto de educación a distancia en la República Dominicana: El caso de CENAPEC', in J B Oliveira and G Rumble (eds) (1992) *Educación a Distancia en América Latina: Análisis de costo-efectividad*, World Bank, Washington DC.

Muta, H and Sakamoto, T (1989) 'The economics of the University of the Air of Japan revisited', *Higher Education* 18 (5), 585–611.

Muta, H and Saito, T (1993) 'Economics of the expansion of the University of the Air of Japan', in Asian Association of Open Universities, *Economics of Distance Education: AAOU VIIth Annual Conference*, Open Learning Institute of Hong Kong, Hong Kong.

Muzio, J (1992) 'Distance-taught computer education for managers and professionals at the University of Victoria', in G Rumble and J Oliveira (eds) *Vocational Education at a Distance: International Perspectives*, Kogan Page, London.

National Board of Employment, Education and Training (1994) *Costs and Quality in Resource-based Learning On and Off campus. Commissioned Report no 33*, Australian Government Publishing Service, Canberra.

Nettleton, G (1992) 'Distance training for telecommunications managers: The TELECOM/Telematique International Course on Project Management', in G Rumble and J Oliveira (eds) *Vocational Education at a Distance: International Perspectives*, Kogan Page, London.

Nielsen, H D and Tatto, M T (1993) 'Teacher upgrading in Sri Lanka and Indonesia', in H Perraton (ed) *Distance Education for Teacher Training*, Routledge, London.

Nielsen, H D and Tatto, M T with Djalil, A and Kularatne, N (1991) *The cost effectiveness of Distance Education for Teacher Training*, Basic Research and Implementation in Developing Education Systems (BRIDGES) Research Report No 9, April. Harvard Institute for International Development, BRIDGES project, Harvard.

Nipper, S (1989) 'Third generation distance learning and computer conferencing', in R Mason and A Kaye (eds) *Mindweave: Communication, Computers and Distance Education*, Pergamon Press. Oxford,

Oliveira, J B and Orivel, F (1982a) 'A Madureza project in Bahia', in H Perraton (1982) *Alternative Routes to Formal Education: Distance Teaching for School Equivalency*, Johns Hopkins University Press, Baltimore.

Oliveira, J B and Orivel, F (1982b) 'The Minerva project in Brazil', in H Perraton (1982) *Alternative Routes to Formal Education: Distance Teaching for School Equivalency*, Johns Hopkins University Press, Baltimore.

Oliveira, J B and Orivel, F (1993) 'Logos II in Brazil', in H Perraton (ed) *Distance Education for Teacher Training*, Routledge, London.

Oliveira, J B and Rumble, G (eds) (1992) *Educación a Distancia en América Latina: Análisis de costo-efectividad*, World Bank, Washington DC.

Open University (1975) *Review of Academic Staff Working Group: Report of a Group to the Department of Education and Science and to the Council of the Open University*, Internal paper, June, Open University, Milton Keynes.

Open University (1988) *Delivery Technologies*. Internal paper VCO(88)20, Open University, Milton Keynes.

Orivel, F (1987) Analysing costs in distance education systems: A methodological approach, Institut de Recherches sur l'Economie de l'Education (IREDU), mimeo, University of Bourgogne, Dijon.

Panda, S K, Satyanarayana, P and Sharma, R C (1996) *Open and Distance Education Research: Analysis and Annotation*, Indian Distance Education Association, (IDEA), Warangal.

Perraton, H (1982) *The Cost of Distance Education*, International Extension College, Cambridge.

Perraton, H (ed) (1993) *Distance Education for Teacher Training*, Routledge, London.

Perry, W (1976) *Open University: A Personal Account by the First Vice-Chancellor*, Open University Press, Milton Keynes.

Phelps, R H, Wells, R A, Ashworth, Jr, R L and Hahn, H A (1991) 'Effectiveness and costs of distance education using computer-mediated communication', *The American Journal of Distance Education* 5 (3), 7–19.

Pillai, C R and Naidu, C G (1991) *Cost Analysis of Distance Education: IGNOU*, Indira Gandhi National Open University, Planning Division, New Delhi.

Psacharopoulos, G (1985) 'Returns to education: A further international update and implications', *Journal of Human Resources* 20 (4), 583–604.

Robertshaw, M (1993) 'The importation and adaptation of distance education courses: Is it an expensive option?', in Asian Association of Open Universities, *Economics of Distance Education: AAOU VIIth Annual Conference*, Open Learning Institute of Hong Kong, Hong Kong.

Robinson, B (1990) 'Telephone teaching and audio-conferencing at the British Open University', in A W Bates (ed) *Media and Technology in European Distance Education*, European Association of Distance Teaching Universities, Heerlen.

Rowntree, D (1991) *Teaching Through Self-instruction*, Kogan Page, London.

Rumble, G (1976) 'The economics of the Open University'. Paper presented to the Anglian Regional Management College/Organization for Economic Co-operation and Development, International Management Development Programme for Senior Administrators in Institutions of Higher Education, Danbury, Essex, 1976–7. Open University, Academic Planning Office, Milton Keynes.

Rumble, G (1979) 'Planning for distance education', in J R Hakemulder (ed) *Distance Education for Development: Report of an International Seminar, 13–15 September, Addis Ababa*, German Foundation for International Development, Bonn.

Rumble, G (1981) 'The cost analysis of distance teaching: Costa Rica's Universidad Estatal a Distancia', *Higher Education* 10, 375-401.

Rumble, G. (1982) 'The cost analysis of learning at a distance: Venezuela'a Universidad Nacional Abierta', *Distance Education* 3 (1), 116–40.

Rumble, G (1986a) *The Planning and Management of Distance Education*, Croom Helm, London.

Rumble, G (1986b) *Costing Distance Education*, Commonwealth Secretariat, London.

Rumble, G (1986c) *Activity Costing in Mixed-mode Institutions:A Report on a Study of Deakin University*, Deakin University, Geelong.

Rumble, G (1987) 'Why distance education can be cheaper than conventional education', *Distance Education* 8 (1), 72–93.

Rumble, G (1988) 'The costs and costing of distance/open education', in J Jenkins, *Commonwealth Co-operation in Open Learning: Background Papers*, Commonwealth Secretariat, London.

Rumble, G (1989a) '"Open learning", "distance learning", and the misuse of language', *Open Learning* 4 (2), 28–36.

Rumble, G (1989b) 'On-line costs: Interactivity at a price', in R Mason and A Kaye (eds) (1989) *Mindweave: Communication, Computers and Distance Education*, Pergamon Press, Oxford.

Rumble, G (1990) 'Open learning and the misuse of language: A reply', *Open Learning* 5 (3), 50–51.

Rumble, G (1991a) 'Topic 3: Financial management in distance education', in Deakin University (1991) *Management of Distance Education*, Deakin University, Geelong.

Rumble, G (1991b) 'Topic 4: Budgeting in and economic analysis of distance education', in Deakin University (1991) *Management of Distance Education*, Deakin University, Geelong.

Rumble, G (1992) 'The competitive vulnerability of distance teaching universities', *Open Learning* 7 (2), 31–45.

Rumble, G (1994a) 'Mixed modes of teaching and learning: Structures, resources, and developments', in M Thorpe and D Grugeon (1994) *Open Learning in the Mainstream*, Longman, Harlow.

Rumble, G (1994b) 'The competitive vulnerability of distance teaching universities: A reply', *Open Learning* 9 (3), 47–9.

Rumble, G, Neil, M and Tout, A (1981) 'Budgetary and resource forecasting', in A Kaye and G Rumble (eds) *Distance Teaching for Higher and Adult Education*, Croom Helm, London.

Rumble, G and Oliveira, J B (eds) (1992) *Vocational Education at a Distance: International Perspectives*, Kogan Page in association with the International Labour Office, London.

Schramm, W (1972) *Quality in Instructional Television*, University Press of Hawaii, Honolulu.

Schramm, W (1977) *Big Media, Little Media: Tools and Technologies for Instruction*, Sage Publications, Beverly Hills.

Schultz, T W (1971) *Investment in Human Capital: The Role of Education and Research*, Free Press, New York.

SCIENTER (1994) *DELTA Concerted Action on the Economics of Flexible and Distance Learning*, DELTA Project D 2104, SCIENTER, Bologna.

Secretaría de Educación Pública, Consejo Nacional Técnico de la Educación, Dirección General de Programación (1981) *La enseñanza media básica en México y el Sistema Nacional de Telesecundaria en televisión y enseñanza media en México*, Consejo Nacional Técnico de la Educación, Mexico. Cited in E Arena (1989) 'Actualización del cálculo del costo de la Telesecundaria Mexicana', in J B Oliveira and G Rumble (eds) (1992) *Educación a Distancia en América Latina: Análisis de costo-efectividad*, World Bank, Washington DC.

Shamsher Ali, M, Enamul Haque, A K and Rumble, G (1997) 'The Bangladesh Open University: mission and promise', *Open Learning*, 12(2) in press.

Shanmugasundaram, M (1995) 'Private costs incurred by learners in distance education and regular university classroom-based education', in S K Panda and R C Sharma (eds) *Indian Distance Education: Contemporary Research*, New Delhi.

Sharma, R D (1983) 'The economics of distance education in an integrated tertiary education system', in Australian and South Pacific External Studies Association, *Papers of the ASPESA Sixth Biennial Forum, Toowomba, 11–15 July,* ASPESA, 163–75.

Sharratt, R (1993) 'Costing of open and distance learning (ODL): is it worth it?', in Asian Association of Open Universities, *Economics of Distance Education: AAOU VIIth Annual Conference,* Open Learning Institute of Hong Kong, Hong Kong.

Shears, A E (1992) 'Developing distance education courses on a shoestring', *Open Learning* 7 (3), 51–6.

Showalter, R G (1983) *Speaker Telephone Continuing Education for School Personnel Serving Handicapped Children: Final Project Report 1981–2,* Indianapolis Division of Special Education, ERIC, ED 231 150, Indiana State Department of Public Instruction, Indianapolis.

Silphiphat, S and Tamey, J (1993) 'The comparison of graduate studies cost per student and government budget allocation: STOU case', in Asian Association of Open Universities, *Economics of Distance Education: AAOU VIIth Annual Conference,* Open Learning Institute of Hong Kong, Hong Kong.

Smith, D and Saunders, M (1989) 'Costing part-time provision', *Open Learning* 4 (3), 28–34.

Smith, D and Saunders, M (1991) *Other Routes: Part-time Higher Education Policy,* Society for Research into Higher Education and Open University Press, Milton Keynes.

Smith, R C (1975) 'A proposed formula for Open University expenditure in a plateau situation', in Open University, *Review of Academic Staff Working Group: Report of a Group to the Department of Education and Science and to the Council of the Open University,* Internal paper, June 1975, Open University, Milton Keynes.

Smith, R C (1986) 'A comparative study of some performance indicators for a UGC funded university, a polytechnic and the Open University', mimeo.

Snowden, B L and Daniel, J S (1980) 'The economics and management of small post-secondary distance education systems', *Distance Education* 1 (1), 68–91.

Sparkes, J J (1984) 'Pedagogic differences in course design', in A W Bates (ed) *The Role of Technology in Distance Education,* Croom Helm, London.

Stone, J (1975) 'Alternative organizational structure for developing multi-media instructional materials', *Educational Technology* 15 (10). Cited in E G McAnany, J B Oliviera, F Orivel and J Stone (1982) 'Distance education: Evaluating new approaches in education for developing countries', *Evaluation in Education: An International Review Series,* 6 (3), 289–376.

Swinerton, E N and Hogan, T P (1981) 'A tested budget model for a non-traditional degree program', mimeo, University of Wisconsin, Madison, Wisconsin.

Taylor, J C and White, V J (1991) *The Evaluation of the Cost Effectiveness of Multi-media Mixed-mode Teaching and Learning,* Australian Government Publishing Service, Canberra.

Temple, H (1991) *Open Learning in Industry,* Longman, Harlow.

Teswanitch, J and Thanavibulchai, N (1993) 'Educational investment for distance education: Unequalization that needs to be changed', in Asian Association of Open Universities, *Economics of Distance Education: AAOU VIIth Annual Conference,* Open Learning Institute of Hong Kong, Hong Kong.

Thurow, L (1975) *Generating Inequality: Mechanisms of Distribution in the US Economy,* Basic Books, New York.

Trow, M (1973) *Problems in Transition from Elite to Mass Higher Education,* Carnegie Commission on Higher Education, Berkeley, California.

Tsang, M C and Levin, H M (1985) 'The economics of over-education', *Economics of Education Review* 4, 93–104.

UNESCO (1977) *The Economics of New Educational Media: Present Status of Research and Trends*, UNESCO Press, Paris.

UNESCO (1980) *The Economics of New Educational Media. Volume 2: Cost and Effectivenss*, UNESCO Press, Paris.

UNESCO (1995) *World Education Report*, UNESCO Publishing, Oxford.

UNESCO/ICDE (nd, c 1990) *Developments in Distance Education in Asia: An Analysis of Five Case Studies*, np, UNESCO/ICDE.

Van den Brande, L (1993) *Flexible and Distance Learning*, John Wiley & Sons, Chichester.

Wachtel, P (1975) 'The returns to investment in higher education: Another view', in F T Juster (ed) *Education, Income and Human Behaviour*, McGraw-Hill, New York.

Wagner, L (1972) 'The economics of the Open University', *Higher Education* 1 (2), 159–83.

Wagner, L (1973) 'The economics of the Open University: A reply', *Higher Education* 2 (1), 71–2.

Wagner, L (1975) 'Television video-tape systems for off-campus education: A cost analysis of SURGE', *Instructional Science* 4 (2), 315–32.

Wagner, L (1977) 'The economics of the Open University revisited', *Higher Education* 6 (3), 359–81.

Wagner, L (1982) *The Economics of Educational Media*, Macmillan, London.

Wei, Runfang and Tong, Yuanhui (1994) *Radio and TV universities: The Mainstream of China's Adult and Distance Higher Education*, Yilin Press, Nanjing.

Wells, S (1976) 'Evaluation criteria and effectiveness of instructional technology in higher education', *Higher Education* 5 (3), 253–75.

White, V J (1992) 'Responses to Greville Rumble's article "The competitive vulnerability of distance teaching universities"', *Open Learning* 7 (3), 59–60.

Wolff, L and Futagami, S (1982) 'The Malawi Correspondence College', in H Perraton, *Alternative Routes to Formal Education: Distance Teaching for School Equivalency*, Johns Hopkins University Press, Baltimore.

Woodley, A (1983) 'Why they declined the offer', *Teaching at a Distance* 23, 2–7.

Woodley, A (1990) 'Some preliminary results from the 1990 survey of dormant students', mimeo, September. Institute of Educational Technology, Open University, Milton Keynes.

Woodley, A (1995) 'The experience of older graduates from the British Open University', *International Journal of University Adult Education* 34 (1), 37–48.

Woodley, A and McIntosh, N (1977) 'People who decide not to apply to the Open University', *Teaching at a Distance* 9, 18–26.

World Bank (1994) *Higher Education. The Lessons of Experience*, World Bank, Washington DC.

Subject Index

Name Index